Liberal Nationalism for Israel

Liberal Nationalism for Israel

Towards an Israeli National Identity

Joseph Agassi

JERUSALEM ♦ NEW YORK

Copyright © Gefen Publishing House
Jerusalem 1999/5759

All rights reserved. No part of this publication may be translated, reproduced, stored in a retrieval system or transmitted, in any form or by any means, electronic, mechanical, photocopying, recording or otherwise, without express written permission from the publishers.

Translated by the author
Typesetting: Marzel A. S. — Jerusalem
Cover Design: Grossman / Daedalos
Cover Photo: Nili Kook

Publication of this book was made possible by a grant from the Institute for Mediterranean Affairs

Edition 9 8 7 6 5 4 3 2 1

Gefen Publishing House
POB 36004
Jerusalem 91360, Israel
972-2-538-0247
isragefen@netmedia.net.il

Gefen Books
12 New Street
Hewlett, NY 11557, USA
516-295-2805
gefenbooks@compuserve.com

Printed in Israel

Send for our free catalogue

Library of Congress Cataloging-in-Publication Data
Agassi, Joseph.
[Ben dat u-le'om. English]
Liberal nationalism for Israel: towards an Israeli national identity / Joseph Agassi.
    p.   cm.
Includes bibliographical references and indexes.
ISBN: 965 229 190 0
1. Zionism. 2. Religion and state—Israel. 3. Jews—Israel—Identity. 4. Israel and the diaspora. I. Title.
DS149.A5913 1999
320.54'095694—dc21
99-14061
CIP

To Hillel Kook,
alias Peter Bergson

As a rule the man who first thinks of a new idea is so much ahead of his time that everyone thinks him silly, so that he remains obscure and is soon forgotten. Then, gradually, the world becomes ready for the idea, and the man who proclaims it at the fortunate moment gets all the credit.

(Bertrand Russell, The History of Western Philosophy, p. 624)

Contents

Preface to the English-language Edition 7
Preface to the First Edition 20
Acknowledgments 24
Preface to the Second Edition 25
Prologue: Hillel Kook 29
Introduction: On Political Normalization 37

PART ONE	*Foundations: The Israeli Nation and its Judaism*
Chapter 1	Concerning Public Responsibility 47
Chapter 2	The Social Contract Theory 55
Chapter 3	The Reaction and Chauvinism 65
Chapter 4	Liberal Nationalism 77
Chapter 5	On Wars of Independence 87
Chapter 6	The Jewish Problem 94
Chapter 7	The Birth of the Jewish Nationalist Movement 106
Chapter 8	Political and Practical Zionism 111
Chapter 9	Zionism and Independence 120
Chapter 10	Faith, Nationality And State 129

PART TWO		*A National Tragedy*
Chapter 11	In The National Military Organization	141
Chapter 12	The Bergson Group	144
Chapter 13	Stateless Jews and the Jews of the United States	150
Chapter 14	The Wave of Hostility	155
Chapter 15	For the Rescue of European Jews	161
Chapter 16	National Self-Determination	165
Chapter 17	Peter Bergson to Chaim Weizmann, April 2, 1945	175
Chapter 18	In the Zionist Establishment	183
Chapter 19	The Hebrew Committee for National Liberation and the Irgun National Military Organization	192
Chapter 20	Then and Now	198

PART THREE		*An Updated Program for the Israeli Nation*
Chapter 21	Decades of Internal Exile	205
Chapter 22	The Root of the Evil	212
Chapter 23	Is Israel Today a Nation-State?	221
Chapter 24	The Purpose of the Change	227
Chapter 25	The Alternative Plan	236
Chapter 26	Concerning National Minorities	243
Chapter 27	The Need for an Israeli Initiative to Establish Peace in the Middle East	252
Chapter 28	Political Initiative Towards Peace in the Middle East	261
Chapter 29	Israel and the Jews of Other Nations	269
Chapter 30	The New Zionist Myth	278

PART FOUR		*Conclusions*
Chapter 31	Personal Summary: Concerning Israeli National Identity	286
Chapter 32	Cultural Conclusion: Concerning the Unity of the Jewish People	293
Chapter 33	A Political Conclusion: Towards a Transition Period	299

Notes	306
Name Index	327
Subject Index	330

Preface to the English-language Edition

The Hebrew versions of this book appeared in 1984 and in 1993. This is my fairly literal, sentence-by-sentence translation. It offers an unusual solution to Israel's political problems (normalization; separation of church and state) from the viewpoint of an unusual political philosophy (a consistent liberal nationalism). This book has a dual character. It is a presentation of a theory of liberal nationalism, with Israel as a case study. It is also a study of Israel's ailments from a liberal viewpoint that is as sympathetic as possible, but also as critical and hard-nosed as possible.

A variety of books appeared since then on the question, how, if at all, is liberal nationalism possible? This is so perhaps because of the great influence on the study of nationalism in the fairly recent book *Nationalism* (London, 1983), by the leading social philosopher and scientist Ernest Gellner, that presents the history of nationalism as initially a liberal movement. Perhaps it is because of the dreadful new phenomenon of ethnic cleansing. Some books follow the tradition of individualist liberal philosophy, whose rejection of nationalism is uncompromising. One of them is *For Love of Country: An Essay on Patriotism and Nationalism* (Oxford, 1997), by Maurizio Viroli, a professor of politics at Princeton University. He contrasts nationalism with patriotism and advocates only the latter; I share with him the view that for two centuries now popular nationalism is illiberal and thus also unpatriotic; but in my view it is important to support patriotic, liberal nationalism. Of the recent books which advocate this, let me single out *The Construction of nationhood: Ethnicity, Religion and Nationalism* (Cambridge, 1997), by Adrian Hastings, an English historian of religion. He rightly dwells on the importance of the distinction between nationality and ethnicity. My appreciation of this book, however, does not take away from my stress on the value and originality of Hillel Kook's idea, here developed and advocated. He has suggested that a nation is liberal only to the extent that membership in it is a matter of choice — of both the nation and the individual citizen. This choice is constrained, and so is the liberalism that stands behind it: we must learn to present theories of the world that take into account its unavoidable imperfections.

Though I am a philosopher, as an Israeli patriot concerned with the future of my country, I express in this book more concern about the case study than the theory. My initial aim in writing this book was to contribute to local politics: my hope was (and still is) that it contribute to widening the debate about the political and legal structure of my country, a debate that so far is damagingly narrow, as it is conducted within the confine of a myth. (A myth is inherently vague: taken literally it is obviously absurd.) It is the New Zionist Myth that (contrary to Zionist doctrine) equates being Israeli with being Jewish. The damage is self-inflicted due to the corruption of public administration and of political life in general, and is rooted in the narrowness of Israeli politics, international relations, and state of mind (bewilderment and frustration).

An offshoot of this myth is the view, popular here (in Israel), that some rabbis impose religious practices on an unwilling population. The situation is represented as a complex matter of power politics. It obviously is not the full story, since countries where religious parties have full parliamentary support may, nonetheless, be quite liberal. Religious life there is run by religious establishments in religious communities separately from political life, which is run by political establishments in political arenas where religious freedom is defended. In Israel, religious life is run by the state, and the people argue about religious freedom and support laws that force rabbis to impose religious practices on a reluctantly acquiescent population.

The source of the trouble seems to me to be national discrimination in the guise of religious differentiation. The western model of a normal country is that of a nation-state: one nation ruled by one national state. There are alternative models, bi-national and multi-national. Their merits and defects will not be discussed here, except to say that they are preferable on all counts to the model of a nation-state with a national minority. This invites a comment. There is all the difference in the world between a cultural minority that belongs to the same nation and the national minority that does not. The national minority is discriminated against, often under the guise of being granted cultural autonomy. This is the situation in Israel. The non-Jews here are not members of the nation. They may be elected to office but not to bear arms. So it is obvious that in Israel an armed man is stronger than a legislator. This is an endless source of demoralization. Also, the Israeli non-Jews who are exempt from military service, are not officially exempt: they are only not called to serve. This makes the law something to circumvent by understandings. Also, exemption from military service is not desired, as it leads to discrimination: many job advertisements include the clause: people with no military record need not apply. Non-Jews live in ghettos not by choice but by a myriad of regulations that trap them there. This is very dangerous.

My effort in raising a public discussion here has met with little success. Local discussions concerning basics are scant and superficial, overlooking the flagrant, prevalent discrimination against non-Jews and against women. These are legally sanctified, though they are unconstitutional. (Israel has no constitution, but its Declaration of Independence and fundamental laws have quasi-constitutional force.) Israeli law is thus a farce and will remain so until basic changes are enacted. To this end, we should separate state and church. A discussion of the distinction between nation and congregation may facilitate this. Israel rejects the distinction and officially judges the nationality of most Israeli citizens to be Jewish and that of most of the rest to be Arab. This renders citizenship an administrative fiction. Consequently, the official aim of the State of Israel is not to serve its citizens, but rather the ingathering of the exiles. Since the Diaspora is here to stay, the claim that it is our aim to eliminate it is sheer propaganda. Yet it is taken seriously here; it is an axiom of the national consensus.

The Israeli national consensus is steadily weakening, due to deep disagreements about the peace process, which is the center of the political scene, at least today. The country is at risk of disintegration. The risk is met with efforts to strengthen the uncontested items in the national consensus, chiefly the New Zionist Myth and its corollary, the idea that the task of Israel is to facilitate the ingathering of the exiles and to show hostility to any criticism of the national consensus, especially to any criticism of the New Zionist Myth.

Criticism is allowed to be vicious here, as long as it is kept within the consensus and prevented from leaking out. Most English-language studies on Israel that have come my way, pro or con, are highly misleading, in that they quietly endorse the consensus. The consensus is that descriptions of our country intended for outside consumption must be idealized. We may admit that it suffers from small defects, but only if we stress that they will be remedied soon. We also admit our dire need for clothing and shelter for our new immigrants, and for state-of-the-art weapons for our armed forces. But nothing more. In a recent Tel Aviv University public meeting in memory of Premier Yitzhak Rabin, Henry Kissinger reported what Abba Eban, Israel's most famous Foreign Minister ever, had told him when both were in office: "What we mean by objectivity is one-hundred percent agreement with us", Kissinger quoted him to say. "I thought he was kidding", he added, raising nervous laughter.

While trying to prevent internal criticism from leaking out, we listen keenly to external criticism, trusting it to be unfair. Criticism from foreign Jews we repudiate as covert excuses for defection. We do not expect immediate massive immigration of millions of Jews; so we reluctantly permit them to stay out, on condition that they extend to us lavish financial aid and unqualified political support. Criticism from non-Jews we treat here as covert anti-Semitism. We still expect the international community to help us, despite our regular misconduct and inept propaganda, and despite the constant flow of hostile propaganda (anti-Semitic and anti-Israeli). Our expectation that the West will indulge us rests on the Allies' disgraceful heartless indifference to the tragedy of the Holocaust when rescue was possible.

The New Zionist Myth is spreading a deep mistrust of democracy. Democracy is inherently vulnerable. This is illustrated by the failure of the inter-war (Weimar) German democracy. Most Israelis take this case as proof of the innate inability of democracy to curb anti-Semitism. This blocks cooperation between Israeli and western Jews, as they are patriotic defenders of democracy, and Israelis judge this as a defection that they will regret only when the next Holocaust arrives. When challenged, this judgment is dismissed as excessively bluntly stated, but with the insistence that the world is against us. This is the Masada Complex.

The Law of Return that keeps Israel's gates open to all Jews is thus considered here to be its *raison d'être*, the justification for its very existence as an independent state. This is dangerous, as independence never invites justification. The justification is endorsed here, because it provides an excuse for religious discrimination against non-Jews (Israeli and Palestinian in particular). A counter-proposal is made here, not to repeal the Law of Return but to reword it, with the intent to remove from it reference to religion, and to affirm instead our readiness to provide refuge to those persecuted as Jews and our preference for immigrants of Jewish heritage.

This book depicts two obvious distinctions: between nation and congregation, and between liberal and illiberal nationalism (the version of nationalism as taken for granted in the West *versus* the chauvinist versions). To confuse these is to allow or even condone the religious discrimination practiced in most trouble spots, including Northern Ireland, the Balkans, the Middle East, the former Soviet Union and the Indian sub-continent (01).

The expression "separation of state and church" does not translate comfortably into Hebrew. The Hebrew word for church is reserved to denote the Christian house of prayer. The expression may then be translated as "separation of state and synagogue", or "separation of state and rabbinate". This does not reflect the applicability of the expression to all religious authority. A better translation is, "separation of secular and religious authorities", yet it harbors another difficulty. The word "secular" refers to what lies outside the religious dimension. It was used by some atheists to denote hostility to religion and this usage became standard in modern Hebrew. So the usual translation here is "separation of faith and state". This separation, almost all Israeli Jews agree, is inapplicable to Judaism; since a Jew is affiliated to a creed as well as to a nation. As the Jewish people is ancient and nationality is modern, it is absurd to view the Jews as affiliated to a distinct nation. Only Israel supports this absurdity; no trend in modern Judaism does. Of the non-practicing Jews, some view being Jewish as an ethnic and cultural characteristic; others, such as the Russian Jews, who constitute a national minority, view themselves as such, regardless of any matter of faith. All organized Jewish congregations reject it. The various conservative and reform congregations characterize themselves as a creed and a sub-culture. Orthodox Judaism, as developed in Europe in the last two centuries, ignores the modern world. Its leaders in Israel have managed to convey contempt for all versions of Judaism except for the orthodox, though they unwittingly render to increase the unpopularity of orthodox Judaism too. They hardly mind this, as their extremely conservative attitude makes them disregard all criticism.

The illiberal New Zionist Myth is operative. For example, it has allowed Israel to request the United States to block migration of Russian Jews to America. It still pretends that all Jewish communities are Orthodox. Objection to its conduct is understandably restrained, partly due to indifference, partly due to a reluctance to embarrass. On occasion some foreign celebrities, some of them Jewish, have objected to its harshness to Palestinians. Non-orthodox Jewish leaders are now slowly showing readiness to censure its hostility to their congregations. They still refrain from demanding that it should cease adjudicating and speaking on behalf of all Jews on matters religious and political. Though Judaism is a very low church, the Israeli Orthodox establishment is a government agency. This forces it to behave increasingly like an authoritative center of a high church. In this it has much popular support here, though an increasingly reluctant one, since most Israeli Jews are non-practicing. This is confusing. I was myself confused about this before I met Hillel Kook (Peter Bergson), whose tenets this book describes. He has helped me see the damage due to Israel's view of its nation as a congregation: it is a damage to its political independence.

This book addresses the Israeli Jewish majority. As our politics involves religion, most of us express our frustration by developing contempt for our tradition and more so for defenders of our parliamentary system. The distinction between congregation and nation should lead to the separation of church and state, and thus to the improvement of attitudes to our heritage, and to the reduction of our sense of frustration.

The political situation here is explosive. The efforts to overcome frustration by appeals to goodwill and to the love of peace that will lead to no improvement, cannot but increase frustration. The instability of the situation guarantees a deadlock. Even if Israel and the Palestinians were to find a stable settlement,

Israel's discrimination against its non-Jews is sure to destabilize it. The experience of confessional strife in other countries should serve as a warning: Israel cannot be stable while openly discriminating against a substantial national minority. Even without discrimination, as long as aspirations of non-Jews are regularly frustrated, as they are here, it is only a matter of time before this will lead to outbursts of destabilizing activities.

This book does not address Israeli non-Jews. The idea of a secular state should appeal to them, as the status of second-class citizens is not exactly to their taste. It does appeal to them, as I saw on occasion. (Encounters between Jewish and non-Jewish citizens are uncommon in my country, as it is officially ghettoized: sales of most of the land is restricted to Jews, and so non-Jews live in separate villages or small towns. Consequently, Jerusalem is divided, as Hebron is, despite all declarations to the contrary. So, almost only a peace-activist meets regularly individuals who are members of the other community.) Israeli non-Jews are unable to do much to alter their political situation, though; initiative must come from the responsible among the Jewish majority here.

This book does not address Palestinians, and refers to them only to report their having the start of a national movement. After a long delay we officially admit this, though feebly and intermittently, and without respecting it. We should respect this movement. Instead we hardly converse with its representatives. This is hard, because of segregation and of a tremendous cultural and educational gulf, and, poignantly, because of bitterness: their situation is much more desperate than ours. (Even financial aid faces many obstacles on its way to their suffering population.) Their leadership is that of the Palestine Liberation Organization, which was not democratically elected: it was very weak after the collapse of the Communist block and more so after the Gulf War — which is why the Israeli leadership agreed to cooperate with them, despite their inability to revoke their charter, the Palestine Covenant, which declares the destruction of Israel a part of its target. (Later on, the United States of America exerted a tremendous pressure on them to omit expressions of the desire to destroy Israel from the Palestine Covenant. It still stands, though perhaps in modification, and it still claims ownership over the whole territory of formerly British Palestine, east and west of the River Jordan. Extravagant claims are politically legitimate, and should be met with reasonable offers, such as the one to exchange them for Israel's recognition of their right to have a territory of their own.)

Local elections legitimized their leadership somewhat. It is not for outsiders to advise them on their leaders. What one can say from the outside about the predicament of the Palestinians is not very different from what this book says of the Israeli predicament, only more emphatically: a nation must come to terms with its past and choose leaders who are not afraid to face basic challenges and conduct public debate on a master-plan concerning the national future, dwelling on more than the immediate future and less on the very distant one. This is even harder for the Palestinians to do than for the Israelis: even the admission that in 1948 they missed a golden opportunity as their leaders refused to declare independence and enter into a peace treaty with their newly-founded neighbor. It is, of course, no good crying over spilt milk, but it is also no use pretending that it was not spilled. As long as the Palestinians are not ready for this admission, they are and will remain handicapped until the twentieth century will recede well into the historical background.

Israel is torn over the Palestinian problem. Is there a Palestinian national movement? If yes, what right might it claim? Unfortunately, this is examined here in Israel not politically but philosophically, or more precisely, theologically. This reduces the hope for peace. We should admit, instead, to a boundary dispute between nations: experience shows that compromise over land is more likely than over religion. Though the Palestinians are becoming increasingly a nation, their situation is no less confused than ours. This is partly due to our confusion, partly due to different factors, including a Palestinian Diaspora in the not too liberal Middle East, an Arab nationalism that curbs the growth of local national movements, and a confusion between legitimate struggle for national liberation and terrorism, a confusion enhanced by the erstwhile terrorist character of the Palestine Liberation Organization. This confusion promotes terrorism. As a precondition for effective peace negotiations, Israel demands that terrorism be eliminated. This demand is reasonable but not realistic.

The view of the Palestine Liberation Organization as a terrorist organization gives repeated cause for annoyance and distraction. It is countered by an erroneous claim and by a correct observation. The erroneous claim is that as heir to the Irgun National Military Organization, the present Israeli

Government also has a terrorist ancestry. The correct observation is that the view of the Palestine Liberation Organization as a terrorist organization is used as an excuse for Israel's own terrorist activities. It is a pity that complaints about terrorist activities are linked to a historical allegation, particularly a false one, since history is no excuse for Israel's present (official) use of torture and of death squads and of occasional terrorist activities abroad, not to mention its segregation and closure of the Palestinian population that seeks employment in menial work here.

This is not to condone guerilla warfare: at most, it is legitimate after all peaceful avenues were tried without success. Nor is it to deny that, almost inevitably, guerilla warfare involves terrorism. Nevertheless, the distinction between guerilla warfare and terrorist activities is imperative, as they differ significantly: terrorism is directed chiefly against civilians, and guerrilla warfare is directed chiefly against military targets. The view of both the Irgun National Military Organization and the Palestine Liberation Organization as terrorist is thus misleading: The Palestine Liberation Organization regularly practiced terrorism in addition to its guerilla warfare and officially as a part of it. Public sentiment in the West concerning violence changed radically twice, with the rise and decline of the popularity of the New Left, which condoned terrorism in academic publications and in the mass media, including popular novels and movies (like the acclaimed cheap movie *The Lost Honor of Katharina Blum*, based on the cheap novel by Nobel laureate Heinrich Böll).

Unlike terrorist activities, guerilla warfare should be recognized, particularly during a war of independence. The Palestinian Uprising, the *intifada* (a corruption of "independence"), is justified as a struggle for independence: in general, not in detail. Particularly not its religious character nor its terrorism, even though they are admittedly dictated by the religious character of Israel's political establishment and by Israeli terrorism against Palestinians. Compromise is only possible between nations ready to respect each other, not between religious doctrines, nor between parties ready to exercise torture. This fact is shamelessly employed by some Jewish settlers in Judea and Samaria (territories claimed by the Palestinian Authority), who justify their terrorist activities (clandestine and open) by messianic arguments. Were a separation of church and state instituted here, it would be possible to arrange for the settlers to become Jewish Palestinians and thus cease to be the major stumbling block to the peace process that they (intentionally) are: their success is due to the ambiguity of their legal status that puts them above the law. They can be forced to choose one or another legal status and to be law-abiding.

The peace process is lame. The Camp David, the Oslo and the Wye accords or any other move contemplated within the present framework will not be the start of a new era. A successful resolution of a deep-seated conflict needs ample grass roots support from the populations of both sides. This is precluded by the widespread, semi-official discrimination according to religious affiliation.

Early in the twentieth century Jewish workers here were troubled by the incongruity between socialism and nationalism. Moslems (the few locals and the immigrant Transjordanians) competed with Jews for work for a pittance in the few new Jewish plantations. Jewish leaders asked Jewish workers to forego all struggle for better pay. The incongruity was never resolved. To date, Israel sustains scars that this left on its few pioneers nearly a century ago: chauvinist arguments are still used to justify exploitation, and exploitation is the unspoken motive for much of the folly of Israeli politics, though this time it hits the non-Jewish workers. Low-status Jews find it hard to utilize the scant avenues for social mobility or to fight for more; so they naturally tend to support the *status quo* that keeps their socioeconomic advantage over non-Jews.

Western observers deem Israel normal; this confuses them. They do notice the odd, semi-official status of Judaism here, yet they fail to notice its import. Church is not separate from state as in France and in the United States, and it is not a state church as in England and in Denmark. The status of Judaism here is vague. This hinders democratic control and enhances all sorts of underhand discrimination. Vagueness invites clashes regarding the power of the rabbinate and this maintains the *status quo*. The more liberal politicians seek religious reform; their wish must be frustrated, as they cannot use parliament to give vent to their frustration: it is no religious synod. Constitutional laws (legislated in *lieu* of a constitution) are openly sabotaged by (legally instituted) religious courts. The popular reluctance to discuss basic issues prevents directing the state to leave religious practices to the communities and to keep them out of politics. So religious coercion is recognized by all political parties, and this blocks debate on basics. The urgent need must be met, if not for a constitution, then for a debate on constitutional matters, especially on the inconsistency between democracy and religious coercion. The best way to do this is to reconvene the Israeli Constituent Assembly that refused to do its duty and declared itself Israel's first parliament instead.

Western confusion regarding Israel rests on inconsistent Western attitudes to nationalism: democrats and individualists tend to undermine nationalism; liberals and anti-imperialists tend to support it. Although the democratic nation-state is traditional, no consistent traditional philosophy supports it. Tracts devoted to any combination of liberalism and nationalism are scarce and hardly ever consistent. This is achieved in this book. Liberalism and nationalism are presented here as matters of degree, rather than in the usual abstract (utopian) manner, and also as matters of some choice. Though the traditional Social Contract Theory is an idealization, it points in the right direction: the desirability of freedom of choice, and the greater the better. Since all this is commonsense, discussion of it is rather academic for successful democracies; but countries which struggle in efforts to evolve into smoothly functioning democracies may benefit from a consistent liberal nationalism, such as the one this book advocates.

This is of some concern even in the developed countries of the world, since every national agenda is increasingly dominated by the global agenda. This agenda requires world peace and security; it should be coordinated by some powerful central authority compatible with national sovereignty. I have discussed this in some detail in my book *Technology: Philosophical and Social Aspects* (1985). However problematic the coordination between the rich nations is, it is rendered more problematic by the poor nations. Soon after World War II, in the early days of foreign aid, Sir Arthur Lewis observed that aid rescued tottering corrupt regimes, causing untold damage. It was irresponsible, however unintentionally so. Offering aid on reasonable conditions improves matters, but it demands that benefactors learn about their intended beneficiaries. Ignorance keeps the peace process in the Middle East in a fragile situation; better results demand the neutralizing of the causes of instability, chief among them are the abject living conditions in parts of the Arab world and Israel's impolitic discrimination against her minorities. The discrimination is an unspoken major item in Israeli politics, lowering the general level of politics to the point of paralysis. Yet we are content to observe that ours is the best political system in the region.

Unfortunately, the region is backward. The chief obstacle to peace and prosperity is the heartbreaking backwardness of the whole region, educational, socioeconomic, and political. Israel must then undertake a political initiative with the intent of advancing the region as much as possible without violating international conventions. Thus far Israel is indifferent to the region's problems, that it carelessly even aggravates. The only exception is the suggestion of one Israeli political leader, Shimon Peres, that the developed countries should contribute to a regional economic recovery plan akin to the Marshall Plan. This is a slogan, not even an outline for a preliminary proposal. It is in everybody's interest to declare a switch from the waste of local resources on weaponry to economic investment. At the very least, an international declaration of intent is required, perhaps also the intent to devise a global Marshall Plan financed by savings due to disarmament. There is no escape from responsibility to one's neighbor, even though responsibility to one's own people comes first: one can do little for one's neighbor as long as one's home is in poor shape. And the house of Israel is in poor shape, as it discriminates against its own citizens, on the tacit excuse that they prosper by comparison to all other populations across her border. As long as non-Jewish Israelis have the right to be elected to its legislature but not to bear arms, Israel tacitly endorses the view that weapons are more powerful than words. This is a dangerous philosophy. An example is the Gulf War. The temptation and the excuse for Iraq's dictator to invade Kuwait rested on the discrimination against Kuwaiti Palestinians. This is why so many of them supported the invasion, and why so many of them had to flee for their lives after the Kuwaiti Government was reinstated by the Coalition, and also why so many of them have demonstrated in favor of Iraq contrary to their own interest. The Palestine Liberation Organization lost its prestige during the Gulf War and yet the Palestinian Authority still has no choice but to support Iraq. At the time, the Israeli Government came to their rescue; today they are taking greater risks, as the Israeli Government is looking for excuses to break obligations that were accepted at the Wye conference.

We must keep trying. My aim is to raise a public debate concerning the desirability and necessity for Israel to normalize and become a Western-style nation-state. The peace process is frustrated, and Israel cannot activate it, as it does not recognize its own nation, confusing nation with creed, hoping to house practically all and only Jews. This will be learned sooner or later, but the cost of the lesson is constantly on the rise. I wish that the transition to normal life will be not too painful, that we will soon proceed with the important real tasks that our abnormal situation is blocking. To normalize Israel would not solve any of her problems but will ease the process of tackling them and enable us to move on to newer and more exciting tasks. Is this too much to hope for?

— Herzlia, Hanukkah, 1998.

P. S. This book is full of loose ends. Some of them are taken up in other works of mine; see Notes below; see also my "The Notion of the Modern Nation-State," in I. C. Jarvie and S. Pralong, *Popper's Open Society After Fifty years*, London: Routledge, 1999, my review of *Israeli Judaism: The Sociology of religion in Israel* in *Philosophy of the Social Sciences*, 28, 1998, and my "The Impact of Auschwitz and Hiroshima on Scientific Culture," in the forthcoming Imre Toth Festschrift. It should be noted, however, that Kook's tremendous impact is rooted in the dreadful blunder that was the opposition of the Zionist leadership to mass immigration, a blunder that persisted despite the approach of the Holocaust. See Hava Eshkoli, *Silence: Mapai [Palestine Labor Party] and the Holocaust — 1939-1942*. Jerusalem: Yad Ben-Zvi, in Hebrew, pp. 18 ff. and 363-34. See also Louis Rapoport, *Shake Heaven and Earth: Peter Bergson and the Struggle to Rescue the Jews of Europe*, Jerusalem and New York: Gefen, 1999. Hopefully, Hillel Kook's influence on post-war political life will soon raise public attention. His march on Washington links with the initiation and character of later marches. His mass appeals to public opinion prodded the United States to recognize lobbies, thus boosting pluralism. It also replaced the traditional partiality for secrecy with the publicity that accompanied the trail-blazing affair of the illegal immigrant boat "Exodus."

Preface to the First Edition

This book was written mostly in the spring and summer of 1980 after many lengthy discussions with Hillel Kook (or Peter Bergson as he was known when he was working in the United States) and in collaboration with him. I extend my gratitude to him. This book presents his political plan for normalizing Israel. To this I have added a theoretical discussion, which I found necessary.

The immediate purpose of this book is the opening of a comprehensive public debate on the matter both in Israel and abroad, and that the debate should concern a comprehensive political plan; the final purpose is a comprehensive political change that would transform Israel into a normal nation-state. But the first step ought to be a political debate. Naturally, such a debate may alter the political plan proposed here or put forth a practicable alternative to it. What is significant about the plan proposed here is not any detail. Its significance is in the ideas which this book presents: that Israel today needs a political master plan, that such a plan is absent from the Israeli political arena, and that it analyzes the causes of this sorry state.

Israel was born of a dream — the dream of national liberty renewed in the historical fatherland. This is the Zionist dream. I am not a party to that dream, but I do not disagree with the claim that this dream was one of the major factors that brought about the development of the theory and practice of Zionism. (Another central factor, no less significant, is rooted in the ever-growing intolerable suffering of the Jewish people.) The dream, the nebulous idea, became at one stage a plan that crystallized into Israel's Declaration of

Independence. The history books on Zionism do not clarify what this stage was, because they refuse to consider the contribution made by the Committee for the Liberation of the Hebrew Nation, founded and headed by Hillel Kook.

The importance of this Committee is in its having shown the significance of the principle of one-sided initiative — a principle that is still unknown in Israel — as the plan of the Committee was to declare the existence of the Hebrew nation and to declare unilaterally a transitional government. This plan rested on the assumptions that such a government could raise public sympathy that would permit its recognition, and that by the achievement of recognition from diverse governments it would gain validity and thus be able to act politically and independently. My purpose is not to rectify the history books, but to make a proposal to discuss the topical ideas — the roots of which are in the plans of this Committee, which was the first to overcome the vagueness of the Zionist dream. The vagueness of the dream permitted the Zionist movement's systematic political oversight of the very existence of a local population in Palestine. The proposal of the Hebrew Committee for Liberation to found the Hebrew Republic of Palestine, in which there would be a separation of faith and nationality, was made, among other things, in order to permit the members of the local population to join the nation and to see themselves as Hebrew Moslems or Hebrews of Arabic descent or something like that. The Committee for the Liberation of the Hebrew Nation estimated that a part of the population would accept this option, and another part would be ready to stay in the country as resident aliens. I do not know what was the likelihood of the Committee's solution to succeed, but it was a practical solution and a humane one, the first ever proposed to meet the burning problem of the political nature of Israel — a problem that still ought to be put on the national agenda. Hillel Kook's plan was updated to fit new conditions, since in the meantime new facts had been created: Israel was founded as an independent state and the Palestinian nation has begun to crystallize. There is, therefore, a need for a master plan that recognizes these facts. In this book such a plan will be presented as a solution in which mandatory Palestine — that is to say, Palestine on both banks of the river Jordan — will be divided between the two nations, the Israeli and the Palestinian, since the Jordanian nation does not exist, but the territory of Jordan is settled by a kernel of a nation, the Palestinian nation. An Israeli initiative seems possible towards peace between the two nations and their states on the basis of the solution of the resultant boundary conflict between them.

This is not to claim that this is the best possible solution, but only that it is a proposal of a master plan based on the principle of unilateral political initiative, taken in consideration of different possible responses of the other sides in the contest.

A similar plan will be proposed concerning the relations between Israel and the Jews of other nations. Israel requires that they settle here. Hillel Kook proposes a plan for improving the deteriorating relations between Israel and the Jews of other nations: the declaration of the separation between faith and nationality, which would be a recognition of the right of the Jews of other nations to remain in their countries or to migrate to Israel, as they wish. This would serve as a means for developing honest, normal relations between Israel and Jews of other nations.

Israel faces severe fundamental problems, the source of which is an impossible situation: the deterioration of the inner moral and outer political situation, the absurd legal and political status of the national minority within, the permanent state of war, and the tense relations between Israel and Jews of other nations and between it and Western nations. A possible solution to these problems is present in Hillel Kook's master plan, the principle of which is the idea of normalization and the need in Israel for the separation of faith and nationality. This separation is no solution to Israel's problems, but it makes a solution possible. And in the present conditions, in a desperate situation in which even the very possibility of a solution seems a distant dream, this is no minor detail.

The Constituent Assembly was elected in 1949 to establish a constitution, or at least discuss the basic problems of the nation, and to direct the transition period from an abnormal Jewish existence to a normal, democratic national existence in its country. This Assembly violated its mandate and became the first Israeli Parliament, the first Knesset. Hillel Kook, a member of the Constituent Assembly, claims that the time has come for an attempt to make a sharp turn and return to May 15, 1948, and remedy the defect established at that time: as a substitute for the establishment of the state of the Jews, a new Israeli republic should be founded, on the proclamation of the Israeli nation as the political heir of all the political aspirations of the Jewish people, the one to reap the fruits of the national war of liberation. And instead of recognizing the scattered Jewish people as the sovereign people of the state, the years that have passed since 1948 should be considered a transitional period, with the declared intent of having Israel transform rapidly into a normal nation-state. Perhaps there was no escape from an attempt to found Israel as a state without a nation, and that only now, after the failure of this attempt, the time has come to try the idea of the normalization of Israel. For if we shall wait for a complete failure, it will be no longer possible to adapt and seek another solution.

This is my appeal to the reader. Whether you agree with me or not, please start with a public debate concerning the master plan presented before you.

— Herzlia, Passover, 1981.

P. S. This book went to press two years after it was completed, except for minor corrections, some deletions, and the addition of footnotes. In these two years our national condition has greatly deteriorated, partly due to the war in Lebanon and its tragic complications, including the report of the national commission of inquiry concerning the massacre in the refugee camps. The national crisis has sharpened but its cause remains unchanged. Therefore, this book seems to me to be more topical today than when it was written, since the causes for the deterioration are rooted in the abnormal state of Israel, a country which allows for a constant state of war and for the regular use of force as the means for solving political problems.

This state is inhuman and impractical. Therefore, the need for normalization seems to me ever more urgent today than when this book was written.

— Herzlia, February, 1983.

Acknowledgments

My gratitude to the many friends, colleagues and acquaintances, who read this book in manuscript in its various stages and who made various comments which I found very useful even when they were very critical or hostile.

As a book which includes results of some research, it should include their names but as this is a political book it is better to name no names, since not all of them will be happy to see their names here and since I do not wish to rely on the authority of important people. So I will not mention them and plead for their understanding.

Preface to the Second Edition

The publication of a second edition of this book suggests that there is an increase in the public interest in the discussion it presents — in the problem of the Israeli national identity. Possibly this increase may invite an exception to the pessimistic tone on which this book ends. But, in part at least, this increase in the interest in the ideas expressed here is rooted in the increase in the public awareness of the deterioration of the military-political condition of this country, since the deterioration is so rapid, that it is daily increasingly more difficult to overlook the bewilderment and confusion in which the Israeli public is immersed. The urgent question is, whether there is sufficient time for action against this confusion, or perhaps, when we will finally be free of it, time will have run out? I do not know, and I stress yet again that the chief aim in having this book published is to point at the danger of the abnormalcy of Israel and at the bigger danger of the general oversight of the despair that is broadening and deepening among the Israeli public, since the despair is rooted in the absence of political initiative in Israel, which is the absence of all initiative, and this absence is explained in this book as rooted in Israel's abnormalcy. It is therefore my aim to repeat and suggest most emphatically that a broad public debate be urgently initiated in Israel concerning the question of national identity: is normalization possible? and is it desirable? All of the proposals to be found in this book come solely to illustrate the possibility of detailing the proposal for normalization into concrete proposals, but each proposal and solution is open to revision and replacement. The only irreplaceable detail in this book is its basic claim that Israel and its citizens should not overlook one burning problem:

that the urgent need in Israel today is to open as soon as possible a comprehensive public debate on the national problem there.

Public and private discussions about this book (as well as about its follow-up, *Who is an Israeli?*, which I published together with Judith Bubber Agassi and Moshe Berent in Hebrew in 1990) give the impression that interest in the national question is increasing among Israeli youths. Even that the proposal that Israel should recognize the Israeli nation excites them, precisely because it defies the remnants of the Israeli consensus that was defective from the very start. I do hope that this excitement is characteristic and serious, and I found this corroborated by the fact that, together with the increase of the interest in normalization and the desire for it, an awareness is increasing that normalization is no wonder-drug, but an outline of an idea towards a detailed master-plan that should be developed in stages — both because there are difficult problems on the way to normalization that have to be met, problems that intensify with each postponement of its realization, and because it still meets with legitimate hesitation, especially concerning the question, how will the recognition and strengthening of the unity of the Israeli nation influence the unity of the Jewish people? (That is to say, is there a conflict or a complementation between the unity of the Israeli nation and that of the Jewish people?) This hesitation is a healthy challenge for those who wish to have a serious public debate. Naturally, it should also be recognized that the same hesitation is likewise a challenge for those who prefer the current abnormalcy of Israel, because they lack the fortitude required for recovery from the New Zionist Myth, which finds an excuse for Israel's abnormalcy in the very existence of Jewish communities in other countries. That this myth encourages inaction is clear to all, as Israel cannot possibly abolish these communities, nor is this in Israel's national interest. But the excuse and the moral weakness have a whiff of justification in the possibility to misuse the proposal made here as support for the proposal to disown the Jewish character of Israel. There is a very small number of Israelis who prefer to substitute Israel's abnormalcy with another, the abnormalcy of a nation disowning the local religion, of disowning the Jewish character of Israel. I am glad to observe that confidence in this justification is decreasing, and the advocates of normalization are well aware of the Jewish character of Israel (02). The religious parties in Israel are regularly blamed for Israel's abnormalcy. There is some encouragement in the growth of awareness in Israel of the fact that this accusation is baseless. And with the decline of the popularity of the baseless accusation of one or another political party, frank complaint is on the increase against the damage that Israel's abnormalcy brings. For this abnormalcy disgraces also the Jewish community — which is the fault of all of Israel's political parties. It is the fault of the Israeli political system as a whole, including the national leadership, and it is based on the refusal to accept responsibility for the current state of affairs and to put the national problem on the public agenda.

There is an increase in the recognition of the import of the demand to reform the Israeli Law of Return, both in order to prevent harm to those who have no intent to use it, and in order to have some guarantee for its continued implementation, in order that this implementation will not depend on the goodwill of bureaucrats and on the popularity of a myth devoid of political significance. An effort was made to hide these facts. The rise of interest in the normalization of Israel and in Israeli national identity need not constitute a fall in the interest in the Jewish people and in the Jewish character of Israel, and in its Law of Return; this fact is gaining recognition here, however minute. This is encouraging, since my aim is not to convince my reader of the justice of any accusation, but to contribute to the placing on the national agenda, as an urgent, central item for public debate, the discussion of the possibility of the separation of the (political) Israeli national identity and the (apolitical) Jewish religious-ethnic-cultural identity in a manner beneficial to all.

To conclude: the aim of the presentation in this book is to bring to public discussion the national problem, so as to enable Israel to show political initiative concerning its future, since its governments do not show political initiative because of their inability, which is imposed on them by their very attitude to the national problem. For in their opinion, Israel will be a normal nation-state only when the Jewish communities outside Israel will practically cease to exist. This opinion prevents Israel from any normal activity until the completion of this process, over which it obviously has no control.

This second edition includes all the material from the first edition with many corrections, some of them of minor errors and most of them corrections of poor expressions and of misprints, in addition to a few explanatory sentences. I have added a few details of updating, especially in the reference to the literature that appeared after the publication of the first edition. Each addition is placed between asterisks. I have also expanded slightly the passages cited out of Peter Bergson's letter to Dr Chaim Weizmann (Chapter 17). I recommend to the interested reader to be dissatisfied with this chapter and read the original (03).

Prologue: Hillel Kook

The purpose of this book is to present a political platform that rests on the ideas of Hillel Kook. The platform in this book includes far-reaching proposals concerning the national political structure and the social structure of Israel, and as to the relations between Israel and its neighbors, its members who are not Jews, and with Jews who are not its members. As background material, Part One includes theoretical chapters — philosophical, political and historical — and Part Two includes biographical material about Hillel Kook, a description of his activities in the United States of America during World War II. The plan itself appears in Part Three.

The philosophical aspect of the platform requires a much broader discussion. It is hoped that readers interested in this aspect will discuss, at length, the philosophical innovations which are discussed in this book much too cursorily. This book does not address philosophers, and its discussion of philosophical aspects will be limited to one and only one purpose: to explain to the reader Hillel Kook's revolutionary innovations, in the hope that the reader will thereby understand the difficulty that traditional thinkers have to understand and master them. In this way, readers can also decide what in this book is contrary to their opinions, as well as what the significance is of accepting or rejecting the opinions and proposals presented here.

The same holds for the historical aspect of this book. A vast literature has been written about the history of the Jewish people in modern times and on the history of the modern political ideologies that have played significant roles in the turbulent events experienced by the Jewish people. Many political and cultural historians have studied these ideologies. Yet I presume that historians who would read the following chapters — whether they agree or disagree with Hillel Kook's ideas — will become more aware of the problems that theoreticians have passed over in silence, and the problems about which historians have written only incidentally while clinging excessively to marginal historical details for want of a broad theoretical background. Historians are cognizant of the fact that peoples, nations, and national groups, evolve through historical processes in which their national awareness plays an important role. Political philosophers do not discuss the theory of such processes, because these have no place for them in traditional political and social philosophical theories. My hope is that the historians who read this book, whether they agree with its content or not, will come to change their historical outlooks concerning the formation of nations and view the processes with a critical eye and deal with them with a comprehensive, theoretical grasp.

This book makes no pretense at providing a history. Many books will be written concerning the history of national movements in general and of the Jewish national movement in particular, as well as on the period after World War II, in which nations were created intentionally by the international community. The purpose of this book is different: to provide a new socio-political master plan for the Israeli nation, and thus even for the Jewish people as a whole. The historical material here is meant to serve only as background material for the presentation of this plan.

Just as philosophical and historical matters will be presented only intermittently and merely to the extent that they are needed for the sake of a clear presentation, so too biographical details on Hillel Kook will be presented only to the extent that they will help explain his ideas. It is surprising that Hillel Kook is almost not recognized in Israel. In the United States, during World War II, he was recognized by his alias, Peter Bergson (04). During that time he was the head of a small group that started out as the delegation of the Irgun Zvai Leumi — the National Military Organization — and became an independent body and a significant political factor in public life.

This body became known by the name "the Bergson Boys" and "the Bergson Group." They organized the Emergency Committee for the Rescue of the Jewish People in Europe and the Committee for the Liberation of the Hebrew Nation. Kook-Bergson entered public life in America as a mere emissary from Palestine, yet he won notoriety while there. His public activities excited the American public, but the Jewish establishment there fought him ferociously. The first Zionist Congress after the war, assembled in 1946, took the trouble to denounce the Committee for the National Liberation (of the Hebrew nation), accusing it of splitting the nation (the Jewish nation). It is odd to discover Americans who remember him (their number is decreasing, of course), and who become excited to this very day when they hear the name Peter Bergson, while in Israel his name is almost entirely forgotten. Similarly, the public bodies that he founded and directed are forgotten. I admit I had never heard of them myself until a very short time ago. How did this happen? Why was it consigned to oblivion that there was a delegation of the Irgun Military Organization to the United States? Why are the Bergson Group's diverse committees, which had caused much excitement, so completely forgotten? Why, with all the history about Israel that we have been fed in the last few years, is this affair almost entirely skipped? How did it happen that a citizen like myself did not bump into this significant historical phenomenon until I met Hillel Kook personally? Clearly, these matters have been forgotten intentionally (1).

I first met Hillel Kook in the mid-seventies at a meeting of the council of the Movement for Citizens' Rights (in which I was active for a few years). Hillel Kook, together with his old friend Shmuel Merlin, presented their political plan to that council. I have a very sad memory of that meeting, perhaps because of the sympathetic impression that Hillel Kook the individual left on me, but more particularly because, though I was a party to his liberal approach, I was not very impressed by his political program. It took a long time before I met him again. I began to study his ideas while seeking a practical political plan, and I came to the conclusion that his plan is of great importance on diverse levels, from the practical political to the philosophical.

It was very strange. I am a philosopher. I have published a few works in social and political philosophy, and I found very few teachers who could instruct me in my work. And here appears Hillel Kook, the amateur, and teaches me a lesson in political philosophy — an important lesson at that — one whose significance far surpasses the horizon of Israel's current problems.

Hillel Kook had conceived an idea that might arouse wide and broad public interest and perhaps bring the political leaders of Israel to wise political action. Where did such a strange fellow come from?

If Hillel Kook had a past public involvement that might gain him a place in Israeli public awareness, it would have to be the tragic affair of the weapons boat Altalena. The details of the Altalena affair are not sufficiently clear to the common Israeli citizen. The details of the story were intentionally confused by official historians of the Irgun Military Organization and the Israeli Defense Force as well as by biographers of David Ben-Gurion, the first Israeli Premier and the Minister of Defense during that period and of Menachem Begin, the head of the Irgun. Therefore, this story cannot be used to introduce Hillel Kook without a detailed study, which will not be discussed here (nevertheless, see below, beginning and end of Part Two).

Another public event, less well known, may serve our present purpose. Kook was a member of the Israeli Constituent Assembly, which was dismantled the day it first assembled, when it declared itself the first Israeli Parliament, the first Knesset. With one exception, all the members of that Assembly did not react, or reacted positively, to being turned into the delegates of the first parliament of the State of Israel. That exception was Hillel Kook, who reacted from the floor, "This is a putsch!" (namely, a court rebellion). To understand his outcry, a few explanatory words are required concerning the difference between a constituent assembly and a parliament. I should merely observe the fact that a constituent assembly was established, elected, and convened for a single purpose — to author a constitution for the State of Israel. The delegates of the Constituent Assembly, including Hillel Kook, knew that they had been elected and appointed in order to author a constitution. This is why Kook responded so sharply to the reversal and distortion of the purpose of the elections. To this day this distortion remains without correction. There is still a need to gather the Constituent Assembly in order to establish Israel properly, while overcoming the difficulties that at the time caused that putsch (the intentional disregard on the part of the members of the first Knesset of the fundamental problems of the Israeli nation).

Till such time, Kook's membership in the Constituent Assembly will be of no value.

An earlier public involvement of Kook, and the most important one from the viewpoint of this book, is his leadership of the Committee for the Liberation of the Hebrew Nation in the years preceding independence. What was this Committee?

To repeat, until I met Hillel Kook, I did not even know of the very existence of this Committee. Was it perhaps a merely marginal phenomenon? I do not know. Yet the fact is that four former members of the Committee were members of Israel's Constituent Assembly (in a party of fourteen out of one-hundred-and-twenty members). How come? The Committee and its activity will be described in Part Two of this book; let me say here very briefly that it was organized as a representative national body for the Hebrew Nation, calling for the immediate establishment of a transitory Hebrew government in exile. Before that, the same delegation organized an Emergency Committee for the Rescue of European Jews, which met with the sharp hostility of the American Jewish leadership, Zionist and non-Zionist alike. (This is a tragedy that invites special research.) But the broad public did not know this, since the official Jewish and Zionist organizations silenced every detail related to the mass murder of the Jews and among the committees that Hillel Kook established there were those that undertook to make the tragic situation publicly known so as to awaken it to put pressure on their leaders to act for the saving of the Jews of Europe. At that time, the Irgun National Military Organization overlooked the activities of these committees. I myself, a rank Palestinian adolescent, considered the Irgun National Military Organization the military arm of the Revisionist Zionist political movement, founded by Vladimir Jabotinsky, and I considered it a chauvinist, romantic, and anti-rational movement — as I still do. The little I read of the writings of Jabotinsky confirmed my conclusions. Today I see things slightly differently. I see a fundamental difference between mystic chauvinist philosophy and a nationalist liberal one. The fact is, Hillel Kook himself, the diverse committees founded by the delegation he headed, and his political plan, then as now, all share a liberal nationalist character. This fact is the major reason for the silencing of the events I wish to note in this book. All this is due to the Israeli pretense that one cannot present a practical plan based on a philosophy that is nationalist yet liberal and thus also rational. This pretense, that liberal nationalism is impossible, seems to me today the root of the severity of Israel's condition, as it encourages hostility to methodic thinking.

In my meetings with Hillel Kook during the seventies, I was profoundly surprised, as rarely before, and at least on three levels: he taught me political philosophy, a political plan, and an historical chapter that had been consigned to oblivion, in which he was one of the main characters, of events that took place in the United States during World War II and up to the day when Israel gained independence. I was surprised to find a person so enlightened and so liberal, so free of all militarism and contempt for the masses, considering that his origin was precisely in those circles that, to the best of my knowledge, did not and still do not excel on this score. How did this happen? I do not know.

My conversations with Hillel Kook between the years 1976-1979 showed me, despite many differences in opinion, some of which are still sharp, how much we share in our attitudes towards our national predicament, and in our desire to see Israel as a normal, enlightened society. I hope that I have succeeded in learning from him many important details, and for this opportunity he has my gratitude. Ever since I met him, Hillel Kook speaks only about the severe national crisis in which Israel is immersed and laments the fact that the country that pretended to offer a solution to the Jewish problem has become an added Jewish problem, if not the most severe one. On this I agreed with him, since like him I assumed that there is no solution to Israel's problems within Israel's current national consensus and that this is the cause of the frustration that is spreading here and of the despair that captures many (whether they leave or stay).

I do not know whether Hillel Kook has a practical solution to Israel's problems. But I did see at once (before I agreed with him on many issues) that his opinions transcend the current Israeli national consensus. In addition, I learned of his plan for an Israeli unilateral political initiative, something which I crave since the very day on which independence was declared. We agree thus not so much in opinions, as in the claim that Israel badly needs a comprehensive national debate concerning basics. Only this way can we develop a plan for a national political initiative, to pitch us out of the current ever-worsening crisis.

* Is there still today any likelihood that the basics of the original program of Hillel Kook be executed? As long as the world does not have a reasonable alternative to the structure of the nation-state in the pattern of Western liberal democracy, this question is the same as the following one: Will Israel reach the level of development common in the West? The (erroneously) received opinion in the West is that Israel has already reached the stage of the normal liberal democratic nation-state. This error causes many disappointments and, at the very least, the erroneous impression should be corrected and not reinforced, as is done by all of Israel's representatives in western countries, be they delegates who represent the nation or the state, or those who represent bodies which justify their very existence with the aid of the New Zionist Myth, and especially bodies that perpetuate the existence of the Zionist movement, that was the Israeli national liberation movement. This way they deny the very independence of Israel and thereby endanger its very existence. Had Israel openly admitted it not being normal, then there possibly could be some likelihood that this situation be put on the agenda for public debate at home and abroad. Such a public debate would, of course, be a debate on the question placed in the opening of this paragraph: is there still any likelihood that the basics of Hillel Kook's program be implemented?

* Another question is thus asked here: why is there no recognition of the fact that Hillel Kook has proposed to try and establish Israel as a nation-state in the pattern current in the West? The public should force Israel to recognize officially this political thinker. Since his activities were officially denounced in the last Zionist Congress prior to independence (see below, end of Chapter 18), it is incumbent on every organization that had denounced them to rescind this denunciation. Since the denunciation was official, its removal has to be official as well. This will remove a stigma and offer the public the opportunity to rethink both the sad affair of a damaging attitude towards one of the contributors to Israeli thought, and in the option he has raised, regardless of whether it is still manageable or not — as it stands or with this or that alteration — or whether it invites a reasonable substitute. The present scandal is the total oversight in Israeli politics of root problems and this must be rectified, regardless of the

different views extant concerning the answers to them: they are burning problems and they urgently invite deliberation. **An official quick rehabilitation of Hillel Kook will greatly facilitate the placing of root problems on the national agenda, and so this rehabilitation should be demanded forcefully and in different ways and on different platforms, political, academic and communal.** *

Introduction:
On Political Normalization

The idea presented for consideration in this book is revolutionary in its very simplicity: Israel should be reconstructed as a normal republic along the pattern recognized in the western world, a republic in which nationality and citizenship are identical, on the one hand, while nationality and faith are separate, on the other. This proposal raises a few difficulties, both general and Israeli. Generally, this proposal is known in the western liberal world as the separation of church and state. This term is translated into Hebrew to read, "the separation between state and religion". The expression is awkward because state and religion are not comparable. One can compare politics and religion or political and religious institutions. Indeed, in western languages one speaks of the separation between church and state. Yet it is not customary to refer to the institution of Jewish religion as a church. The term must, therefore, be translated into Hebrew as "the separation of state and rabbinate". It is merely a theoretical question, whether it is possible and/or desirable to distinguish between politics and religion and separate between them? It seems easy and desirable to distinguish between politics and religion in the sense of understanding the difference between them. It is not at all clear, however, whether it is possible to separate them in the sense of blocking the possibility of mutual influences, or whether it is desirable to keep them too much apart. Religious thinkers have something to say about politics and political thinkers have something to say about religion, and why should they not say what they have to say?

But, of course, it is accepted in the modern democratic world that the institutional authority of the state, which is a political institution, and the institutional authority of any religion or religious community (whether church, rabbinate, or any other), should be kept separate.

Nor is the separation itself a sacred principle; its aim is merely to prevent a conflict between democracy and religion for all concerned parties, those that support this or that religion and those who do not, those which are in power and those which are in the opposition.

* When I wrote the previous paragraph it did not occur to me that the proposal to separate religion and politics will ever be entertained as an option of a platform for some political party: I took it for granted that the reader will notice easily the absurdity that it is. To my surprise I was refuted in 1990: in a debate at a convention of the Israeli Labor Party concerning "the separation between state and religion", which was an accepted slogan in that party for ages, the proposal was made to take this slogan seriously and seek ways to implement it. This proposal was rejected, and the slogan to replace the rejected one was, "the separation between politics and religion". The absurdity of this slogan did not trouble those who were proposing it, as they were seeking a merely empty slogan, one that has no practical implications, since it is clear that its application would require of every religious person to relinquish politics. The debate concerning the separation must be purposeful: the separation should prevent conflicts, especially existential conflicts, namely such that otherwise they do not avail themselves of compromise solutions. *

It is no accident that the expression "separation between state and religion" is awkward. Admittedly, the expression in the European languages is more precise, since it refers not to religion and the state but to religious institutions and the state. That is to say, the separation is in essence institutional and concerns the institutions of government and the institutions and organizations of religious communities. The structure of the western state is that of the nation-state, both the state institutions and the political and social systems are ruled and organized by the state organizations. But there is little literature in the western countries about the difference between the state and the nation-state.

For all discussion concerning the nation sounds like Chauvinism, because the competitor to liberal nationalism, the romantic chauvinist movement (as I will explain at the beginning of Part One of this book), is vociferous and unpleasant. Because the national problem is so central and confused in Israel today, it is impossible to speak about the separation between the state and the religious institutions, which is a formal political distinction (organizational separation), without first discussing clearly the content of the political separation (the separation between existing bodies): the Israeli nation, which acquired its political liberty and its political expression in its state (Israel), and the Jewish faith, which is the prevalent faith in that nation, but which is shared by people who belong to other nations. The conceptual distinction between two groups (for example, a religious congregation and a nation) is always done by pointing at members of the one who do not belong to the other (in the present case, Israelis who are not Jewish and, vice versa, Jews who are not Israeli).

Therefore, to explain the proposed normalization (separation of nation and religion), it is of vital importance to present the fundamental ideas of Western democratic, liberal nation-state in a clearer and more precise manner than the way in which this is done in western countries and in the western literature concerning politics and nationality in general (since there the distinction between faith and nationality is traditional and self-evident). I will not enlarge on the political discussion concerning this clarification any more than is required for the reader of this book. The reader who is concerned with the foundation of this clarification and its roots in general, liberal, social philosophy is invited to consult my philosophical book that deals with the same issue (2). (To my regret, though that book clearly exhibits political concern, it does not include an extensive discussion of practical political questions, because it was written before I met Hillel Kook.)

In order to explain the idea of the nation-state in this book, I found it necessary to explain the political-philosophical ideas on which western political discussion is based, and to present the weakness of these ideas and outline democratic liberal nationalism in a manner acceptable to both scholar and politician, in western countries and in Israel. And, indeed, I have been pleased to observe that a few scholars, philosophers and political scientists, have found much of interest in the material to be found at the opening of this book. A clear presentation of the ideas which served as the foundation of political philosophy and liberal nationalism, theoretically and practically, enables one to see the history of Zionism in a new light and to understand the theoretical and historical basis for the abnormalcy experienced by the Jewish people today. Even some of those who reject this book's proposal — to abolish this Israeli abnormalcy and thus turn Israel into a liberal nation-state in the western style — have agreed that my presentation has shed new light on the history of Zionism.

The first part of this book, which deals with the foundation of political philosophical theory in the west and the history of Zionism, is presented here with one specific aim: to overcome one difficulty that proved to be an obstacle on Kook's road when he tried to explain in Israel the principles of his theory. His audience considered his ideas the way they consider the diverse platforms and plans that appear in Israel — as just another alternative well within the existing Israeli consensus. Yet, in order to understand his ideas, one has to see that they are in quite another perspective.

This difficulty is not specific to Kook's opinions or even to political thinking in general. It is a more general difficulty, and a number of theoreticians of thinking have observed it both in philosophy and in psychology: ideas usually expressed in one framework sound different in another, and this causes a distortion of their content, because the context or framework within which they used to be said has been changed. This is well known to anyone who takes part in public debates. Quite often one party participating in a debate claims that another party has quoted them improperly, even if the quote is verbatim and quite precise, because the quotation is taken out of the context in which it was originally said. Therefore, it seemed vital to me when writing this book, to present a politico-theoretical, philosophical framework and a Jewish historical framework — not in sufficient detail to stand by themselves, but with the least detail required to prevent the possibility of interpreting Kook's ideas as merely an additional alternative within the present Israeli national consensus. My proposal is that the new framework should be accepted as the framework within which to create a new national consensus. The purpose is the presentation of a nationalist intellectual framework, free of the slightest hint of Chauvinism, one in which there will be no need to explain repeatedly that there is a difference between the nationalist and the chauvinist, and between the liberal open-minded nationalist attitude and the xenophobic, narrow-minded one.

Responsibility for the first part of the book is mine and not Kook's. I am grateful that he has provoked me to present these ideas, which he created and developed, in a philosophical framework congenial to me, and that he has helped me present the history of Zionism accordingly. Of course, Kook's ideas developed in a different way, under the pressure of events that, as a participant in political activity, he could not overlook.

These events are presented in Part Two of this book, and for the same purpose. I am not Kook's biographer. Since I have already published a book that comes close to being biographical (3), I am aware of the enormity of the effort that has to be invested in biographical writing. It would only be proper that a suitable person should invest energy and thought about the topic and write a suitable biography that would suit its subject. I hope that such an author will be found in the near future. My purposes are different and here only a historical presentation of the development of Kook's ideas is included, since such a presentation may help change one's intellectual framework — as is well known among those who study the question, how do intellectual frameworks change? In other words, the first part of this book is a theoretical examination of the difference between old and new frameworks, and the application of this to the study of the history of the Zionist movement. The second part presents the development of Kook's ideas and their clash with the Zionist consensus. This presentation is not complete or satisfactory, except for our single purpose of offering a suitable background, the presentation of a new framework, for Part Three of this book.

Part Three of this book presents in some detail the plan for the normalization of Israel. The proposal has many layers: there is an essential, theoretical part, and there is a practical part that depends on time and place and which, with any significant change in the political situation, will become obsolete, and this would create a need to seek an alternative to the obsolete part. This is not to say that such changes are desirable. On the contrary, it seems to me that the deterioration of the political situation in Israel is clear today to an ever-increasing portion of the Israeli public, which shows increasingly that there is no alternative within the existing national consensus. Since common Israelis justifiably refuse to abandon the nationalist framework, and since they are not researchers who can seek nationalist alternatives beyond the national consensus, they naturally feel frustrated and desperate. But, of course, a nationalist solution that transcends the existing national consensus is possible, and the solution presented here does indeed transcend it. The solution is both nationalist and liberal.

Therefore, if the proposal will be adopted, it could become the new national consensus that would put the nation on the road to a solution for Israel's basic problems, which are increasingly becoming a heavy burden for its citizens.

I originally wrote a Part Four to this book that aimed to illustrate the fact that the proposal to normalize Israel (namely, render Israel a liberal nation-state on the western model) opens a broad field of activity for every reader who finds this proposal sufficiently interesting and promising to attempt to implement it and to analyze the results of the attempt. But I decided that it was too early to publish it, since the present book calls for one and only one activity: the opening of a public debate on the national problem. Instead, then, Part Four of this book presents some conclusions. This book proposes the agenda for the debate and the critical discussion of the thesis that is central to Israel's national consensus today: that the Israeli people are of necessity abnormal. This is the received opinion, the opinion that the Israeli individual, as well as the State of Israel, of necessity belongs to the Jewish people and that there is no freedom of choice in this matter, since it is the duty of all members of the Jewish people to settle in Israel, whereas the duty of those already settled there is, first and foremost, to maintain the possibility that non-Israeli Jews will migrate to Israel one day. I will venture to show that this thesis is false and that it precludes any reasonable solution to Israel's increasingly pressing national problems.

PART ONE

*Foundations:
The Israeli Nation
and Its Judaism*

This part is a discussion of the national problem and its implication for the Jewish problem. There is a difficulty involved in this discussion; it is rooted in the following fact. Historically, the national problem was raised among European Jewry in the manner in which it was found among the European nations, where it was raised in a distorted fashion. The distortion begins with the refusal of liberal political thinkers to recognize nationality as a political fact. This was shared by all the liberal thinkers who studied political theory from the early modern age until the French Revolution of about two centuries ago, and by many liberal political thinkers since then, to this very day. They were not uninformed, as the existence of nations and nation-states is general knowledge, but they were not happy with this fact, since they refused to recognize discrimination. In their battle against discrimination, especially religious discrimination, they also tried to fight national discrimination. Therefore, in their discussions about political theory they ignored both religion and nationality (as well as race and aristocratic origin or the lack of it; perhaps they also tried to overcome discrimination against women, I do not know).

Their chief question was this: by what right does one person rule another? What duties do the ruled have towards the ruler? And what duties does the ruler have towards the ruled? There is no need to consider answers to these questions in order to see at once that they are based on a special approach, a specific philosophical approach — one that we have inherited from the philosophy of the Enlightenment Movement. This approach was common among the educated public in Western Europe already three centuries ago, and came to be accepted gradually also in Eastern Europe, including the large Jewish communities in Poland and Russia.

This distortion of political theory (the disregard for the very existence of nations) led quickly to a distortion in the opposite direction. When Enlightenment political theory was defeated with the failure of the French Revolution (whose leaders spoke in the name of Enlightenment), it gave way to a reaction (that is to say, the reaction to the Enlightenment, the Reaction for short). This movement, also known as the Romantic Movement, saw itself as a nationalist movement but was Chauvinist in that it emphasized the significance of the nation as a whole and undervalued the worth of the individual. In part it sought freedom — not individual freedom but national freedom; it was thus anti-liberal, at least in part. Consequently, a distinction has to be made between liberal nationalism, which maintained some Enlightenment tenets, and illiberal nationalism or Chauvinism — where Chauvinism is by definition anti-liberal and thus opposed to the ideals of the Enlightenment Movement. Regrettably, confusion reigns between these two nationalist movements, the liberal and the illiberal, since both the Enlightenment Movement and the Romantic Movement had broad philosophical foundations and broad foundations in political philosophy, but not liberal nationalism. This fact calls for a correction that should prevent the continuation of the confusion between liberal and illiberal nationalism, or between liberal nationalism and Chauvinism. Foundations for the liberal nationalist movement are required, so that it may stand clearly between the non-nationalist liberal movement (the Enlightenment Movement), and the illiberal nationalist movement (Romanticism, Chauvinism).

In order to present the principles of the liberal nationalist philosophy, it might be useful to say that its philosophical foundation is to be found in the principle of self-determination both of the nation and of the individual with respect to the nation. This principle I have learned from Hillel Kook. This principle has a broad philosophical grounding in liberal philosophy, which is the continuation of the idea of Enlightenment with an addition that makes an important difference: the recognition of the existence of societies, national and other. This recognition is a modern addition and correction to the traditional liberal idea. It is an extremely important amendment, as it will help us understand the confusion in Israel regarding nationality. In the last century and a half the Jewish tradition fairly justifiably mixed Enlightenment and Romantic ideas — justifiably so because these two movements have complemented each other. Yet the mixing was not systematic and permitted confusion between anti-liberal Chauvinism and liberal nationalism. Consequently, in Israel the fear of Chauvinism grew and led to the underrating of nationalism. The baby was thrown out with the bath water — the principle of nationalism with the anti-liberal principle of Chauvinism. Thus the state was underrated too, since the modern state is a nation-state. And then the situation was reversed: the value of the state was emphasized while the nation was overlooked. And when the state was considered a supreme value, Chauvinism erupted forcefully in the Israeli political arena. In what follows, this process will be clarified. Here one might simply notice a tragicomic fact. Israel's labor movement, the movement that was socialist, and so it follows the principles of the Enlightenment Movement, including the underrating of nationality, unwittingly fell prey to the Romantic Chauvinist movement. It did so while emphasizing the uniqueness of Judaism as a faith-nation. The movement was not deterred by its irreligious, at times even anti-religious, ideology. All this resulted from the absence of a clear idea about nationality.

Chapter 1: Concerning Public Responsibility

The purpose of this chapter is both theoretical and practical. It presents the central idea of all social sciences — the idea of the one-sided initiative — which regrettably is neglected even by social scientists themselves.

The social sciences generally vacillate all too often between discussions of everyday concrete matters imbued with commonsense and abstract discussions that are theoretical, odd, and distant from the everyday. Consequently the function of science is undermined, since its function is to build a bridge between the abstract and the empirical, between the earthly and the ethereal, between the theoretical and the everyday. This is not to say that the social sciences do not include such bridges. A particularly deep and significant innovation exists in political theory, and it is the principle of representative democracy, including the idea of a legislature whose function is to update and rectify the laws of the state. These two ideas grew in the political daily life of the western world and evolved on the basis of a very rich intellectual background. (They will not be discussed here.)

Efforts to overlook the wealth of details in order to gain a more general picture, a bird's-eye view, render the picture increasingly philosophical. The more limited and erroneous the philosophical principle that guides observers, the more limited and erroneous the observers' grasp of the few details that appear in their field of vision, since the facts are integrated within a mistaken system.

In addition, very often the guiding idea does not permit the existence of certain everyday facts, which common sense upholds. In such cases, observers tend mistakenly to add these facts to their picture of the world. Consequently, the picture becomes logically inconsistent, and then it must be rectified. For, an inconsistent opinion lends itself to the effortless deduction of whatever conclusion one wishes, and such exercises have no value whatsoever, since one might deduce a conclusion that one finds desirable, and another will deduce the opposite conclusion. In such a case, the guiding idea will not direct the choice between the two conclusions and therefore it will be utterly worthless, both theoretically and practically.

The fact that a guiding idea may mislead, and even systematically so, led the architects of the scientific revolution of about four hundred years ago to the view that one should not accept any guiding idea unless it is proven. The conclusion from this might be that every debate about any idea whatsoever is a preliminary debate, since after an idea has been proven, there is no appeal concerning it, except from quarters hostile to science. This was the guiding idea of the Enlightenment Movement.

Concerning the Enlightenment Movement, only two significant items will be presented here: first, it was individualist; second, it is untenable, at least in practical political matters where constant disagreement is inescapable. The following expands a little on these two items and then offers a discussion of the philosophical movement that succeeded the Enlightenment Movement.

The Enlightenment Movement was individualist because it saw every tradition as a collection of errors and confusions, a collection of mere hypotheses and unfounded beliefs. Its followers saw the existence of different traditions as the source of dissension and of war. They saw in science the unanimity that prevents dissension and war, a rational way for human beings to seek their place in their world. According to the teaching of the Enlightenment Movement, since ideas and proofs are matters of the intellect, and since the intellect is individual property and the most important thing that human beings possess, the human individual stands at the center of our world. Therefore, individuals, the subject-matter of the Enlightenment Movement's teaching, are presumed to be brave enough to extricate themselves from the limitations of their traditions, to think independently, and to decide for themselves what their opinions should be and accept their own responsibility concerning them. And, indeed, the morality of the Enlightenment Movement is rooted in individualistic ethics and therefore, as we shall soon see, the social and political theory of the Enlightenment Movement is individualistic as well. That is to say, the Enlightenment Movement finds it necessary to explain how individuals ever find themselves in societies and belonging to nations.

It turns out, then, that individuals are responsible each to themselves and to other individuals. And when members of the Enlightenment Movement recognize public responsibility, they recognize it only because they see the public as a collection of individuals. Naturally, the Enlightenment Movement valued the intellect both as the most important of the factors which bring individuals to create and maintain a society and a state, and as what creates science when put to proper use. The sound society, then, is one guided by the light of science and hence it is an ideal society. A long time passed before it became clear that the ideal society, especially when founded on science, is not the democratic society of the familiar liberal parliamentary sort. A few decades ago, *The Origins of Totalitarian Democracy* by Jacob Talmon appeared and caused a sensation in the learned world, because it explained just this fact and gave it historical foundations (4).

Since the teaching of the Enlightenment Movement presents proper society as grounded on science and science as grounded in the individual intellect, it is clear to it that individual responsibility should suffice. Therefore, according to the teaching of the Enlightenment Movement, there is no room for public responsibility proper. When the philosophy of the Enlightenment Movement brought about the French Revolution of about two centuries ago, and this Revolution failed to bring about a sound society, a reaction to the Enlightenment Movement emerged, known as the Reaction Movement. The Reaction Movement was Romantic and its starting point was the reverse: generally, individuals can hardly live except in the sort of the society in which they grew up. The individuals of the Enlightenment Movement, observed the Romantics, lack in historical background, are uprooted, isolated, never quite social animals, belonging neither to an ideal society nor to any other. Society is a given, they said, and individuals are social products.

This is the exact opposite of the Enlightenment Movement's teaching. The Enlightenment Movement said, individuals get together and create society. The Reaction Movement or the Romantic Movement said, society creates individuals in its own image and this is the source of the national character: individuals are products of national characters, or else they are without character, or they are utterly exceptional. This is the collectivist philosophy. It perceives the human collective as an organism, as a society that is also a state, an economic organization, and a religious community, etc., etc. It values the collective and takes it as prior to the individual. Collectivist ethics takes responsibility away from the individual, and even the political leadership does not have any moral responsibility beyond that of representing the collective and serving the collective interest.

This philosophy is plainly irrationalist, anti-individualist and chauvinist. In particular it should be noted that collectivist philosophy leaves no room for individual responsibility, but for public responsibility alone, placed on the leadership of the national state-society-market-religion — on the national leadership.

What, then, is the place of public responsibility of the rank-and-file citizen? For, the ordinary citizen remains devoid of public responsibility both according to the Enlightenment Movement and according to the Romantic Movement. Since World War II many researchers — philosophers, sociologists, political scientists and historians — are seeking a new philosophy that should unite the desirable in the two traditional modern philosophies, that should serve as a possible alternative to both, and notice the public responsibility of common citizens.

The proper place to start from, it seems to me, is the principle of public responsibility of the individual as an individual. This principle has a tradition of its own, of course, but not in the two guiding philosophies of the modern world. Without discussing this tradition in general, it may be noted that the Jewish tradition, according to which all Jews are responsible for each other, presented public responsibility as an ideal. But this ideal, which to me seems so basic, does not look that way in its specific Jewish formulation. For, in its specific Jewish formulation, the collective towards which the individual is responsible, appears in two polarized ways. On the one hand, practically, the public in question is the

Jewish community to which the individual belongs; on the other hand, abstractly, it is the scattered Jewish faith-nation which includes all Jews, past, present and future.

The concept of public responsibility should be updated, and this can be done by reference to a specific public, or, more precisely, to specific publics. For, as is recognized in all the social sciences, in all societies that are not primitive, the same individual may belong to different publics. This is a key factor for the understanding of the present book. Public responsibility, to repeat, is taken as a basic quality both by modern moral philosophy and by modern political philosophy and the meaning of this responsibility is conditioned on the public to which it refers. Therefore, neither the individual is prior to society nor is society prior to the individual; hence one must reject both classical philosophies in which until recently modern social and political thought sought its foundations.

It is difficult to find the place of recognized facts in a unified philosophical system. Let me offer as an example for this from my personal experience. As I have already observed, I was active both in studies of social and political philosophy and in Israeli politics prior to my meeting with Hillel Kook, from whom I have learned what I wish to present in this book. A detail which he takes particular cognizance of, one which I too was aware of before we met, concerns the basic difference between the individual responsibility of political leaders in western democratic societies and the principle of political collective responsibility of the diverse Israeli governments. I always saw the principle of collective responsibility as an escape from personal public responsibility. Hillel Kook goes further when he explains the supremacy in Israel of the principle of collective responsibility: he claims that the Israeli abnormal political situation does not permit the Israeli public to demand of its government that it cater for public welfare and peace. For, he claims, the Israeli abnormal political situation requires of Israeli citizens that they view as top priority the responsibility of the Israeli government towards the Jewish people as a whole, or the Jewish nation as a whole, namely to all of its sons and daughters, past, present and future. The principle of the abnormalcy of Israel — the principle according to which Israel belongs not to a specific nation but to the scattered nation cum religious community — relieves the Israeli government of any public responsibility towards its own nation and renders it irresponsible. This irresponsibility is then cloaked with collective responsibility. Hence, things would be different were the members of the Israeli nation to require that responsibility be directed towards them and not towards the amorphous and atemporal Jewish nation, the nation that cannot be placed in space and time. For then, it would require specific responsibility of specific individuals and would not be content with a collective responsibility, which is also amorphous and even metaphysical (abstract, ethereal).

The principle of public responsibility has a specific meaning when applied to a specific individual with reference to a specific public. It is customary to consider the definition of that public as the definition of that responsibility. For example, when the individual is a teacher and the public is pupils, one speaks of educational responsibility. When one speaks of the public of consumers one speaks of the economic responsibility of the individual. The same holds for social responsibility, religious responsibility and political responsibility, all of which the Romantic philosophy, we may remember, fuses into one.

This fusion is disastrous for two reasons. First, a political order of priorities differs from a religious order of priorities. Second, public persons, individuals active in a public, whether voluntarily or in appointed or elected roles with responsibilities towards specific publics, have to take into account the preferences of their specific public. How can one know what is the order of priorities of that public? Is it not enough to take account of disagreements concerning the order of priorities, which is economic, or social or religious or political? How can we know what is the public universal order of priority? Citizens are unable then to fulfill their duties and reveal their sense of responsibility when they refer to the collective to which they belong in a general manner, as a public which is educational, as well as economical, social, and religious, on top of being political, not to mention artistic and other. The confusion of all these publics destroys all sense of responsibility.

Collectivists will not disagree with this. They will add that the role of the leadership is to mold the general order of priorities and the public has to accept this order of priorities without deliberation, since it is not possible to discuss such complicated matters. And if we ask, how will the leadership know what is the overall order of priorities, then the Romantics will answer that the leadership has to rely on tradition, or on strong individual intuitions which cannot be controlled. Public responsibility, according to Romanticism, is transferred from the individual to the public through the leadership, and therefore no public responsibility is operative, except that which lies in the hands of the public, the collective as a whole: in the hands of the national leadership.

Contrary to the Romantic view, according to the democratic view, the right and duty of individual citizens is to use their intellects, to show initiative, and to act responsibly. But their ability to act in accord with the democratic view is conditioned on their ability to decide what they should do and how they should act according to their own understanding and on their own responsibility. This book appeals to individuals who have a sense of political public responsibility, with the aim of bringing about a discussion of the question, what they should do, in the hope that this discussion will bring some action.

It remains to explain the principle of unilateral initiative, because it is generally confused with the principle of originality — because Romantic philosophers confuse the politician with the national political leader and deems that person a religious mentor, an educator, an artist, and more. This is why Romantics demand of leaders to act according to strong intuitions. All this is nothing but confusion. Initiative emerges as the individual decides on an aim, and then considers possible alternative lines of action towards that aim and then chooses one of them.

In the social sciences this is known as the rationality principle. Yet usually it is not properly formulated there. When considering the possibilities of a course of action, the individual has to take account of the reactions of others to the choice of that action, particularly if the desired end is not attainable without cooperation.

The first rational move, then, is the call for negotiations which might lead to action. It is customary, especially in Israel, rather than plan for the response of the other, to try and guess what would be that response which the other may make to this or that intended step. Allegedly, this is rooted in a sense of responsibility. But in general it is rooted in confusion, since what is required is to guess not what will be the reaction of the other but what are the different alternative reactions of the other, and to propose in advance different reactions to each of these reactions.

In other words, there is no initiative except that which leads to a plan of action; and there is no plan of action that is properly called a plan, except that which takes account ahead of time of the alternative reasonable reactions of others and of the possible reactions to them.

This does not suffice, because the claim that Israel has to undertake the initiative is not in itself an initiative. For, what should be done if Israel will not undertake an initiative? Initiative, thus, even political initiative, stems from individuals. And in the present case, the readiness to show initiative is expressed by the decision of readers as to what they can do, and what they will think of their chosen activity if it will prove to be only partly successful or even if it fails. The aim of this book, then, is not the presentation of a plan of action, but the inauguration of a political debate concerning the need for political initiative. And if the reader will find in the plan of action purposed here a merely negative value, and will start arguing against it, whether in an academic setting or in an intellectual circle or in a public political debate, then I will consider my activity initially successful and hope that this step will lead to another step, and that the common Israelis who have given up hope of participating in responsible political activity, will find themselves engaged in such activity. Of course, if the reader will agree with ideas presented in this book and will try to spread them expecting a renewal, then perhaps in this may raise hope.

Chapter 2   *The Social Contract Theory*

Let us return to the questions previously asked, ones that constitute the starting point of the political philosophy of the Enlightenment Movement: by what right does one individual rule another? What are the rights of the ruler and what are the rights of the ruled?

Peculiar to this philosophy is the fundamental assumption that all humans have the right to freedom and that all rule deviates from freedom, which is thus either justified or a transgression that is no different from armed robbery. Also peculiar to this philosophy is the idea of the justification which grants both the ruler and the ruled rights and obligations towards each other. This looks like a sort of exchange of rights and obligations. Because of that, it is assumed that this exchange is a matter of agreement between ruler and ruled. Therefore, this Enlightenment theory is called the Social Contract Theory. The present account is inaccurate in a manner that might disturb readers familiar with political philosophy to some extent, but not readers more concerned with the national problem than with political philosophy. The inaccuracy is two-fold. First, in the circles of the advocates of the Social Contract Theory a problem was raised: was there really one day a convention where the initial social contract was signed, similar to the receiving of the Law at Mount Sinai but without divine intervention? That is to say, was there at any time a gathering of humans, or of some pre-humans, who had no government and no ruler, in order to establish government by the original contract between ruler and ruled? This question is still disputed. Among those who think that indeed the original contract has been drawn are some that engaged in another controversy: when and how was the contract drawn? For, it is clear to all that the contract was not drawn by literate individuals who signed the declaration of the foundation of the first state. The question, then, is, how was the original contract drawn? Different advocates of the theory of the original contract gave different answers to it. These are of no concern here. Some of the opponents of the theory of the original contract endorse the Social Contract Theory nonetheless: the justification of the state is the contract that citizens corroborate daily and hourly in their very conduct as law-abiding citizens. Others say, common citizens are unable to leave their particular place and particular form of social life, and so they accept the government not in order to honor a contract but as social creatures. From the viewpoint of the followers of the philosophy of the Enlightenment, this controversy may be of supreme importance; from the viewpoint of the present book it has no importance. Therefore, the Social Contract Theory will be presented here without discussing the question of whether an original contract ever took place, and without discussing the question, is it possible to cancel the social contract the way it is possible to cancel any other contract, or is it so deeply rooted in human nature that every human being will want to abide by it anyway?

It is important to notice, however, that members of the Enlightenment Movement looked for a just government and assumed that the governed knew what they wanted and what they did not want. That is to say, members of the Enlightenment Movement looked for a way to establish a government that would take account of the will of the governed as much as possible. From the very start they looked for as liberal a government as possible, under the assumption that citizens would be as free as possible — free to decide what freedoms they were willing to yield to the government and in return for which benefits. No doubt, the philosophers of the Enlightenment Movement exhibited both a very great faith in the ability of individual citizens to make decisions and a high degree of sensitivity to their suffering.

As to individual suffering from existing conditions, even with all of our sympathy to this suffering, and accepting the assumption that this suffering is caused by injustice inflicted by the rulers, even then we may not overlook the possibility that the injustice that causes the suffering results from the stupidity with which individuals run their affairs, such as the stupidity with which the government is tolerated. For example, subjugated nations suffer from the yoke of foreign rulers, and free nations may suffer from the stupidity and helplessness of their own governments. The difference between the two cases is so well known that it demands neither explanations nor examples. Moreover, it is customary and accepted in the enlightened world that every independent agent, a person or a public, not to mention an independent nation, has the right to suffer without, thereby, sacrificing the right to independence and allowing strangers to impose their help and goodwill. This is a most important detail, since foreign conquerors have no difficulty finding justification for invasion by reference to the interest of the conquered. The modern imperialists are not the only ones convinced that they have the duty to take care of the inferior world; this is "White Man's Burden", the obligation to subjugate the rest of the world. Already the ancient Romans did; they began their intervention in Judea under the pretext that they came to implement peace between fighting brothers, just as they generally justified their cruel rule by the claim that they were imposing peace on the world, the famous *Pax Romana* so-called.

Some suffer because of their stupidity and some suffer because their independence is violated. It is important that only the suffering caused by others is unjust and was viewed so by the Enlightenment Movement. This is the starting point of modern political philosophy for the last four centuries. Hence, the philosophy of the Enlightenment Movement consciously overlooked the question, is one who violates the independence of another a brother or a stranger to the other? The question asked by the philosophers of the Enlightenment Movement was most general: what is generally the justification of one individual's rule over another? Where does the right to rule come from? They disregarded the national component in government out of principle, out of the objection to the suffering of every human as a human. What justification is there, they asked, to violate the liberty of the ruled?

This way of posing the question looks most reasonable, and it is difficult to see how one can contest this wording of the question and to the view of it as a basic question in all political philosophy. As is the case with every other question, this question also rests on a prior assumption. But this assumption is of the right of the individual to liberty, and it is difficult to see how one can challenge this assumption. Indeed, assuming that every individual has the right to liberty and agreeing that in every government there is an element of bondage, be it ever so slight, then it is our duty to see in every government some violation of some individual right. It seems, therefore, that the violation is either justified or not. There is no other option.

Generally, civilized people tend to admit that there are diverse sorts of justified imposition and justified violence, as, for example, in the case of a patient who lies in hospital and has to accept the rules governing that hospital; or in the normally justifiable violence of surgeons who assault patients and hurts them. The question is, what kind of justification is it?

We all agree that government without any violence is impossible. Police violence that limits the movements of criminals is the most obvious example, one that is regularly compared to the violence of surgeons. But some say that government violence is never justified. Among those who voice this opinion are those who advocate government despite the lack of justification for its violence and those who oppose it unconditionally, on the grounds that it is never justified.

The opponents of all types of government are anarchists. The word "anarchy" means, no ruling. In modern languages the word "anarchy" is often used to mean lack of order, or chaos. One says, for example, the government lost its control and anarchy ensued, when one means, the government lost all control and order disappeared. This is an improper use of the word. For the question is, does the lack of government lead to chaos? Those who say that order without government is impossible are opposed to anarchism, of course, for, nobody advocates chaos. Indeed, anarchists also detest chaos, and so it is unjust to anarchists that their opponents do not admit this fact. Anarchists wish to have no rule, within a well-ordered organized society. Anarchists suggest that this state is ideal, and it stems from the awareness of the injustice involved in every use of force and every act of violence, as well as the awareness of the truth that government without violence is impossible.

Imagine a government that has some normal power to impose its will. Imagine further that all its power to impose its will is lost, and yet the governed continue to follow its orders, willingly and not for fear of punishment. This is an image of an organized anarchy, whereby the government goes on functioning only as an administration which uses no coercion, not as a government proper, namely, not one that applies force.

During the time of the Enlightenment, in the Age of Reason, most of the political thinkers held that anarchy is the ideal, though not fully realizable. The most important among them was John Locke, a personal friend of the celebrated physicist, Sir Isaac Newton, and a party to the opposition of the government of his time. (Locke even went into exile and participated in the English Glorious Revolution of 1688.) Of the same ilk was Adam Smith, who in the middle of the eighteenth century wrote his famous book, *On the Nature and Causes of the Wealth of Nations*.

This is not to say that Locke and Smith were anarchists, since they expected that the ruler would have some kind of police force to impose proper order, particularly that it should impose the honoring of civic duties, including the honoring of contracts and of promises. The key point, however, is that they demanded of rulers that they should limit themselves to policing functions alone and that they should keep policing functions to the barest minimum. (Their theory is called "the model of government as a night-watchman".) The intelligent reader will see at once that to add the national dimension or any other dimension to a model of government of so narrow a compass is quite impossible. Indeed, when Karl Marx claimed that in the West in his time the government had a mere night-watchman's function he concluded that the regime then (he called it "capitalism") had no place for a recognition of nationality. But he made a mistake, since there never was a regime so narrow as described by the model of government as a night-watchman.

Not all were anarchists who denied all justification of government violence. Already in antiquity the celebrated philosopher Plato described a thinker who claimed that there is no justice, that might is right. This thinker claimed that the democratic regime is but the association of the weak in order to overcome the strong, and that it should therefore be no surprise that the strong tend to oppose democracy. And he concluded that neither democracy nor anti-democracy is morally superior in any way. Government, in his view, is justified not by morality but simply by the ruler's power over the ruled. He thus viewed every strong regime as sufficiently justified as long as it is strong enough to keep going. According to this view, rulers, however tyrannical, will be justified in their tyranny by their political activities — until their subjects succeed in demoting them. This way, however, the righteous become villains, since on that day the inability to sustain a position by force makes it wrong. According to this view the violence of the ruler is justifiable not by words but by brute force alone.

So much for the extremists. At one extreme are the anarchists and the near-anarchists who advocate government as a night-watchman and who eye governments with suspicion. At the other extreme are the supporters of every regime that meets with success, even when that success rests on violent oppression. Between the two are the moderates, who agree that there are rulers whose activities are justified and rulers whose activities are not justified. But, again, the activities that require justification are only the activities that involve violence. For, when taxes are paid voluntarily, then they constitute no problem, and there is no reason to prevent the ruler from collecting them. Hence, the problem is of the justification not of taxes but of their imposition by force. How can we justify exacting taxes by violence? How can one justify any imposition?

Governments usually justify the taxes that they levy from the citizenry with arguments concerning the budget. But every reasonable person knows that every state justifies its budget, despite the very obvious fact that not every budget is just. Does this not prove that justification by itself will not do? Moreover, assuming that this justification alone will not do, but that sometimes it is accepted and then it is just, and sometimes not, then the question arises, who decides when a budget is accepted or acceptable or to be accepted? And since it is well known that sometimes an unacceptable budget is accepted, the question arises, when is it acceptable? What makes a budget acceptable? Which government argument is acceptable and which is not? Generally, what is the standard for acceptability that rulers use to justify their actions?

Amazingly, these questions are not to the point, since, it has already been observed, it is the right of every independent individual to do the stupidest thing, just as it is the right of every independent state to run its economy unwisely. For, to repeat, withholding agreement on this invites every foreign invader to come and conquer a state in order to improve its budget after the conquest in accord with the conqueror's own judgment. It should therefore be agreed that whenever the population accepts their government's budget, this should do, since the imposition is then no longer imposition but a matter of agreement.

This is the Social Contract Theory. This theory, it should be stressed, indicates not that one regime is better than another, but that any government whatsoever exerts violence that is not justified or that is justified by the consent that the ruled accord to this violence. What is the level of violence that is required? To this question many answers were given, from one extreme to another. The most liberal of the advocates of the social contract thought that only a minimum of violence is required, and no more, the minimum being nothing more than the task of the police (and raising the taxes that cover their wages). The most anti-liberal among the advocates of the social contract was Thomas Hobbes who wrote in the period of the Great Rebellion, the mid-seventeenth century civil war in Britain. In his view the purpose of the ruler is to prevent civil war. The ruler who fails in that assignment thereby invites a rebellion. Rulers who manage to prevent civil wars have the right to rule according to their own understanding and will (for, if we start bargaining about the limits of the rights of the king, a civil war may ensue). Though Hobbes allowed kings everything under the sole small condition that they prevent civil wars, the tyrannical king in power after the civil war did not like him, precisely because he conditioned the right of the king to tyranny by the agreement of the people to accept it in exchange for internal peace.

And, indeed, this is at once the strength and weakness of the Social Contract Theory. Its strength is in its objection to all imposition and in its grounding of the ruler's right to use force, on the readiness of free citizens to acquiesce and submit to the ruler's yoke. Its weakness is in its consequent denial of the right of the ruler to coerce in any real sense of the word: nobody will call coercion the demand to fulfill promises, and any imposition complying with the theory of the social contract is of this sort. Worse still, people usually know what they have promised their neighbors, why they have promised what they did, and what they expected to receive in return. It is therefore reasonable to demand of them that they fulfill their promises. And if they say they could not have known what they had promised, whether because they had made promises under some mistaken supposition or under the influence of drink, and so on, then they can appeal against the demand that they fulfill their promises and begin with negotiations or litigation with their neighbors, as becomes rational civilized human beings. Nobody could claim that the same holds true concerning relations between the individual and the state. Individuals do not know what they had promised, when they had promised, or how they had promised. Nor do they know what benefit they may expect to receive in exchange. Moreover, an agreement between two individuals is made usually voluntarily, that is to say, under the assumption that each of them could avoid undertaking an obligation or concluding a deal. But is the same true concerning the deal between the individual and the state? Sometimes this is how things look, when there is an agreement between the citizen and the state, as when the citizen voluntarily joins the regular army as a soldier. But sometimes it is not at all like that, as when the individual is inducted into the army under compulsory mobilization in times of emergency.

This is the major criticism of the Social Contract Theory. The idea already appeared in Plato's early work in which his teacher, Socrates, accepts the rule of the state and refuses to escape jail even though he was sentenced to death in a flagrant violation of justice. For, Socrates says, I agreed to stay here till now because the conditions were agreeable to me, and it is unfair that precisely when the conditions are not agreeable to me I should clear out. I have an agreement with the laws of Athens, says Socrates, and I have to fulfill my part of the contract. Individuals could have cleared out if they wished, but in not doing so they express agreement to accept the good and the bad, and then they cannot legitimately complain about receiving the bad while ignoring the fact that sometime earlier they had accepted the good. The question asked by students of the Social Contract Theory, Adam Smith included, was this: as common citizens have no choice, as they have no real option to migrate (both because of ignorance of foreign languages and because of the difficulty they have selling their meager property and purchasing travel tickets), how then can its advocates assume that common citizens have a choice?

This is not the place to discuss the finer details, as it is clear that though the prohibition against migration is a form of subjugation, the freedom of emigration does not suffice. The social contract is invalid, since if it were valid, then the obvious conclusion would be that the freedom to emigrate should suffice, and it would be clear that in every country where there is no prohibition against emigration, the very refusal to choose to emigrate is a tacit acceptance of all imposition from the rulers and hence, in essence, that there is no imposition in that country at all. This is an entirely intolerable conclusion. It is known that unjustified impositions exist even in countries from which it is very easy to emigrate. Unjustified impositions are the very items that legislators and other reformers of the legal and administrative systems try to reduce; all their labor is nothing but a silly joke if all impositions are anyway justified by the social contract which is validated by the fact that not all citizens leave their homeland.

Nevertheless, the Social Contract Theory is of enormous significance. The most convincing argument in its favor is true and important and possibly self-understood. (It is self-understood in the sense that one who does not see that the following argument is true suffers from a defective political perception). The argument is already introduced in the writings of Jean-Jacques Rousseau, the author of the classical book *On the Social Contract.* In that period it was shared by even some of the opponents of the Social Contract Theory. The argument is very simple: no government can be stable without some sort of support from the population at large. No ruler can rule by the force of bayonets alone.

One way or another, the ruler is a minority with insufficient power to hold in real cages the majority that is ruled. Therefore, it is necessary that the ruled accept the authority of the ruler. But the acceptance of this authority (and this has to be repeatedly emphasized) applies equally to states such as the Soviet Union, where there is no right of emigration. Hence, if this argument provides sufficient justification by the social contract, then it should be accepted as justifying also the Soviet Union, as well as any occupation, as long as it is stable — except for the Nazi rule over Warsaw Ghetto during the Warsaw Ghetto Uprising and its likes. The argument, then, if valid, justifies almost every rule as in principle not violent.

And so, in the final appraisal, the philosophy of the Enlightenment Movement has failed in its assignment. It began with an attempt to justify good governments but not bad governments, on the assumption that every imposition is evil, except the imposition that is accepted on a truly voluntary basis. Yet in the end this attempt either justified all government as such or no government at all. That is to say, Enlightenment political theory failed to demarcate civilized government that serves its subjects from the government that subjugates and conquers. It is no surprise, therefore, that the Enlightenment Movement did not distinguish between foreign and local subjugation. And, indeed, at the beginning of the nineteenth century many Enlightenment thinkers justified the foreign subjugation by Napoleon in the hope of seeing him as an expression of the ideals of the French Revolution that were inherited from this movement. Consequently, the Enlightenment Movement was severely damaged.

Nevertheless, despite the failure of the Enlightenment Movement in its attempt to demarcate between just and tyrannical rule, and despite its consequent failure to demarcate the difference between self-rule and foreign rule, it had an inner logic. This inner logic was very important, for it includes a single corollary that has been forgotten: the negative aspect of foreign conquest is not in its being foreign, but in it's being subjugation. And so we have come to an awkward situation in Israel today. We are subjugated despite our having freed ourselves from foreign rule, for we have no national liberty, since Israel still does not legally recognize its own nation. And if the reader insists that subjugation needs a foreign ruler and asks who that foreign ruler is, I reply that it is the anti-Jewish myth.

But it is better to leave the question of who the ruler is. The next chapter will discuss the view of the anti-liberal nationalist movement, according to which it is important only to be free of foreign rule and individual liberty itself is of no importance. The chapter after that will discuss liberal nationalism. In that discussion readers will see clearly that the possibility of losing liberty rests on the possibility of a subjugation that is not dependent on the existence of foreign rule. This possibility is reasonable enough and one should therefore beware of it. Wherever it is realized, as it has been realized here, it should be fought against. This is no minor matter.

Chapter 3: The Reaction and Chauvinism

The Enlightenment Movement was idealistic. It attempted to see all humans as equal and to erect a political philosophy on the principle of the liberty of every human as human. This theory was unrealistic and this contributed to its failure.

The Enlightenment Movement thus was followed by the Reaction Movement, which deemed ordinary people as uneducated and therefore unable to govern themselves, as devoid of autonomy. That is to say, the Reaction Movement did not consider ordinary people as deserving of liberty thus reestablishing both class discrimination and national discrimination. It demanded national discrimination allegedly in order to protect national unity, and national unity allegedly in order to protect national liberty. Its demand to protect national liberty seemed to its opponents (as it does to the author of these lines) as a mere excuse for its rejection of individual liberty.

The Reaction Movement adopted the Romantic philosophy, according to which the nation is a society and society precedes the individual, who is nothing but an organ, a cell in the body of society. The exceptions are the geniuses who in their splendid isolation prove themselves worthy of autonomy — of intellectual independence, of liberty, and of national leadership. The proof that they are geniuses is naturally rooted in their having managed to take the helm despite all opposition. This is certainly an inhumane philosophy, dangerous and fraught with disaster since in this way Romanticism recommends conformity and its sweeping imposition, since the common citizen should abide by it and the genius should rebel against it.

The adherents of the Enlightenment Movement who believed in the rule of reason did not all endorse the Social Contract Theory. Some of them, such as Adam Smith, claimed that membership in a society, and thus citizenship, is a fulfillment of natural need; hence it is a matter of neither choice nor contract. But what all the members of the Enlightenment Movement did hold in common was the view of reason as the navigator in all areas of life. Thus they held that every human being is rational — a being with the inalienable right to liberty. It is difficult today to imagine just how revolutionary was the liberal attitude to every problem — from abstract learning to daily life. The abolition of class distinction and religious discrimination was for the members of the Enlightenment Movement not only a basic principle but also the immediate, clear corollary to all that bestows value on human life in general. The readiness to discriminate, against a peasant or a Jew, seemed to the Enlightenment thinkers a puzzling phenomenon, a phenomenon that required explanation because it is so irrational, and thus unnatural and even perverse. The fact that the greatest majority of humanity behaved in such a perverse manner only increased the sense of puzzlement.

The influence of the Enlightenment was first felt in Britain. That country suffered religious wars at the end of the first half of the seventeenth century. Puritans had suffered persecution, and some of them escaped to foreign lands. But most of them stayed, and towards the middle of the seventeenth century they started a civil war known as the Great Rebellion. After that war, Jews were accepted in Britain no less than Catholics. Soon the kingdom was reestablished and in 1688 a Catholic succession to the throne was prevented in a bloodless revolution (this is why it is known as The Glorious Revolution) and religious freedom was maintained. Obviously, class distinctions were not abolished in Britain and remain to this very day; even universal suffrage was an achievement that Britain reached only after many stages of development; the process was concluded only after World War I.

France was the classical land of the Enlightenment. In the eighteenth century, the diverse sciences flourished there and the ideas of freedom and equality were very popular. Members of the Enlightenment Movement belonged to the upper classes and even to the high aristocracy. They preached equality and thus introduced the new spirit that brought about the French Revolution which abolished all privileges and even the titles of nobility, and gave complete freedom for political action to all citizens in indifference to their origin or religion.

The United States gained its independence a few years before the French Revolution and preached the same ideas of individual liberty, received from the philosophy of the Enlightenment. The principles of Enlightenment, including those of individual freedom and of human rights, found their best and strongest expression in the United States, and were written into the Declaration of Independence and into the Declaration of Human Rights and in the original Constitution there.

The Hebrew reader of this book need not be told that the European Enlightenment failed as a political revolutionary movement. This failure is the fundamental assumption of the Zionist Movement, with which practically all Hebrew readers are familiar. The European Enlightenment Movement promised Jews total equality, but, of course, did not keep that promise. Were that the case, then perhaps there would be no urgent need for Zionism in any enlightened country, that is to say, in any country where the principles of the Enlightenment Movement were popular.

What has happened? Enlightenment philosophy suffered weakness on two counts, both already alluded to. The first was its inability to legitimize any coercion. The second was the inability to recognize national rights.

The first weakness is expressed very clearly in Jean-Jacques Rousseau's classic book, *On the Social Contract*. He was the intellectual father of the French Revolution. In that book he discusses coercion and recognizes the fact that coercion within the bounds of the contract is not real coercion. In that book Rousseau asked, what should be done to an individual who refuses to accept the terms of the social contract?

The answer to this question is given early in the book, in a terrifying and disastrous sentence, "He is forced to be free." This imposition of liberty means, of course, jail, and jail is coercion, not liberty. To consider jail the imposition of liberty amounts to an outright lie of the sort that became increasingly popular in the nineteenth century and reached its peak in the twentieth century in the Nazi theory of the Big Lie. In order to justify coercion, Rousseau not only had to appeal to the will of the majority of the people but also to the general will. What is the general will? How is it possible that such an entity as the generality exists? The abstract generality in which the general will resides is a mysterious entity, beyond the individuals who partake in it. What is this entity? How does this entity express any will?

These are philosophical questions. The plain historical fact is that they carried amazing weight in the development of the theory and practice of European politics between the time of the French Revolution and World War II. It is difficult to assess the extent to which these political developments were ruled by accidents, and to what extent by the inner logic of the situation. But this inner logic of the situation constitutes several sufficiently clear facts: the philosophers who opposed the Enlightenment Movement claimed that the generality, the collective, exists above and beyond its members, and it possesses the collective will; this will has priority over any individual's will and even against the wills of the majority, and there is a way to discover it with no need to consult the people.

The French Revolution was led by the members of the Enlightenment Movement whose political views were naive beyond measure. In their opinion the desire to think freely without prejudices is a necessary and sufficient condition both for the abolition of the old regime and for the foundation of a new, enlightened one. This naiveté is very dangerous, though not necessarily disastrous.

In North America this naiveté led the United States of America to develop as a modern state, to the separation of state and church, and to the view of the state as a mere instrument — even as an instrument for the realization and protection of human rights and liberties (namely, individual rights of citizens and of non-citizens alike). Society was deemed an association of individuals, and the state the instrument of society and no more than that, an instrument available for the service of individuals as individuals. The very same idea and the very same naiveté failed in France, causing enormous disorder, a tragic and desperate bloodbath known as the reign of (French) terror. The tragedy was that this terror was rooted in the desire to salvage the French Revolution by cementing national unity. In addition, when no other way to create national unity was found, attempts were made to effect it by the force of the guillotine. This terror worsened the situation desperately, since the guillotine eradicated, among other things, the best children of the Revolution, thereby destroying all chance of getting out of the disorder quickly, with honor, and in an orderly fashion. Napoleon then conquered the defeated France with a very small force, while giving rise to false hopes of imperialist glory. Napoleon's idea was a pathetic and very simple lie. Despite the decisive failure of the French Revolution, it remained a symbol of human liberty and in countries that suffered limitations on individual liberties it became a fascinating, attractive and exciting symbol. In the name of this fascination and excitement Napoleon attempted to subjugate the whole of Europe and to put himself and members of his family on the thrones of diverse European countries. Anyone who thinks that this attempt was doomed to failure is a naive optimist. In any case, whether Napoleon was identified as the bearer of the ideals of the French Revolution or not, the idea of liberty, in whose name the French Revolution was carried out, excited educated European youths, and the authorities looked for ways to repress them. Thus the Reaction Movement was born. The reaction of the Reaction Movement was to Napoleon, and to the ideas of progress in whose name he spread destruction across Europe. The Reaction Movement responded with hostility towards the movement for political liberty and expressed this hostility as opposition to the movement for human rights. But, in order not to appear as the enemy of freedom, the Reaction Movement appeared in a grotesque fashion as the bearer of the banner of the movement of national liberty, the liberty threatened by Napoleon. National liberty and individual liberty turned thereby into competitors for the sympathies of the naive confused young European freedom fighter.

The anti-liberal national movement inherited from the liberal Enlightenment Movement an abstract question, a question of the legitimacy of government: what right has one human to rule another? To repeat, Enlightenment thinkers saw this merely as a matter between individuals: if one individual rules another with right, then this right depends either on the validity of a contract between them or on the validity of the interests of each and every individual in the political system. Questions pertaining to the geographical limits of government were left open as was the question of membership within one political system or another — questions like the following: who is a citizen and who is not? How long should one settle in a foreign country before losing one's citizenship? Is dual citizenship possible? Such questions were considered in the Enlightenment Movement as not touching the central question of the rights of government.

This is why these questions were not discussed in the Enlightenment Movement. The members of the Enlightenment Movement required that citizenship should not be subject to any religious or class discrimination, and they assumed that this should do. But the very same questions that did not interest the thinkers of the Enlightenment Movement became central to the discussion within the Reactionary thinking of the Romantic Movement.

The first assumption of the Reaction is true: the Enlightenment theory of individual liberty had failed. The second assumption is also true: a society without government is impossible. The interest in government showed by the Enlightenment was rooted, it will be remembered, in the desire for individual liberty. This concern with government was endorsed by the Reaction Movement despite the contempt it showed towards individual liberty. The concern with government turned, therefore, into an excuse for the idea that society and state are one and the same entity.

Since the Enlightenment Movement assumed that the individual precedes society, the Reaction Movement reversed the order and assumed that society precedes the individual, concluding from this that the state precedes the individual. The Reaction, therefore, demanded liberty for the state, not for the individual. This changed the question, what is the legitimacy of government? This question was turned in the teachings of the Reaction into the question, which society has the right to its own state, to an independent national government? And so the idea of national self-determination developed, though dimly, as a part of the teaching of the Reactionary anti-liberal movement; for, the liberal Enlightenment Movement did not consider this subject-matter at all.

Prior to the French Revolution the right of self-determination of a class was recognized, as well as that of a society or a sub-society, but not that of a nation. After the French Revolution (which came in the wake of the philosophy of the Enlightenment Movement) the right to self-determination was recognized as the right of any collection of human beings. For, according to the philosophy of the Enlightenment Movement, every group of humans has the right to associate, the right to become a society, and if they were deemed members of a given society their right was recognized to separate from it so as to found a new society with its own government. The Reaction denied this idea and returned to older ones, ones which accorded the right for political independence only to a collection of human beings that has a certain degree of crystallization, socially and culturally. Therefore, the philosophy of the Reaction became an integral part of Romantic philosophy, since the latter considered the ideal individual as one linked by roots to a crystallized organic society.

The Romantics claimed that only a crystallized society with roots in history and a sound tradition has the right to be called a nation or a national entity and thus the right to self-rule and national political independence.

The question which the Romantic philosophers considered most important was, therefore, what turns a collection of human beings into a nation? For, only a nation has the right to liberty, self-rule, and national independence. What qualities of a collection of human beings grant them this exalted right? The answer, of course, lay in the national tradition. This includes the national language, the folk culture, and the ability to organize into an independent state. For many, the answer also included the idea that the state needs the national religion, in contrast to the precedent practiced in the United State and in France of the separation of state and church.

Romantic philosophy made light of the ideas of individual liberty, recommended their suppression and taught that individuals had no rights except to sacrifice themselves to the collective. Nevertheless, this philosophy caused great excitement and tremendous enthusiasm. The reason for this was in the appeal to the national sentiment that had been developing for centuries in Europe, and that had been neglected and lacked proper expression before the Romantic philosophy bloomed. Here is an interesting example of it: The English Puritans, who escaped from religious persecutions in England to North America at the beginning of the seventeenth century and founded the colonies in New England — that in due course became a new independent country — the United States of America. These people were not eager to cross the ocean, but did so with great courage under intolerably difficult conditions and undergoing many perils. It is not surprising that they first escaped not to North America but to tolerant Holland, where they were allowed to worship their God in any way that pleased them. But their children began to speak Dutch and something rebelled in them, that was strong enough to change their attitude towards the forces of nature and enabled them to take the risk, to cross the ocean and to settle in the New World. This was their sense of belonging to a given culture, the germ of the national feeling. Nevertheless, the American Revolution underestimated the national sentiment and even used the word "nation" as synonymous with the term "state".

The Enlightenment Movement overlooked national sentiments; the Reaction excited them. For these two errors the world still pays a high price. National sentiments and the nation are two very different things, since the state of the nation is a political matter, whereas national sentiments are a matter of emotional and social character. Thus, for example, when Abraham Lincoln, the celebrated President of the United States, declared Civil War against the Confederation of the southern states of the United States, he did this not in order to free the slaves, even though he very quickly made their liberation a war objective. Nor was it a response to the southern states as they had launched hostilities. Lincoln declared the Civil War against the Confederation because the south seceded. In this way, he declared, they violated the national unity.

Still, the question of the identity of a nation has not yet been clarified. What kind of national unity should be preserved according to Lincoln's opinion even at the cost of a civil war, and what kind of unity permits or facilitates separation? These questions were left open and were even carelessly disregarded because the national movement did not receive a proper expression, since the expression it did receive was that of the Reactionary philosophy of the Romantic Movement, which busied itself with national liberty not out of interest in nations and in national aspirations, but out of the effort to sabotage the inquiry of the Enlightenment Movement into the question of the legitimacy of government.

The question of the legitimacy of government is also called "the problem of sovereignty". Enlightenment thinkers of the seventeenth and eighteenth centuries considered this question one that follows from the fundamental assumption that every individual is necessarily autonomous (independent). If the ruled are independent, why should they permit the rulers to constrain them? The fundamental assumption of the autonomy of each individual was rejected by the Reaction, which is, of course, what made the Reaction reactionary, and thus conservative, anti-liberal, anti-individualist, and collectivist. Individuals are not free of the limitations of the space and time in which they live, the Reaction said, nor is it desirable that they should be free of the limitations of the society in which they live. If they were, they would lose normal contact with their environment and become alienated, estranged from their own people. When this happens on a large scale, society becomes atomized; from the one coagulated unit society then turns into a heap of isolated single items, inviting foreign conquest to come and impose an external, artificial order as a substitute for the internal, natural order destroyed in the process of atomization — a process caused by the pursuit of individual liberty.

As this discussion illustrates, according to the Reaction's teaching, individuals have no autonomy; only collectives do; that is to say, groups possessing the capacity for self-rule. Such a group has, in addition to all the wills of its individual members, the will of the collective or the general will that is above and beyond the individual wills of all the individuals whom it encompasses. This collective will, because it is the will of the organized collective that is not a mere collection of individuals, exists above and beyond the collection of individual wills.

It is therefore clear, again, why it was so important for reactionary Romantic philosophers to ask the question, what collection of human beings has the right for autonomy? In addition to this question another was raised and placed on the agenda: Who is the individual on whom the collective imposes the duty of government?

This is an entirely secondary question, and in principle so. For, according to the Romantic philosophy of the Reaction, an autonomous collection of people is a well-organized collection, a collective proper, and so it is also ruled justly. The question that these philosophers preferred to ask, therefore, is not, who has the right to be the ruler? Rather, it is, what are the properties of the group or the social organization, or of the political unit, that give it the right to autonomy? They recognized only a group or social organization or political organization that has the right to autonomy as having the right to be called a nation, and only a nation has the right to autonomy. The supreme question of the political philosophy of the Reaction is, thus, What unit constitutes a nation?

This question is not at the root of nationalism, nor of nationalist movements, nor does it characterize these movements. But it was the central theoretical question that engaged the Reactionary philosophy professors in Germany in the early period after the French Revolution. They identified the nationalist movement with the collectivist and anti-liberal ideology of the Reaction; they identified this ideology as concerned with the question, What characterizes a nation? They identified the character of a nation with that of a collective and thereby with hostility to liberalism. This is a most important historical detail in the history of both political thought and nationalism in the nineteenth century. This question still has important projections to the life of Israeli society.

To this day spokespeople of the Enlightenment Movement are wholeheartedly hostile to the nationalist movement. Among the most important and popular of them are Elie Kedourie and Karl Popper. The former was originally an Iraqi Jew and the latter an Austrian of Jewish extraction. They were both British and for decades after World War II they served as professors in the London School of Economics and Political Science, famous for its influence on political life all over the world. Both opposed nationalism on two grounds: because of its anti-liberalism by its very definition in the philosophical writings of the Romantic Movement, and because of their wholehearted support of the unqualified autonomy of the individual. They deemed it threatened by the nationalist movement, which they considered collectivist. That is to say, they saw as dangerous the opinion that autonomy is possible only to a human collection but not to an individual (5).

But, contrary to their views, one might claim that autonomy is possible both for the individual and for the collective. Contrary to their opinion, national and individual liberty is not necessarily in conflict: nationalism is not necessarily the oppression of the individual. The national liberation movements of the nineteenth century sought liberation from foreign rule. It was not always clear who were the local people and who were foreign. For example, it is no more than a historical accident that there is no such country as the State of Piedmont which lay mostly in today's Italy and partly in today's France; to a large extent this is the result of the fact that most of the inhabitants of Piedmont considered themselves Italian and their king became the first king of the unified Italy in order to strengthen this feeling and prevent separatism. There is no inherent cause for the fact that the vast area of North America is divided between only three states, whereas Central America, which is relatively small, is divided into many. There is likewise no inherent reason for the failure of the idea of pan-Slavism, that there is no Slavic nation but a few Slavic nation-states, each having its own national culture and national language. And there is, likewise, no inherent reason for the absence of an Arab nation, for failure of the idea of pan-Arabism, except perhaps that the idea of nationalism has not acclimatized in the Arab world. And indeed, to date only a few Arabic-speaking states have reached the stage of modern nation-states (and none of them in the western liberal democratic pattern). Hence, it is not *a priori* clear, it is not inherent (as the Romantic philosophers claimed), who is a local and who is a stranger. It is clear that when the rulers of a regional city are too constrained by the rulers in the capital city, then the regional city may rebel and claim to be the capital of a nation subject to foreign rule and demand independence, and then develop a nationalist movement of the region. Sometimes this happens and sometimes not.

Why? How? What factor turns a human group into a nation, and what causes the development of this factor? Philosophy could not come up with answers to these questions, though much ink was spilled on the many debates in which attempts were made to answer them. These debates had no positive value; they only helped whip up hatred towards anyone who could be considered alien, that is, not a member of the nation. The questions led to the desire to consider the source of national unity in the uniformity of the customs of the members of the nation. In its turn this led to the desire to oppress the individuals who were different because of their difference and to call them aliens.

Romantic philosophy claimed that the right to freedom belongs not to every human collective but only to a nation, and that in order to count as a nation certain conditions must be met.

Thus this philosophy encouraged interest in and study of the question, what are these conditions? Under which conditions does a human group become a nation? This question obscured the fact that every human group has the right to self-government. It soon became one whose significance is self-evident, one divorced from the concern with liberty. It led to inquiry in two different directions. It is possible to assume that certain groups constitute nations and look for the conditions that they satisfy. It is possible to assume that certain conditions make a group a nation and attempt to apply these to a given group. Thus, it is possible to assume conditions that Jews do not fulfill, namely territorial concentration, and conclude that Jews do not constitute a nation. It is also possible to assume that the Jews constitute a nation, as a matter of fact, and to look for conditions that will justify this assumption.

Liberal politicians who advocated religious equality claimed that Jews do not constitute a nation. Some Reactionary politicians who advocated religious discrimination did so on the claim that the Jews constitute a nation. These politicians have caused the rise of the Jewish nationalist movement whose ideologists agreed that indeed the Jews constitute a nation.

Moreover, they agreed that a nation occupies a national territory, and so they promoted the idea of the speedy return to Zion.

The debate concerning the conditions that turn a group of people into a nation is lengthy and protracted; it did not come even to a partial conclusion. It was admittedly impossible to deny the existence of the ancient Jewish people. But it was possible to assert that Jews do not constitute a nation, that they are merely members of a religious congregation, or a group characterized in any other way, other than the way a nation is characterized. Indeed, some Romantic philosophers claimed that the Jews are an aberrant case: in their view Jews are neither a nation nor members of the nations within which they dwell. And the status of the Jews is still unclear, since Israel clings to the declaration that the Jews are at once both a nation and a religious congregation, and refuses to ask, what makes the Jews a nation in a manner that makes them necessarily also share a faith? And, perhaps, there really is no need to go into details, as it is clear that this declaration is mistaken, despite its being repeated in Israel time and again. For, as is well known, some Jews are members of different nations and some Israelis are members of different religious communities. But a fundamental confusion in Israel prevents Israelis from recognizing these familiar facts. (See Part Three of this book.)

Chapter 4 — *Liberal Nationalism*

The Enlightenment Movement fought for the freedom of the individual and overlooked national liberty, considering it a mere corollary. The Romantic Movement fought for national liberty and considered individual liberty as limited to service for the nation. The outcome was upheavals and wars and civil wars that took place in Europe from the French Revolution and until the middle of the twentieth century — the period that was fought with the ideological struggle between these two movements. In addition to this ideological struggle, debate raged about the theory and practice of socialism, which was partly the continuation of the liberal movement and partly an innovation, namely, Marxism. This ideology will not be discussed here because it does not belong to any discussion about nationalism. (According to Marx there are no nations but only classes, and there is no possibility of individual liberty except in the communist society, which would develop by itself out of the socialist revolution.)

The liberal Enlightenment Movement contributed by mistake to the rise of the Romantic, anti-liberal Chauvinist Movement by its oversight of the national sentiment, of national societies, and of nation-states. In addition, the Enlightenment Movement preached the application of science to the treatment of political problem; it viewed science as proof, as the finality and generality that permit no dissent. Thus it contributed also to the struggle against democracy and liberalism (as Jacob Talmon shows in his classic *The Origins of Totalitarian Democracy*) (4).

It is strange that the Enlightenment Movement, which contributed to the world the recognition of common people's desire for liberty and for enlightenment, thereby laying the foundation of national liberal enlightened democratic regimes, did not support either democracy or nationalism. Democracy was rescued because the Movement had a liberal democratic tradition and because in this way it permitted the development of liberal nationalism. But neither the Enlightenment nor the Romantic philosophy offered any foundations for democracy, except that, by and large, the goal of the followers of the Enlightenment Movement was democracy and of the followers of the Chauvinist Romantic Movement was nationalism. Members of the Enlightenment Movement supported democracy since they supported enlightenment, toleration, and the exchange of ideas that characterized democracy best.

The Romantics supported nationalism, finding in nationality an instrument with which to attack the desire for individual liberty and also to develop the reactionary form of nationalism that they advocated. The one erroneous impression was that democracy is basically scientific and that science is always right. The second erroneous impression was that nationalism is always reactionary and anti-liberal and always risking individual liberty and human rights.

The deeper reason for this was that the Enlightenment and Romantic Movements agreed on an abstract idea according to which all human sciences should be based either on the assumption of the existence of the individual, explaining the existence of society as a collection of individuals, or on the assumption of the existence of society, explaining the individual as a member of society and thus as having this or that national characteristic. The assumption that both the individual and society exist did not appeal to the classical thinkers, since it may have led to the conclusion that there is a conflict of interests and a permanent conflict between individual and society. The assumption therefore looked obvious that only one of these two really exists.

This assumption is a castle in Spain, as every social science has to assume the existence of both individual and society. And if this leads to the conclusion that friction between individual and society is possibly unavoidable, then this conclusion fits real life better than the Utopias of both the Enlightenment and

Romantic Movements. I will not discuss this further in this book since I have dedicated to this topic a book devoted to the social sciences in general (2).

The development of modern, national, liberal democracy, and of democratic theory without a suitable ideological and intellectual framework, clearly underscores the possibility of practical and even intellectual developments without sufficient ideological foundation. But this does not make it desirable. On the contrary, the crises that have frequently assailed democracy have arisen because it had no clear foundations in social and political philosophy and because attempts to supply it with foundations in the philosophy of either the Enlightenment or Romantic Movement frequently failed. A similar crisis frequently assailed nationalism. Its advocates had to explain repeatedly that nationalism is not the same as Chauvinism, since nationalism can be liberal whereas Chauvinism is by definition anti-liberal nationalism.

This indicates intellectual difficulties. In addition to these was the practical difficulty to find a clear demarcation between liberal and non-liberal nationalism. Even those who explained this fact met this difficulty, and many of them were troubled about it.

Perhaps the most outstanding example of this trouble appears in the writings of Vladimir Jabotinsky, who certainly was influenced by diverse liberal ideas, as he confessed and as is anyway clear from his writings and correspondence. Despite this influence on his ideas, he repeatedly used Romantic arguments and language. And if he himself was or was not a Romantic, many among his audience considered him one.

Specifying the most important differences between liberal nationalism and Romantic Chauvinism should facilitate the study of the phenomenon of nationality from the liberal viewpoint, both in order not to get entangled in a reactionary world-view and in order not to ascribe to nationalism uncritically a reactionary or Romantic attitude. This facilitates discussion of the existence of nations and of national aspirations, in both reactionary and liberal manners, without confusing these two *a priori*, while examining them in fact and deed. What differentiates between them is not necessarily the presence or absence of liberalism — since the acceptance of a Romantic claim one may unwittingly shift from liberal nationalism to reactionary Chauvinism — but rather the readiness to recognize national aspirations and accept their legitimacy unconditionally.

To repeat, at the base of the classical theories of political philosophy was the problem of the legitimacy of government, or the problem of sovereignty: what right has the ruler to rule?

The answer to this question turns government into government by right, and therefore, usually unwittingly, to an ideal government. The answer has to be Utopian — whether a Utopia of the Enlightenment Movement, according to which individuals are free because they are ruled voluntarily and in their own interests, or one of the Romantic Movement, according to which the national society rules itself by virtue of its being a nation. Modern liberal democrats should refuse to answer this question precisely because the answer to it renders the state a Utopia, an ideal state. Instead, liberal democrats should recognize the existence of government as a matter of fact and consider our task not to justify it but to make it as liberal and democratic as possible. For, the desire for liberty also exists as a matter of fact, and this fact should win as successful an expression as possible (6).

The advocates of liberal nationalism not familiar with what has been said in the previous paragraph, may easily be swayed to accept the Romantic answer, which, to repeat, raises the dangerous question, What makes a group of humans into a nation? What characterizes a collection of people that deserves self-rule? This question is dangerous because it is the question of the conditions of the nation's right to national liberty.

In European history of the nineteenth century, a very important place is allotted to the national liberation movements that were dragged into this controversy. There were nations in Western Europe, for whom the national question was not important, because it did not raise questions except that of the exact boundaries of the nation-state. The national question raised in Germany and in Italy the simultaneous desire for national liberty and national unity, whereas Switzerland remained outside the picture altogether. Outside Switzerland, those who studied the national question preferred to overlook its existence — since it was a democratic nation-state, a fact that refuted all the theories about national character. Switzerland itself preferred not to be dragged into the stormy dispute about the national question. The East was ruled by empires, the Austria-Hungarian, the Russian, and in part also the Ottoman, all of which were under threat of dissolution by the nationalist movements.

A special place was allotted to the Jewish problem. According to Enlightenment theory, Jews should have been given full civil rights, at once, and unconditionally, that is to say, they should have been granted total emancipation, complete liberation. According to the Romantic theory, Jews are not totally equal unless they are members of nations, but how can it be that a Christian nation should have a member who is not a Christian? Therefore proposals were repeatedly made to deprive Jews of the right to emancipation and to lock them up in ghettos as a national minority (aliens, members of a different nation), until they would agree to convert to Christianity. But how is it possible to consider them members of another nation, when they lack such major national characteristics as a national territory?

Inconsistently, Marxist leaders too studied the national question. According to Marxism, nationality does not exist at all, but Marxists could not overlook the existence of nations and tried to take it into account — of course while studying the Romantic question: What characterizes a nation? As a conspicuous example, Joseph Stalin wrote a book dealing with the national question. His central thesis was that the Jews do not constitute a nation because they have no motherland. Ironically, this claim was no novelty at all, since it had already been made at the beginning of the nineteenth century in Germany, from whence it spread to all the places reached by the nationalist movement, which was, to a large extent, a confusion or a mix of liberal nationalism and Chauvinism.

Therefore, anyone who wishes to belong to a nationalist movement without being a chauvinist has to recognize as a fact the very existence of national sentiments, and the assumption that there are factors that enhance its development, including the desire for national liberty. The fact that nations exist has to be recognized, and the fact that diverse human groups develop the desire for national independence, thereby becoming nations. These facts should be accentuated as much as possible: the Enlightenment Movement did not recognize the existence of nations, and the Romantic Movement did not recognize the development of nation, but presented the existence of a nation as an accomplished fact, which justifies its self-rule and its desire for self-rule. By contrast, the liberal national movement considers the nation a dynamic entity whose development might be helped and which it is desirable to help develop so that it should progress and liberate itself and its members. And thus, today, after the defeat of Romanticism in World War II, it became fashionable to speak about nation-building as a desirable process, and even as a matter of course.

This is a most significant fact — intellectually, from the viewpoint of the study of the rise of political ideology, and practically from the viewpoint of the politics of the twentieth century after World War II. This was the period of the United Nations Organization, when the idea of building and recognizing new nations came to be adopted by this organization. Regrettably this idea came incidentally and without much thinking or planning invested in it, so that it went into decline.

The Enlightenment Movement was contemptuous of human history. Its thinkers saw in history only a failed beginning, a collection of facts about tyrants who belonged to some local traditions, who imposed on their subjects prejudices received from their local traditions, to serve the political oppression of their brethren and neighbors. The Enlightenment Movement viewed the true beginning of human history in the acceptance of the rule of reason both over human thinking — the development of the sciences — and over all areas of social and political life — the development of rational society. The Romantic Movement saw history as the most important and essential human science, since, contrary to physics and chemistry, the sciences that assume the existence of atomic matter, the laws of politics and of psychology are limited to historical conditions and assume the existence of organic societies. Therefore, the Romantics sharply criticized the outlook of the Enlightenment Movement as lacking an evolutionary historical dimension in its description of the world, as if every state in it was fixed and stable rather than a process. One might say that according to the Romantics, the error of the Enlightenment Movement was in looking at the cinematic film as if it was a collection of single isolated stills. However, this very same criticism should be leveled at Romantic philosophy itself, especially because it too is unable to explain the development of nationalist movements, or the development of the nation-state. This inability is concealed behind the claim that the most important principle is that the nation has historical roots. (Indeed, every social structure is rooted in history, including the structures that support the natural sciences.)

Let us take again the example of the United States. Officially there is no American nation, only citizens and the state. American individualism required that the state be given only the role of an instrument for the service of individuals (citizens) who inhabit it. Nevertheless, the country had a national liberation movement at the time of its War of Independence, a movement whose ideas did not disappear after the Declaration of Independence and recognition of which was expressed in the official slogan "one nation under God", and later even with the slogan "one nation indivisible", and even in the anti-individualist slogans of some of the leaders of its War of Independence. Indeed, due to the absence of a sufficiently appropriate expression to American nationalism, the national sentiment often received a religious expression, because the United States seemed, quite rightly, to be a Christian country, or a Christian nation. But this view is of accomplished facts and not of a process. It does not even account for the legal fact that grants some legitimization to this or that political or religious institution. Nevertheless, when the wave of immigration, which was to a considerable part Jewish, grew at the beginning of the twentieth century, legislation was enacted in order to limit it and this limitation discriminated between immigrants according to the country of origin: in fact immigration from English-speaking countries was never limited. The limitation was made on the basis of the claim that the national character of the United States had to be maintained. Half a century later, in the 1970s, this immigration law was declared contrary to the Constitution of the United States (which was based, we may remember, on the idea of human rights), and the law was abolished. There still are immigration laws in the United States, as well as a law permitting the authorities there to deport a criminal who is an immigrant, but not a criminal who is born a citizen. The excuse for the existence of such laws is not satisfactory, due to the lack of a satisfactory theory of the nation-state. Thus the United States, which is a nation-state, is often recognized as a state but not as a nation, and this was the case even in periods in which American national pride became so excessive as to bear on Chauvinism and despite the fact that American national pride is a well-known fact.

The source of this difficulty is this: the principle of a national right to self-determination has no appropriate formulation within liberal philosophy, despite all the discussions concerning the principle and despite the fact that even the very mention of this principle brings about a very favorable and even a very emotional response. The two precise formulations that it might be given cancel it altogether.

One is the liberal, Enlightenment formulation, according to which every human collection can declare itself a nation, and that renders joining as well as leaving the nation no more than a mere administrative matter. In this way, nationality, and joining one nation or another, is considered no more than joining or leaving a sporting club or a commercial establishment. The Enlightenment formulation does not grant any content to nationality but gives it a mere administrative framework for the sole purpose of the convenience of government. The other formulation is Romantic, and it requires that there be content to nationality and that this content should be fixed *a priori*. This formulation contains the claim that the content of nationality is a compound of a few clear defining characteristics. Yet, as a matter of fact, these defining characteristics are not clear, and the Romantics themselves still quarrel about the list of the characteristics required to define a nation as a nation. (It is not clear which components are, and which are not, vital for integrating into a national unit.) Nevertheless, it is important that nations exist and that their existence is recognized, with or without a definition. If a nation does not exist, we can further ask, is it desirable that it should exist? And if the answer to this question is in the affirmative, we can ask, how is it possible to accelerate the process of the formation of a nation (7)?

The principle of self-determination, therefore, seems different from what the two traditional intellectual frameworks recommend. National self-determination may be viewed as the height of a process of national crystallization. We have to admit several points, including the following. This process is not sharply delineated. Its product is not complete. We do not quite know what the factors are that bring about this process of nation building and which of the factors that participate in the process constitutes a considerable and significant part of it. Similarly, it should be recognized that not every part of the nation can detach itself and declare itself a separate nation, for this may conflict with the principle of national unity. Therefore, those who seriously endorse the principle of national self-determination have to clarify for themselves (more precisely than has been done thus far) how the principles of national unity and of national self-determination complement and limit each other. In addition, it has to be fully and explicitly admitted that the Enlightenment Movement was mistaken in viewing the process of joining a nation as akin to joining a commercial firm, since naturalization is not a mere administrative process. And it also has to be fully and explicitly admitted that the Romantic Movement was mistaken in considering membership in a nation as something given and unalterable.

The principle of national self-determination should be clarified in the light of all this: it should be worded, in accord with the proposal made by Hillel Kook, as the principle of self-determination both of the individual and of the nation. As a result, individual membership in the nation will become a right and not a duty, and national awareness and sentiment will not clash with the commitment to liberalism and democracy. Also, national liberty will thus comprise both the liberty of the nation as a whole and the liberty of the individual as a member of the nation.

In conclusion, because the scholarly literature has thrown into doubt the very existence of nations, the question of the definition of the very concept of the nation has been raised, and this has derailed the whole discussion. The theoretical political literature has a chapter on the history of nationalism that centers on the definition of a nation. This chapter is already closed, because the concept of definition itself has changed radically in the modern literature of logic and mathematics — so much so that today most philosophers and scientists rightly refuse to settle disputes with the help of verbal definitions. But a remnant of the traditional passion for the study of definitions still persists and this remnant is the study of criteria for making distinctions. For example, how can we distinguish between groups that belong to the same nation from groups that do not? Usually, criteria invite thought experiments. For example, imagine that two groups declare war against each other. Is this a civil war or a war between neighbors? Assume that an answer to this question was already given. If the first option was chosen then it has already been decided that the two groups belong to the same nation; otherwise it has been decided to the contrary; and if one has difficulty deciding between these two options, then it is a borderline case. The existence of borderline cases is a very important fact, which both classical philosophies reject.

The English philosopher Thomas Hobbes lived at the time of the Great Rebellion, the civil war in Britain in the middle of the seventeenth century. The nub of his political theory was the notion that the role of the state is limited to the prevention of civil war. This notion has lingered in the literature in various forms to the present. In this way, it is natural to assume the very concept of the nation was classically introduced into the discussion and even into political theories that officially refused to recognize the existence of nations. Admittedly, adherents to these theories said that they were opposed to all war, and their demand that the state should defend its citizens against enemies both from without and from within was merely the readiness to recognize a necessary evil. But recognition of the very difference between the (theoretical and practical) attitude of the state to a foreign enemy and its attitude to an internal enemy constitutes the recognition of the fact that the state is aware of its own nation. And, indeed, the modern nation-state managed to overcome the threat of civil war and bring internal peace, at least relatively so, well before it succeeded in overcoming the problem of international wars and bringing about even a relative world peace, precisely because the nation is a basic component in the nation-state.

Chapter 5 *On Wars of Independence*

The existence of the nation was recognized even by liberals who opposed the nationalist principle: they opposed nationalism in principle, not in fact. They made a clear distinction between civil war and international war, of course, and in two ways. The first was territorial: civil war takes place between groups within the national territory, whereas international war involves either attempts at conquest of foreign territory or boundary conflicts. The second was legal: the prevention of civil war is the task of one government, be it ruled by a tyrant or by the law, whereas good neighborly relations rest on understanding between countries or on non-aggression pacts. A little deliberation will show that this applies to the situation accepted in the modern world, not in tribal societies and not in societies of earlier ages, especially not those that employed mercenary armies. The liberal members of the Enlightenment Movement therefore saw in the rule of law a necessary condition for enlightened rule, and rightly so. What, therefore, in their opinion, is the right attitude of the citizen to the law? All liberal thinkers agreed that as long as the law is given to improvement by peaceful means, it is obligatory, even though it is not ideal. But who decides whether this is so? And how is it possible to act if this is not so? These are open questions. Clearly, when the rulers were speakers of French who behaved in a tyrannical manner towards the peasants who spoke different local dialects, it could be expected that the latter would organize in order to rebel. Before the rise of national movements, this was the situation both in England, where there was no peasant revolt, and in some German principalities, where there was a peasant revolt — one that was suppressed violently and cruelly. The German peasant revolt may then be viewed as the beginning of the German national movement, and the suppression of this revolt as the beginning of distortions that were not rectified for ages if they ever have been. (Possibly the recent unification of Germany will permit rectification of these distortions and then Germany will be able to enter proper cultural life; it is too early to judge this matter, which, anyway, is outside the present discourse.) Even the diverse movements in Russia in the nineteenth century may be viewed as national liberation movements, despite Russia having been an independent state not occupied by foreign rulers.

Hence, according to classical liberal literature, national liberation wars are civil wars in which the ruled view themselves as members of a self-liberating nation. Hence the distinction between wars of liberation and civil wars raises afresh the specious question, what is a nation? The question is almost unavoidable, particularly when account is taken of the fact that members of the ruling foreign nation tend, rationally enough, to find collaborators among the members of the conquered nation.

This question is specious nonetheless; it brings the discussion at once to the mold of Romantic philosophy, which recognizes nations as organic bodies and which provides too simplistic a criterion for their being organic: national liberation movements of real nations must succeed sooner or later (7).

But precisely here the superiority of the liberal nationalist theory is manifest, both as compared with the classical liberal theory which opposes nationalism, and as compared with the Chauvinist, illiberal, Romantic nationalism. For the liberal nationalist theory endorses the principle of the rule of law and the legitimacy of the law on the basis of its endorsement by the nation. This theory deems then as justified any movement for national liberation as one of many possible liberation movements in which the injustice of the ruler is based on discrimination. In this way, those discriminated against are given incentive to unify in order to improve their lot and attain justice.

But the present discussion raises a question that is no less difficult: what is justice and what is injustice? Liberalism, we may remember, views justice as the rule of law validated by a contract between the members of the nation who agreed to accept it, explicitly or implicitly. But this answer was officially rejected during the severe crisis which the liberal movement underwent as the result of the Nuremberg trials immediately after World War II (trials in which war criminals were tried and held responsible despite the fact that they had committed crimes while obeying superior orders). Additional considerations for the mass movements in the West in the sixties and the seventies concerning conflict between morality and the law led these movements to develop a style of passive resistance and they continued to violate the law to various degrees of violence, because in the Nuremberg trials the judges had ruled decidedly against obeying an immoral law.

I have explained in other places, in scholarly (8) and not so scholarly writings (9), why this solution is impossible: if in principle citizens must consult their conscience first, then there is no place for the law, except in matters that do not pertain to questions of conscience; no legal system is possible within this limitation, and yet society cannot exist without a more or less publicly endorsed system. Hence, our attitude towards laws that seem immoral to us, must change, both in the international and national frameworks.

As to international law, the question has been handled in the writings of Yoram Dinstein in a book that is considered a classic on this question (10). I have discussed this question elsewhere, and it does not concern us here (11). As to the conflict between ethics and law within a given national framework, matters are much simpler and in this way modern parliamentary democracy is superior to ancient Greek democracy: the rule is that the law must be respected even during a parliamentary struggle intended to repeal it. In addition, it has been accepted today, and justly so, that in borderline cases it is better to be ready to pay the price of personal resistance, accepting arrest or other penalties in the hope of raising public awareness of the immorality of this or that law, on the assumption that this awareness will hasten the process of legal reform.

This is a positive innovation. We cannot understand some given historical situations except by taking into account the fact that this innovation was not known in those situations. For the sake of clarity, let me stress that this innovation appeared in the time of the mass protest movement during the Vietnam War, and also during the concurrent passive resistance approach of the Black civil rights movement in the United States under the leadership of Dr. Martin Luther King. It is easy to confuse King's position with that of Mahatma Gandhi, who was active in the thirties and in the forties, because both used the slogan of passive resistance. As to Martin Luther King, violation of the law, not passivity, was his main point. As to Gandhi, passivity was his main point; he did not raise any legal question at all. The celebrated theologian Reinhold Niebuhr discusses the question before us in his book, *Moral Man and Immoral Society* (12). He went so far as to charge Gandhi with confusion between passive resistance and no resistance at all, noting that passive resistance was a means of political struggle. Today it is easy to see how right Niebuhr was; had Gandhi been struggling against Nazi Germany and not against Great Britain, he surely would have lost, for the Germans at that period would have been very happy to meet passive resistance with machine guns, and exterminate the enemy at minimal cost.

Gandhi's political power lay, therefore, in his knowledge that the means he had undertaken would help win the struggle against Britain by winning sympathy for and moral goodwill towards his struggle. So, when Gandhi said, as Niebuhr quotes him as saying, that passive resistance succeeds in mysterious ways, he was misleading his audience. In fact, claims Niebuhr, Gandhi agreed that violence is equally valid as a means of struggle, in one case only: when violence mobilizes sympathy and moral goodwill better than passive resistance does. So Niebuhr himself justified violence in any struggle for national liberation.

How do fighters for national liberation justify their violation of the law?

Let us open with the question, When is it at all permissible to violate any law whatsoever? To repeat, social reformers in the new style of Martin Luther King recognize the law and their violation of the law, and they are willing to pay for this by going to jail or accepting any other penalty. It is not the same for any freedom fighters in the old style, be they members of the Irgun — the Jewish National Military Organization — or of Gandhi's Indian national movement, or members of the armed forces fighting for freedom in the American Revolution two centuries ago. For, unlike Dr. King, these three other movements fought against foreign rule. Similarly, in these three cases the rebels claimed that they were not rebels but freedom fighters. That is to say, they refused to recognize the law. They were not fighting for the achievement of freedom, but for the maintenance and realization of an existent freedom.

Readers who follow this discussion in the light of common sense will surely ask, what is the difference between a fighter trying to achieve freedom and a fighter trying to maintain freedom? The answer rests in the legitimacy of the struggle: free individuals do not recognize the law that oppresses them, and their struggle is legitimized by their very liberty. This is a dangerous point; one small step differentiates it from the claim of the reactionary Romantic philosophy that the existence of the nation legitimizes; for, after all, the German nation granted legitimacy to its Nazi Government, and Nazi law accorded highest priority to any edict of the Leader, with no consideration of any other kind, since the Leader required blind obedience. It is no accident that the American Revolution, which took place before the rise of the Romantic Movement and founded itself on the liberal, individualist philosophy of the Enlightenment Movement, used a technical justification: the American revolutionaries argued that the rule of the British Government expired, as far as North America was concerned, because it was illegal to tax people not represented in the legislature. (No taxation without representation, was the slogan of the rebels.) There was an enormous value to the arguments on the basis of which rebels do not recognize their being rebels, since they do not recognize the law against which they rebel. This made it possible, in the period in which the more modern ideas were not available, to distinguish between freedom fighters and armed robbers.

I had a classmate in elementary school by the name of Absalom Habib. After we grew up, we parted ways. He was a member of the Irgun National Military Organization. In the same period I became a Marxist and deemed legitimate only mass struggle, not the struggle of an élite — even if it aims to arouse a mass movement. Habib was arrested and sentenced to death. The British authorities in Palestine knew that his execution would cause them some unpleasant consequences, since it could spark a negative reaction in both the Hebrew public and the British. It did not occur to them that it would be preferable to ignore the verdict and simply not to hang him. So they encouraged him to ask for a reprieve. He refused, for to do so would have been to recognize the British rule. He preferred execution. The story of his colleague, Dov Gruner, who was hanged together with him, was even more shocking: under pressure he asked for a reprieve, but the next day he withdrew his request. This is also true of other young people who faced execution, feeling that there is a difference of life and death between being freedom fighters, who violate a law which they do not recognize, and merely fighting against a recognized law (13).

Does this, then, justify violence? No doubt, Habib and Gruner saw themselves as freedom fighters, and, no doubt, the authorities considered them gangsters. The question is, when and under what conditions is violence of one sort or another justifiable?

Let me begin with the Marxist position which, to repeat, in my youth I endorsed. In Marx's view, when the masses of workers are aware of existing injustice and of the value of the revolution, it is easy to call them to take over the government. The way to educate workers, he added, is by the just struggle for ends which workers will attain only after they will take over the government. The way to educate workers for readiness to fight for these aims, in his view, is by a just struggle for humbler aims, for the aims of the workers as they understand them. That is to say, in the beginning, the aim of the struggle is better pay and better work conditions, and in the end, it is the revolution. Marx's theory is mistaken, of course, although it is most intelligent. But, of course, along with being mistaken, it is limited: it is not applicable, for instance, to the European partisans who, under the yoke of the Nazi conquest, completely overlooked the Marxist theory and agreed to conduct an underground struggle against the rule imposed by the Nazi conquest.

There is no doubt, then, that guerrilla war was considered justified at almost any period of time, even when the fighters in question did not represent the majority of the population. This is equally true in the case of the Maccabees, who fought the conquerors of Palestine, as in the case of the partisans during World War II. In the case of the partisans, there was within the public general sympathy for them and, had the situation been normal, they were the sort of people the population would have supported. Hence, fighters who represent a minority of the population receive legitimization not from philosophical arguments but on a technicality: they claim that were their country free, then the population would willingly accept them and bless them, yet, by virtue of being under oppressive rule, the population is unable to give proper political expression to their aspirations.

In this way nationalist liberal philosophy links political relations at home and abroad. Fighters who represent a minority but claim that were their country free they would have the support of the majority, use the struggle as a political means by which to mobilize public opinion both at home and abroad. This should not surprise, since the state of a war of national liberation is an intermediate situation, between inner liberation, as was the case in the French Revolution, and liberation from a foreign oppressor, as was the case with the struggle of India against Britain or in the struggle of the Jewish population in Palestine against it.

To conclude, by overlooking the fact that passive resistance is a political weapon, Gandhi gave it mystical characterization. In so doing, he generalized his demand for passive resistance to all cases, including the case of the Jews of Europe. He thus opposed the Zionist Movement and demanded that European Jews should fight the Nazis by passive resistance. Of course, this was an unrealistic demand, as Martin Buber claimed in his open letter to Gandhi. And, of course, the required solution had to be a national solution, including mass migration, except that this solution failed and the mass migration began only after Israel declared independence.

The difference, again, was not specific to Israel. World War I was imperialist, and all who partook in it were irresponsible. The founding of additional states in Europe after the War admittedly answered certain demands but did not remove the shame of the War from the participants in it. And the claim that the Versailles Treaty is just as well as the claim that it is not just — the claims that stood behind World War II — both are utterly frivolous. The fact that World War I was gladly joined both by those who pretended to be liberal and by those who pretended to be socialists rendered the theory of the Enlightenment a devalued coinage.

The Russian Revolution, and other revolutions that visited Europe in its wake, and the subsequent war of intervention against Russia, all championed liberty. But it was the readiness to exhibit untold irresponsibility while uttering high-sounding verbiage that gave birth to World War II and to the dreadful disaster that it was for humanity, the German nation and, particularly, the Jewish people.

Chapter 6: The Jewish Problem

The Jews constituted a central issue in the history of all European nationalist movements. The reason for this was simple: the Romantic movement was, we remember, the almost official ideology of the nationalist movements and it advocated not liberal nationality but the anti-liberal Chauvinism that commends xenophobia, the hatred of strangers, and even the hatred of the different just because they are different. In particular, the mark of German Romantic philosophy was its hostility to Jews. Thus, for example, the leading German Romantic philosopher, Georg Wilhelm Friedrich Hegel, contended in his early writings that the Jews had lost their right as a nation, whether because they were too ancient a nation or because in their depravation they had rejected the national hero, Jesus Christ. He concluded that Jews are merely mechanical. In other words, in the private opinion of the young Hegel, the Jews were not human, because they were not members of a nation; for, individuals derive their humanity from society and, according to the Romantic teaching, society is identical with state. (In his later writings Hegel was more cautious but no less venomous.)

That the Jews constituted a central topic in the nationalist debates in Europe in the nineteenth century does not necessarily mean that they constituted a central problem. So it should be noted that, in addition to being the target of hostility, they also constituted a central problem, and that is why they were discussed in all important debates concerning the national problem. The reason for this is that in the nationalist movements and the literature on nationality, discussion concerning nationality centered on politically problematic cases.

Cases that were not politically problematic were simply ignored. The question could be asked, for example, whether the English constituted a national entity despite the fact that England never had a national liberation movement. But generally this question was not asked. Nor was any other question asked about England, because in England no political problem gave rise to it. The thinkers who dealt with the national question generally tended to handle burning political problems. Those who recognized Scotland as a political problem asked the question, are the Scots a separate national entity and where is their national liberation movement? Those who did not consider Scotland problematic, were glad to fuse Scotland with England and even to consider the Scots English for all intents and purposes — an insult to all Scots, even those who did not care about the national problem.

The Jewish problem should be presented as it was presented in the literature of the nineteenth century. But then one should at once add to this the following observation: the term "problem" in the singular is misleading, since the Jews caused different problems for different publics at different times. The present chapter will therefore offer a survey of the diverse problems that could be seen as the Jewish problem, or as parts of the Jewish problem. And it is convenient to begin such a discussion from the standpoint of the various nationalist movements.

At first, to repeat, the theoretical expression of the nationalist movement was received from German Chauvinist philosophy. In early nineteenth century German Chauvinist literature, one question was central and cardinal from the national political viewpoint: should Jews in diverse German states be offered full citizen's rights? This was the question of the emancipation of the Jews. As a result of the French Revolution, the French Jews received full citizen's rights and the Jewish problem was not raised there for a century, until towards the end of the nineteenth century, when the French clericalist reactionary movement expanded and raised the question in an artificial manner in a display of a position that clearly opposed the principles of the French Revolution.

The famous Dreyfus Affair gave focus for the debate, in which the whole nation took an active part. Alfred Dreyfus, a general staff officer, was condemned in 1894 to life imprisonment for allegedly having betrayed military secrets to Germany. This was an error that the French authorities recognized and yet preferred not to correct. The debate about this affair became the symbol of the struggle between the radicals (the heirs of the Enlightenment Movement) and the clericalists (the reactionaries). At the beginning of the nineteenth century, the winds of the French Revolution had blown eastwards, and Jews in diverse German states had received full citizen's rights. These rights had been withdrawn towards the middle of the century as a result of the Reaction, causing a wave of conversion to Christianity among the liberated members of the German-Jewish community and setting the stage for such reactions as accompanied the Dreyfus Affair. Thus there is truth in the Zionist allegation received among the historians of the Zionist Movement, that but for the hatred of the Jews many more Jews would have assimilated into the European nations within a very short time, since those who inflame the hatred of Jews brought back consciousness of their Jewish roots to those who had lost it, and to some of them the consciousness of Jewish identity returned too — national as well as religious.

In East Europe, the national problem became acute towards the end of the nineteenth century because of the fierce competition between the nationalist and socialist movements. Part of the competition concerned those Jewish youths who had left the ghetto and embraced the ideas of the Enlightenment Movement, since they constituted a pool of possible recruits as activists both in the national liberation movements of Eastern Europe and in the socialist movements there. But very soon the nationalist movements rejected the Jews, leaving most of the young Jews with a choice between socialist activity and nationalist Jewish activity.

So far the attitude of European nationalist movements to the Jewish problem at the end of the nineteenth century. What do these have to do with the Jewish nationalist movement? The answer is that from its very start the Jewish nationalist movement accepted its ideology from European nationalist movements.

The Jewish nationalist movement began as a social movement before it received any political expression. It is difficult to understand and know how Jewish nationality looked to East European Jews in the middle of the nineteenth century. The first public expression of Jewish nationality or to Jewish national identity was pathetic. It was the revival of the Hebrew language, that is to say, the writing in stilted Hebrew of novels and poetry whose content was largely borrowed from mediocre European stock. Nevertheless, not to be deeply impressed by this pathetic phenomenon, to be unable to see in it a dimension that is far from the pathetic, a dimension that has in it daring and even a measure of heroism, is to lack — not necessarily national sensitivity but certainly human sensitivity. For nationality is a general human phenomenon, since it answers certain human needs (14).

Significantly, the expansion of the Jewish nationalist movement was the spreading of the Jewish national identity as separate from the Jewish religious identity, sometimes in opposition to it and sometimes in addition to it, and possibly sometimes also as a substitute for it. In one way or another, to begin with, this identity was unoriginal and meager in ideas, lacking in all theoretical dimension. That is to say, it received the few ideas that it had from the European thought of that period. Moreover, the movement received at one and the same time ideas of both the Enlightenment Movement and the Romantic Movement or the Reaction, which caused great intellectual confusion in Jewish Enlightenment in general. Nachman Krochmal's ideas were difficult to comprehend, because they were expressed in florid Hebrew and because he was influenced by German philosophers whose ideas are heavy and cloudy. His writings were published only after his death in the middle of the nineteenth century, and they are classical to this very day; I do not know if they had any influence on the Jewish nationalist movement and what message his writings might have brought to the ordinary Jewish public. It is clear, in any case, that the confusion in his writings of Enlightenment and Romantic ideas was typical of the thought of the Jewish nationalist movement and its offshoots, and continued to be so perhaps up to the present. Similarly, Peretz Smolenskin imitated in his major novel the cheapest part of the anti-clericalist literature of the Western Enlightenment Movement, and just as that literature presented leading religious figures, cardinals and the likes, as womanizers, so Smolenskin presented the Hassidic rabbi, the Zaddik, as a womanizer. This, of course, is very foolish. Yet it is important that he wrote his books in Hebrew. And though he wrote very few novels, in part following the Enlightenment ideology and in part the Romantic ideology, including the idea that a Jew who has a sense of national identity will find a place in a synagogue even after having lost all religious conviction and thereby also all religious identity. Other writers, particularly Mendili, succeeded after a fashion in blending Enlightenment and Romantic thought while relying for inspiration on Russian literature, which at its early stage tended more towards the Enlightenment but very quickly moved to the Romantic camp and remained a mixture of aspirations for progress and nationalism. The nationalist aspirations often received chauvinistic expression, particularly in the writings of Dostoevski. The expression they received in the writings of Tolstoy is more liberal, though still confused.

The present study does not deal with literature and art and certainly not with the history of literature. But one cannot study the history of political ideas in the nineteenth century without studying the faulty foundations given them by the Romantic Movement, and that Movement cannot be presented in disregard of literature and art. The Romantic Movement, as opposed to the Enlightenment Movement, did not attempt to compete with it in intellectual acuity and scientific precision. Instead of appealing to the human intellect, it whipped up deep local sentiments through diverse means — religious, cultural, and artistic. According to the Enlightenment theory, thinking is the essential human quality and all humans share thoughts; there is, therefore, no greater human achievement than science, and science is common to all humans as humans. According to the Romantic theory, there is no bigger human achievement than the genius of a developed nation and of its national leadership, intellectual, political, and military, and this achievement is expressed in national culture, including religion, art, and way of life. The Romantic Movement taught that a flourishing nation should aspire not towards what unifies humanity, but rather towards what unifies itself. And to that end, the nation has to impose and implement what is specific to it, in order to impose it both on its own members and on all of its neighbors. As far as possible, the tendency towards this imposition of one's genius on neighbors became an integral part of the anti-liberal, Chauvinist character of the nationalist movement. And this Chauvinism, to repeat, tended to hold a monopoly on all nationalist movements making it a cardinal duty to steer nationalism away from liberalism as far as possible.

The rise of Jewish nationalism, it bears repeating, had no roots in any internal development within Judaism; Judaism remained the same with but minor changes for almost two millennia, from the destruction of the Second Temple to that time. The origins of Jewish nationalism, therefore, may be clearly traced to the development of the western world. And, indeed, the idea of the Jewish return to Zion appeared first in the nineteenth-century writings of all those authors who did not know what was to be done with the local Jews.

The antecedents to Zionism can be found in the writings of the celebrated seventeenth-century philosopher Benedict Spinoza, who was expelled from the Amsterdam Jewish community, and in those of the famous English philosopher Joseph Priestley, the celebrated discoverer of oxygen in the eighteenth century, as well as in the writings of diverse nineteenth century authors, whose names decorate the early pages of every history of the Zionist Movement.

It was easy for an author unfamiliar with the Jewish problem to solve it with the pretext that it is desirable to send the Jews away, and even to turn this cruel pretext into a humane idea by the additional pretext that they should be sent back to their own motherland. The evidence for this is that even the most extreme Chauvinist movements, which incited the masses to violent hatred of foreigners, particularly to hatred of the Jews, often used the slogan: Jews, go to Palestine! And in this respect there is no difference between the crude, insensitive people who tormented the local Jews and the enlightened noble philosopher, since the Jews had nowhere to go. And, indeed, one who does not appreciate the fact that the Jews did not have the option to migrate to Palestine, is unable to appreciate the great daring of the Jewish nationalist movement, including the Zionist movement at its very inception, which looked at the time like utter madness to many Jews, among them individuals who possessed a very clear national identity. It is clear, then, that the political thought of the Jewish nationalist movement underwent an important change when, instead of praying for the return to Zion, a discussion of its realization emerged, despite all the dangers involved. This change began when the leaders of that movement began to write political treatises instead of novels and poetry in Hebrew. What was this development?

Since Jewish nationalism imbibed its nationalist ideas from German philosophy, it had no choice but to claim that the Jewish nation existed in actuality. And because German philosophy saw the abnormal situation of the Jewish people as proof of their not being a nation, Jewish nationalism demanded normalization in a way similar to the one in which German nationalism had demanded a generation earlier. German nationalism had demanded normalization in the form of the unification of the German states, namely, the unification of some of the German-speaking countries. Jewish nationalism demanded the normalization of the Jewish people by the attainment of a motherland. And this in order that the people should qualify for the status of a nation in the very near future. The logical contradiction between the opinion that the Germans or the Jews belong to an existing nation, and the opinion that the Germans or the Jews belong to a people that very soon will become a nation, is the contradiction that afflicted all nationalist movements of emerging nations, in Central Europe and Eastern Europe as well as in other countries. The Jews, however, had to pay dearly for this idea, because normalizing the Jewish nation was very problematic, and in the process of normalization the greater majority of the Jewish people in Europe were butchered. This is how the central purpose of the Zionist movement — to solve the Jewish problem in Eastern Europe by mass transfer of Jews to Palestine — met with utter failure.

We have to return then to our question, how did the Jewish nationalist movement develop, from prayers for a return to Palestine and writings of novels and poems in Hebrew to planning the return to Palestine? Without accepting the limitations of the Romantic ideology, whose language was used at that period, we should discuss the question, how did the Jewish nationalist movement develop? For this ideology does not enable one to discuss emergence but presents what emerges as if it were an accomplished fact.

The most important detail is that the Jewish problem was the result of the general European nationalist movement. This is so because that movement adopted the reactionary, anti-liberal, nationalist ideology of Romantic philosophy. As is well known, the hatred of the Jews was certainly the common inheritance of Europe throughout Jewish history. But the problem was not the hatred of Jews by itself; it was a constant situation that brought about that hatred, whether in Christianity or Islam. And, indeed, a Jew who converted to the local religion personally escaped this hatred. Whole Jewish communities, however, could not escape hatred this way, as is evidenced by the history of the Jews who were forcibly converted to Christianity wholesale in Spain and Portugal and were still hated there. In places where liberalism was the rule, Jews did not suffer much from this hatred. In places where the Reaction was dominant, the demand was voiced to prevent Jews from having equal rights — emancipation or liberty; it was first demanded that they should baptize, but then the notion developed according to which Jews have to be persecuted even after they were baptized, since, culturally and nationally, they are still alien corn. This notion is anti-Semitism, which is the political transformation of the hatred of Jews, and which has brought about the greatest and cruelest disaster to date in the history of Jews and of Europe and perhaps even of the whole human race.

The persecution of Jews or the suffering of Jews that resulted from this persecution, was not the cause of the Jewish national awakening, since Jews had suffered for millennia without any national awakening. The nationalist movements and the diverse national liberation movements in Europe, especially in Eastern Europe, did increase the hatred of the Jews, but this hatred invited diverse responses. One was simply mass migration (to North and South America and to other immigration countries), as was customary in Jewish tradition. Another traditional response was increased segregation in ghetto life, in increased adherence to tradition through the intensification of the Messianic character of Judaism as intensely as possible in total oblivion to the surrounding world.

In addition to these two traditional responses to the intensification of the hatred of Jews, emigration and adherence to a religious ghetto, new possible responses appeared, the roots of which were in new developments that depended not at all on the hatred of Jews but on the emergence of liberation from religious fetters.

This liberation from religious fetters does not necessarily entail the dismissal of religion. Rather, this liberation is nothing but the readiness to see in Judaism diverse components in addition to the religious one, or perhaps in addition to the religion and the religious community as one component. Other components could be culture, tradition, or perhaps even nation. Without discussing such questions as, whether a nation without a specific religion or without a specific culture is possible, or whether a specific culture without a nation is possible, the very image of Judaism as having diverse components must be seen as an innovation, one that invited new thinking and deciding on which component to accept and which to reject. This way, of course, new options of responses to the hatred of the Jews were raised, in addition to the traditional ones.

One option of a response to the hatred of Jews was escape to the socialist movements. This escape was partly to the sort of socialism which was hostile to all national specificity, including the Jewish one, but there was also the escape to a sort of socialism that does recognize the Jewish specificity as a peculiar culture, a culture devoid of any national political dimension. (This was the Jewish Bund.) The Jewish nationalist movement was but one response among many to the great increase in the suffering of Jews, and, to repeat, it was a rather hesitant response, because it had no political expression and no one was on hand who knew how to give it any political or organized expression.

This, then, is the national problem from a Jewish viewpoint in the period of the end of the nineteenth century in Eastern Europe: the problem of the great rise in the suffering of the Jews. This problem was new, because it appeared in a new context and permitted new approaches to its solution. But no national solution to it was found. Against this background Dr. Leo Pinsker's *Auto-Emancipation* should be understood. In this book he claimed that the Jews should not wait until they are given rights, that they ought to take the rights for themselves. And because the existence of a nation requires a motherland, he proposed that the Jews should take for themselves a motherland. And, he proposed incidentally, because the Jews have a historical affinity to Palestine, they should migrate to that land.

Nevertheless, Pinsker did not become the father of the Zionist movement, but the father of the idea of political Zionism. For, he did see the Jewish problem in a political light, but he did not present his solution in a practicable manner. The translation of his solution to the language of practice, then, was hidden in the possible future as an additional step. It is not surprising, therefore, that there was great confusion among Jews in Europe. To a large extent, this confusion was expressed as the sense of a tremendous appeal of the socialist camp to Jews freed from Jewish tradition. This also is not surprising, as is obvious from the fact that in the much more tolerant West, Theodor Herzl identified the Jewish problem with the problem resting on the fact that Jews played a major role in the socialist movements, which were seen as a cause of social instability. Herzl presented Zionism as a solution in the style of typical Western colonialism similar to what was happening in Kenya and Rhodesia at the same time — even though he did so in a much more enlightened and daring fashion than was acceptable at the time: the idea of settling a colony in an organized mass migration as a solution to a national political problem and not as an attempted external conquest.

It is well known that Herzl was ready to accept Uganda as a new motherland for the Jews. Hence, it is clear that he looked for a practical solution to the human Jewish problem. He argued that, because the masses of Jews were rejected by European nations, and because they had no channel for any social or political activity, except for socialist revolutionary activity, it would be better to provide them with a new motherland to which they may migrate, so as to solve both their own problems and those they caused as unwanted guests in Europe. In Eastern Europe, nationalist ideology obviously had a much stronger influence than in the West — both among the population at large and among the Jews there. For Judaism became an important heritage, in addition to its being a religion, for all those East European Jews who lived in a great concentration of population — because these Jews were often free of religious limitations, whether they remained religious or not, and saw in their Judaism not only a shared religion but also a shared culture, shared history, and shared fate (including being persecuted by the local population and including the desire of the local nationalist movements to reject them). That is to say, under the influence of Romantic philosophy, they accepted Jewish culture as an added or a separate phenomenon that accompanied the Jewish religion, but one that was essentially secular, one whose validity was independent of the question of the validity or invalidity of religion. Thus they saw themselves as a nation for all intents and purposes, although they missed having a motherland. They thus felt a new kind of need: the need for a homeland different from the need to return to Zion felt by the religious Jew not aware of Jewish culture from the secular perspective, from the perspective separate from the Jewish religion. They naturally preferred Palestine, the part of the world on which they already had their eyes focused, even though previously their attention had a mere religious, Messianic character. In brief, the love of Palestine became a secular idea and a secular sentiment — both for Jews who had lost their religious faith and for Jews who remained religious while acquiring a new secular, cultural, national sentiment.

To repeat, Chauvinist ideology did not make room for evolution; it is therefore not surprising that the evolution described here was not clear to those who experienced it and that it is still unclear to Israelis today and to most historians of the Jewish people. There was nothing left for the members of the evolving nation but to claim that they were members of a pre-existing nation, of a nation for all intents and purposes, as an accomplished and authentic fact. This only brought them to an attempt, at an increased pace and with great impatience, to achieve what was missing on the list of the characterizations of a nation. Political Zionism demanded massive migration all at one time, once a motherland had been granted. Practical Zionism, in contrast, proposed that Jewish pioneers should migrate to Palestine at once, without waiting for political developments, both because of the historical ties of the Jews to their land and in order to create the impression that they already had a motherland, even though a large portion of the members of the nation still lived in exile for one reason or another.

This looks like a childish inconsistency, but then all nationalist movements in the nineteenth century suffered this inconsistency. This is even more apparent in many historical cases and in many inaccurate historical details concerning which many modern sober historians bitterly complain, although history cannot be recreated, certainly not with the aid of complaints and misgivings.

To conclude, the Jewish problem was a bundle of problems that looked different to different groups from the national perspective or from the intellectual one. Social scientists are ready to recognize this fact as self-evident. But they overlook it when they discuss the Spring of Nations, namely, the period of the blooming of European nationalist movements in the mid-nineteenth century, because this topic, and this period in particular, is the exclusive property of Romantic philosophy, which points at one problem in one formulation in one way from one viewpoint — from the viewpoint of the dominant trend in the dominant nation — while overlooking all other viewpoints. Because of the enormous influence of Romantic philosophy on the nationalist movement in general and on the Zionist movement in particular, and because historians generally tend towards Romanticism anyway, history books in general and histories of Zionism in particular give a unified image of the history of the nationalist movements, especially of the history of Zionism. Because the Practical Zionist faction was dominant in the Zionist movement, the image of the history of Zionism remained as if the other trends within it were nothing but variants of Practical Zionism. This trend was Romantic and in possession of a cloudy political ideology, one that still rules Israel. Consequently, there is still too little political understanding in Israel and no readiness to view the Israeli nation in a new political liberal manner as is required. It may be worthwhile, therefore, to survey the history of the Zionist movement in a liberal light, free from Romantic, irrational features.

* It is regrettable that this discussion as to the differences between the trends within traditional Zionism still has a practical significance, and that this significance is greater today than when this book was written. When the heirs of Political Zionism, Menachem Begin and his associates, attained power, they displayed agreement with Practical Zionism on all points except perhaps in degree, ones that amount to no more than two mere propaganda items: the stress on the nationalist motive and the rejection of the socialist flavor that most leaders of Practical Zionism had endorsed. Surprisingly, in recent years the extremist chauvinists in Israel follow the Practical Zionists both in their economic activities and in their settlements in Judea and Samaria and in the Gaza strip. This is paradoxical, since whereas the early settlers rebelled against British rule, which had lost its jurisdiction when it betrayed its mandate, the settlers today are rebelling against the government of autonomous Israel, thereby endangering its sovereignty. As is well known, the illegal activities of the settlers have gained a tremendous boost from the support they have received from leaders of diverse political parties, including some members of the government. This detail stresses yet again the fact that diverse Israeli governments refuse to recognize Israel's independence on the excuse that most of its nation is not settled in its territory. This flimsy excuse — the notion that Israel belongs to the Jewish people and not to the Israeli nation — is the very threat to its independence. It is therefore imperative that Israel should recognize its nation as separate and different from the Jewish people, though most of its citizens are Jewish. *

Chapter 7: The Birth of the Jewish Nationalist Movement

In presenting the history of the Jewish national movement, one faces a central difficulty that cannot be satisfactorily surmounted. In speaking of movements, one does not mean political groups or political parties (even though it is clear that usually the carriers of diverse political ideas are political groupings) and not the individuals who create them, as the individual who creates a new idea in obscurity — as was the case with Hillel Kook — is not a political power until the new idea breaks through and reaches its intended public. When speaking of a political idea, it is better to concentrate on its central ideas and not dwell on details. But in the present case, the central political idea of the Zionist Movement is the general nationalist idea of nineteenth-century Europe, based on Romantic philosophy, which treats nations as existing entities that justify the existence of sovereign states, or national liberation movements that aim at the founding of sovereign states. And yet the element distinctive to the Zionist Movement was, in addition to the declaration of the existence of a nation, the awareness of the need for nation building. Exceptionally, the less systematic Zionist thinkers, the less consistent and precise ones, found it easier to reach more interesting and more significant conclusions. The central Jewish thinkers at the beginning and middle of the nineteenth-century, such as Nachman Krochmal and Heinrich Graetz, spoke early on about the Jewish nation as existing and accomplished, and thereby confused religion, nation, and people, just as they confused religion, culture, society, and state — in keeping with Romantic philosophy. They spoke from a comprehensive philosophical viewpoint but said things that carried little weight, theoretical or practical. In contrast, journalists such as Moses Leib Lilienblum achieved sharper and more successful conceptions, but the absence of a general theoretical framework prevented them from clarifying, stabilizing, and successfully implanting their achievements.

Thus their achievements were lost almost immediately. Lilienblum belonged to and advanced the Jewish national movement that preceded Zionism, known as the Lovers of Zion. He spoke specifically of the significant divergence in matters religious, both among religious people (between the more conservative and the more liberal adherents to religious practice) and between religious observant and non-observant Jews (called in Israel "secularists"). The religious variance, he predicted, would receive a cultural character, and would remain within the proper framework and gain manageable proportions, if a different factor — that of national unity — were added to it (15). At the same time, Eliezer Ben-Yehudah wrote that his interest was not in the Jewish faith (which he claimed would certainly prevail in the Diaspora) but in the nation, which, he said needed a national territory and a national language. It is no accident that current Zionist tradition holds the opinion that Ben-Yehudah revived the Hebrew language and the opinion that the Hebrew language never died (usually ascribed to the Nobel Laureate Israeli novelist S. Y. Agnon) so that there is no truth in the claim that there was ever a need to revive it. Here the inconsistency characteristic of many nationalist movements receives a particularly clear expression in the Jewish national movement: at one and the same time the nation exists, including all its paraphernalia and characteristics, and it has to be fashioned and given those paraphernalia and characteristics in order to justify its aspirations and sovereignty.

Of course, it is very easy to settle this inconsistency. Both Lilienblum and Ben-Yehudah distinguished the traditional, historical Jewish religion, which maintains continuity with the distant past, and the new situation, which they did not know how to describe. Lilienblum spoke of the aspiration for national independence and of the need to organize a mass migration that would be facilitated through the collection of large sums of money and the purchase of large terrain from the authorities of the Ottoman Empire. Leo Pinsker even distinguished between the Jews and the Jewish nation, and Ben-Yehudah too distinguished between the Jewish religious community and the Jewish nation. Later, Kook and his associates termed this nation the Hebrew nation. Today he speaks of the Israeli nation.

For the distinction between the nation and what has preceded it, more is needed than the distinction between nation and individuals who belong to it, or between nation and religious community, or between nation and culture, and even between nation and society — that social unit called in sociological jargon the Jewish ethnic group. In order to distinguish between the nation and what preceded it, one must distinguish clearly between the Jewish people and the Jewish (or Hebrew or Israeli) nation, just as one must distinguish between the French, German, Italian, and Russian people, and their nations. For it is clear that nations evolved from the peoples that preceded them, even though this is not a historical necessity. The proof that no historical necessity is involved here is in the fact that the same did not happen for national groups that evolved in migration countries, where the majority of the immigration occurred after the American and French revolutions (16).

Clearly, then, there is room for the distinction between society and state, as well as between an ethnic group governed together and a nation. And, indeed, such distinctions were not agreeable to the nationalist movements of the pre-World War II period. Hence, to avoid the errors of streamlining the past through hindsight, care should be taken to avoid using new distinctions to describe any movement from that era. Thus it should be noted that the Zionist Movement began in a nineteenth-century Europe that was torn by internal wars and revolutionary movements, nationalist and socialist. Likewise it should be noted that most of the activities of the Zionist Movement occurred before World War II.

Against this background the differences stand out between the three or four streams that existed in the Zionist Movement from its very inception to its culmination in the foundation of the desired Jewish state: the Political Zionist Movement was founded by Theodor Herzl and Max Nordau; the Spiritual Zionist Movement, was founded by Ahad Ha'am and Martin Buber; finally, the Practical Zionist Movement, including the Socialist Zionist Movement, to which practically all the senior Zionist leaders belonged, deemed itself the legitimate heir of the movement of the Lovers of Zion and that included the aforementioned Lilienblum, Pinsker, and Ben-Yehudah. An addition to these three streams was the New Zionist Movement, or the Revisionist Movement, founded by Vladimir Jabotinsky, that was officially the continuation of the Political Movement and therefore will not be discussed here. It might be worthwhile to look at each of these three traditional streams in the light of the distinctions made above, surveying the degree of awareness of each stream to these distinctions.

The Spiritual Zionist Movement will be examined in the remainder of this chapter; the Political and Practical Zionist Movements will be discussed in the next chapter. The New Zionist Movement will not be discussed here, as its views did not differ from those of the Political Zionist Movement.

The Spiritual Zionist Movement was essentially devoid of real political interest. This does not mean that Ahad Ha'am and Buber showed no interest in the idea of political Jewish independence. On the contrary, they spoke clearly in favor of independence. Admittedly, Buber sided with the ideal of a bi-national state as preferable to a national state, but this was for him a mere technical concern; when the State of Israel was founded he welcomed it and hoped it would enter into a peace treaty with its neighbors (16a). As Buber was a thinker who had molded his own social philosophy both in general and within the framework of the Jewish national movement, one might expect from him a higher degree of consistency and method. I will therefore speak more about Buber than about Ahad Ha'am, though his influence was relatively even smaller. In a classical article, "Between Society and State", in which he criticizes the classical liberal philosophy of the great philosopher Bertrand Russell, Buber dealt with political philosophy. Russell saw society as a collection of individuals and the state as a mere instrument. Buber, by contrast, though he agreed that a state was a mere instrument, claimed that the existence of society was a different matter, that society was an important and independent entity. Yet Buber rejected collectivist philosophy and all his life he adhered to his anarcho-socialism — a blend or a compromise between individualism and collectivism. He took the social ideal to be not only the decentralization of the liberal state (on this he agreed with the liberal political tradition as did Russell), but even in the decentralization of society into communities based on their communal and cultural life. Thus he deviated from the individualist tradition that did not consider social groups, in disagreement with Russell who generally preferred to overlook the shaping of social life. Of course, Buber also deviated from that collectivist tradition which was anti-liberal and thus centralist.

Concerning Zionism, Buber made two main points. On both of these points — and only on these — he agreed with Ahad Ha'am, who repeated them in different ways. First, Buber said, the concentration of Jews in Palestine will not abolish the existence of Jewish communities in the western countries. To this all other streams in the Zionist Movement agreed, except for Jabotinsky, as we will see later. (The ideology of the State of Israel wavers between the opinion of Jabotinsky and the traditional opinion of the majority of Zionists.) Second, they asserted that the significance of the foundation of Jewish settlement in Palestine is not political but cultural, for it would be no achievement if the Jews had an independent state devoid of culture. This is an expression of the failure to distinguish between society and culture, and even between a nation in the sense of a social unit (that it is to say, an ethnic unit) and a nation in the political sense of the word. This failure to make a distinction blocked the understanding of the political role of the national liberation movement. In praise of Buber it might be noted that he succeeded, almost alone, in creating and developing the cultural renewal movement of German Jewry. Admittedly, German Jewry was almost entirely destroyed during the Nazi period, but his activity was not in vain, since the Jewish organizations that he created constituted an important tool for the rescue of the German Jews. But Buber was not able to participate in the political side of the rescue of the German Jews, nor did he do anything to save the Jews of Europe during the War, even though he clearly declared that their rescue had priority over all other activities (16b). As to Ahad Ha'am, he died much earlier, and his major contribution was cultural and critical — as one can see even today from his classical papers "Truth From Palestine" and "Altneuland" that excel in honesty and courage. After his death they said of him that on his deathbed he changed his opinions and accepted the ideas of Practical Zionism. This story is a myth similar to the Catholic myth about members of the Enlightenment who were heretics but repented on their deathbed. It also raises the most difficult question: in what way did he change his opinion? What is the difference between Spiritual Zionism and Practical Zionism?

Chapter 8   *Political and Practical Zionism*

For the sake of clarity and brevity, it is preferable to discuss Political Zionism, the stream in Zionism founded by Herzl and Nordau, before discussing Practical Zionism. The only difficulty in presenting the ideas of Political Zionism is this: the heirs of Practical Zionism to this very day have yet to understand Herzl and his opinions. For example, Shlomo Avineri, whose representative book, *The Making of Zionism*, (17) was endorsed with great sympathy by the whole of the Israeli public except for some ardent adherents of Jabotinsky, views the history of Zionist ideology as the history of the ideology of Practical Zionism. Accordingly, he declares that Herzl made no theoretical or political innovations and did not excel except as a publicist who managed to get the ear of a broad public — Jewish and non-Jewish alike. This should not be considered an idea that merits criticism, as it is not sufficiently serious. But it merits consideration as an important typical fact, which bespeaks the absence of a normal political sense in Israel today — not only in Avineri but also in the broad spectrum of his readers. I will return to this later in more detail.

The presentation of Herzl's idea should begin by noting that his predecessors had a limited outlook. Initially, Herzl was no adherent of the nationalist idea: he viewed the Jewish national problem as the problem of the sufferings of the Jews; only later did he consider the nationalist idea. His predecessors among East European Jews did not discover the national problem — not as a political problem — even though they spoke about it and referred to it. All that they said was merely an outgrowth of their feeling about it, and no more. They spoke of the sufferings of the Jews and of the causes of that suffering. They even succeeded in grasping that the sufferings of the Jews constituted a deadly criticism of the ideology of the European Enlightenment, since in diverse places the Enlightenment Movement, as well as the nationalist movements, increased, rather than decreased, the sufferings of the Jews. I do not know if there is an answer to this deadly criticism. Personally, I tend to think that in countries in which the Enlightenment ideology was sufficiently well absorbed by the general public, and in which genuine liberal national policy was developed, the Jews did not suffer as much, even while enduring discrimination. Only when the clericalists attacked the (Enlightened) liberals, especially in France, was the hatred of Jews renewed. Hence, conceivably the Jewish criticism of the Enlightenment Movement was somewhat excessive. I do not know. But this is an academic question. Because the Enlightenment reaped minimal success in most of Europe, and because the nationalist movement did succeed, the Jews in Europe suffered — whether because of the success of the Enlightenment Movement or despite its preaching brotherhood and logic, or because of its failure to inculcate brotherhood and logic. One way or another, the suffering of the Jews grew unbearably. Herzl's predecessors described this suffering. They also described the fact that the Enlightenment and nationalist movements did not help Jews and they partly proposed (here and there, in small measure) political solutions to the problem, how this suffering should be mastered, including ideas of national revival, of mass migration, and more. But it was Herzl who discovered anew the Jewish problem as a political problem, not as a problem of what should be done to alleviate the suffering of the Jews of Europe. It is known that Herzl did not overlook the suffering of Jewish individuals or of Jewish communities, or the failure of the Enlightenment Movement and the nationalist movements to alleviate that suffering. But, specifically, he attacked the problem from a political viewpoint. The political expression of the Enlightenment Movement was a declaration of Human Rights, which, when applied to Jews was known as the Emancipation of the Jews, that is to say, the legal recognition that Jews had full citizen's rights. Such emancipation should politically abolish Judaism as a political entity and as a political problem. Emancipation had to remove the political dimension from all that remained of Judaism: the Jewish religion, or the Jewish culture and ethnic group. Herzl saw in the failure of the emancipation a political fact that meant the reopening of the political problem. A group or a socio-religious unit was suffering and that required specific political attention: the Jews who were not welcome and were not satisfied constituted a political trauma, but also a political factor as a group that violated the stability of the political systems of Western Europe, thereby constituting a political challenge. In Herzl's view, anyone interested in political stability was well advised to try to remedy this political situation, and the remedy was to be achieved by political means. This was a major step; it was not simply a matter of finding a context for a human problem.

In one characterization, Herzl transformed the Jewish problem from a problem of the Jews to a problem of the whole of Europe — and an urgent one at that. He could therefore appeal (as he did) to political leaders and institutions with a proposal for a political solution: in order to prevent the threat of a whole European explosion, it was advisable to help the dissatisfied Jews to leave Europe and find a political asylum elsewhere — in their own state, in the State of the Jews.

In Avineri's discussion there is no mention of all this. Avineri discusses, of course, the well-known fact that Herzl appealed to political leaders and institutions. He sees this as a proof of Herzl's daring sense of adventure and personal ambition, even emotional instability in a person who, in Avineri's opinion, was merely a successful master of public relations. There is much truth in this; it is obviously desirable to see the personal dimension of Herzl and not to view him solely as a politician. To that extent, Avineri deserves gratitude, regardless of the acceptability or otherwise of his opinions. But it is sad that Avineri describes Herzl as an unstable individual only in order to obliterate his having been a political thinker and a politician representing a non-existent state. Avineri's hidden assumption, that one cannot represent a state that does not exist, is Romantic and mistaken. It is a fundamental error committed by most historians of national movements.

Looking at the facts in their proper historical context, one sees the conservative and radical elements that played significant roles in Herzl's philosophy. It is difficult for us, children of the twentieth century, in light of the fact that in August 1914 the peace of Europe vanished overnight, to imagine the profound sense of social stability that permeated the end of the nineteenth century, expressed in the politics, society, and even art of that period. In that fateful year, the twentieth century entered with immense turbulence the whirlpool from which it has still not emerged. It is therefore difficult for us to see the force and the significance of Herzl, who spoke in the name of this former stability. He stressed that West European Jews were attracted to revolutionary movements, thus putting the desired political stability at risk. All this means little to modern people, with the exception of a few extreme conservatives. But without joining this extreme conservatism, we can see that, with the aid of political conservatism, Herzl presented the Jewish problem as an all-European problem, just as the Black civil rights fighters in the United States presented racial discrimination as an all-American problem. Politically speaking, the problem of racial discrimination is, like the problem of the discrimination against Jews, a problem with a political aspect. Therefore, it has the right to a political solution: to legislation, to a change of the political status of the discriminated, the persecuted, and the sufferers, to obliging the police to defend their rights, to obliging lawcourts to be at their service and enable them to use them in litigation as they find fit, and so on. Herzl had a choice between two options: an attempt at increasing control over the political apparatus in the Western countries, or the attempt to erect a new political apparatus in a new country. In the light of the Dreyfus Affair and the anti-Semitism that caused it and emanated from it, Herzl gave up hope for the first option and adhered to the second. It is clear, then, that Herzl had a Western image of the Jews and of their sufferings, to which he proposed a Western solution: the erection of a new political apparatus through the means of existing political apparatuses. He appealed, therefore, to *foci* of political power, to Sultans, Kaisers, and heads of states, and to world political public opinion — while trying to create organizations of his own, in order to further his political aims.

Without this political dimension which, as is well known, largely failed, there is no difference between Herzl and the Lovers of Zion Movement, or between him and the heirs of that movement — the leaders of the Practical Zionist Movement. And to overlook every idea that has failed would be to overlook most of human history, since almost every human idea in human history has failed. We can say that, generally, almost every battle and struggle in the effort to improve the lot of humanity has failed. Only the struggle as a whole is continuing, and one can even see signs of improvement in the free world. The same holds for the idea of Herzl, including its transformation in the hands of Jabotinsky and Kook. And so, today, instead of saying that Herzl has failed, some say that he was an adventurer — meaning, his activity was based on no idea whatsoever, but on psychological drives alone. This claim is easy to refute by a perusal of his books and diaries.

In sum, this is the distinction between the Spiritual and Political Zionist Movements. The former saw the center of the Zionist idea in the founding of a spiritual center in Palestine; it considered the foundation of a state a marginal concern. Similarly, this movement stressed the continuity of the existence of the Jewish Diaspora. Herzl, by contrast, saw things differently. He did not lessen the value of the cultural contribution of the future state, whether as a contribution to Judaism or as a contribution to humanity at large. Instead, he stressed the political side of the picture, since he proposed a political solution to a political problem, in particular a solution to be achieved by using existing political means. He also assumed that not all Jews would migrate to their country and that there would be Jews in Europe even after the state of the Jews will be established. He was in agreement with Ahad Ha'am on this: the existence of the state of the Jews will enable Jews abroad to live in greater comfort, because a safety valve was provided by the open option for all Jews to migrate there, if and when they wished, or if and when they were persecuted. No doubt the fact that both these movements accepted both the cultural and political plan does not bridge the chasm between them, since the priority which the one movement granted to the cultural solution, and the priority which the other movement granted to the political solution, were sufficient causes for disagreement and even for an inability to cooperate.

Young Martin Buber, who was a member of the Zionist Movement practically from its inception, and who cooperated with Herzl for a while, managed at one point to dissent from him and even to surrender direct political activity in the Zionist Movement. As for Ahad Ha'am, except for passive participation in the first Zionist Congress, he did not act politically, and was content to be a critic from the outside. Also, Buber diverged from Romanticism whereas Ahad Ha'am remained Romantic and more nationalist in his opinions; this way he was closer than Buber to the Practical Zionists.

The leaders of the Practical Zionist Movement did not grasp the political aspect of Herzl's ideas. They saw in him (as their heirs still do) a successful spokesperson of an East European movement — one who had the talent to organize and manage a successful public relations operation and to stimulate interest in that movement among Westerners, Jews and non-Jews alike. The Practical Zionists accepted the nationalist ideology and the idea of Jewish historical continuity as a heritage from the Lovers of Zion Movement. The major practical difference between Practical Zionism and the Lovers of Zion Movement was that the Practical Zionist leaders intentionally and systematically encouraged the desire to migrate to Palestine and organized the migration of pioneers and the founding of new agricultural settlements. Some of them migrated to Palestine, so that from the beginning the movement had leaders here as well. This is not to say that the Spiritual Zionists, Ahad Ha'am and Buber, opposed migration. Indeed, they themselves migrated, in the hope of finding cultural value in the new settlement. (And, indeed, Buber's most important sociological book, *Paths in Utopia*, examines the cultural and political significance of the kibbutz movement.) Herzl opposed the pioneering movement, but his opposition was merely practical: he was afraid that the Practical Zionists would raise the price of land while he was attempting to purchase the whole of Palestine for as low a price as possible; he was also concerned about the safety of the pioneers.

The two central trends within Zionism were the Political and the Practical. Each developed a political doctrine that the other rejected. This doctrinal difference characterized the two streams and the movement as a whole more than anything else did. The political theory of the Political Zionists was this: the Jewish problem is all-European and so there is room for political cooperation between the Zionist Movement and European governments. The political theory of the Practical Zionists was this: one must intentionally avoid as much as possible, all political, legislative, or organizational activity; instead, one must create accomplished social and economic facts, since these will necessarily bring about genuine political changes. This is the whole of the theory of Practical

Zionism. Its significance is enormous since it places political value only on accomplished facts and on nothing else.

The main accomplished facts were, of course, the settlement of Jews on the land and the organization of many charitable institutions to finance this settlement, especially the well-known ones — the National Fund and Foundation Fund — but there were other funds. But the Practical Zionist leaders opposed the foundation of a national bank, and Herzl took pride, as can be seen in his diaries, in the fact that he used a minor parliamentary trick to overcome this opposition of the Practical Zionists (18). There is no need to say that Practical Zionism ruled the Zionist Movement from the death of Herzl to the foundation of independent Israel. Since the foundation of the state was the central purpose of the Zionist Movement as a whole, it was clear that the character of Zionism of necessity was altered once this purpose was accomplished. Nevertheless, there is justice in the widespread claim that Practical Zionism continued to rule Israel even after independence was declared, since the idea of Practical Zionism — a central Romantic idea in Zionist garb — remained the leading idea of the young state: the creation of social and economic accomplished facts was preferable to taking initiative in political action, and there was no significant political action except the one imposed on the political leadership under the pressure of accomplished facts.

Since no political initiative takes place in Israel, and since facts are accomplished here that sometimes have political significance and that sometimes even impose on the political leadership the need to take some political action, a simple question is thereby raised: does not the situation in Israel justify the theory of Practical Zionism? How can we examine whether this theory is worthy of endorsement and, if endorsed, as Israel's guiding idea?

A critical examination of the theory of Practical Zionism requires that the question be examined, were the political decisions made under the pressure of accomplished facts really decisions caused by the social, economic, and cultural facts created by Practical Zionism?

The answer to this is in the negative, and for two reasons, internal and external. The internal reason is that not all the political activities of the Zionist leadership were dictated internally by the idea of Practical Zionism — beginning with activities that ended with the Balfour Declaration concerning the foundation of a Jewish national home in Palestine and ending with the Declaration of Independence. The external reasons were the political developments in the surrounding world, which influenced the history of Israel more than the accomplished facts created by the Practical Zionist Movement. Nevertheless, the ideology of Practical Zionism rules in Israel to this very day, and consequently fundamental political questions are still neglected here.

The development of the Israeli defense apparatus may serve as an illustration of this. Israel's Army is called the Israeli Defense Force in order to emphasize that it developed organically from the Haganah [= defense] Defense Organization of the Jewish settlement movement in Palestine, which was a most faithful expression of Practical Zionism. The fact that the defense organization developed reluctantly and in stages fits the ideology of Practical Zionism. Critical examination shows two details that transcend the framework of this ideology and oppose its central idea. It is well known that David Ben-Gurion, who increasingly came to the fore as the main leader of the movement, supported diverse steps in the development of the defense apparatus not only for practical reasons, but also through his profound conviction that the unity and harmony of the Jewish settlement in Palestine must be retained at all costs. Out of this conviction he endorsed the Haganah [= defense] Defense Organization even though he had disbanded its predecessor, the Hashomer [= watchman] Organization. He also organized skirmishes with the dissident underground organizations that did not abide by the authority of the Haganah Defense Organization, the Irgun National Military Organization and the Fighters for the Freedom of Israel. These skirmishes went by the odd name "the season" (meaning the hunting season). Alternatively, he allowed an arrangement in which the activities of the three underground organizations were coordinated under the bombast name of "the Resistance Movement". He likewise declared the independence of Israel, despite opposition from within his political group, not in accordance with the idea of Practical Zionism but merely out of fear that the dissident underground organizations would declare independence by themselves, regardless of any decree of the Zionist Board of Directors to the contrary. This idea, therefore, of retaining national unity at all costs, deviated from the framework of Practical Zionism. This idea sometimes took on a communal, ethnic characteristic and at other times a clear-cut political characteristic. In addition, the contribution of the British forces to the development of Jewish defense, especially during World War II, should be considered. At that time an organization of shock troops under the command of the Zionist Board of Directors was organized on British military initiative and functioned as a regular force within the Jewish Defense Organization. And, of course, the British authorities were not guided by any Zionist idea.

Undeniably, the Zionist Board of Directors did undertake political steps, such as the organization of an underground defense organization, the coordination of the diverse underground organizations, the Declaration of Independence, and the organization of mass immigration. Admittedly, also, not much political initiative was expressed in the undertaking of these political moves, and therefore they do not necessarily conflict with the central idea of Practical Zionism. But Ben-Gurion, the leading personality in the Practical Zionist Movement and the first Premier and Defense Minister of Israel, acted to a large extent under the strong sense of the need to maintain national unity at all costs — and thus he certainly deviated from the central idea of Political Zionism. The influence of new political facts, in particular the helplessness of the Jewish leadership during the disaster of the destruction of Jews in Europe, changed the picture radically. The Practical Zionist Movement endorsed — after a tragic delay — the principles of Political Zionism: the idea of mass immigration and the idea of the urgent need for a Declaration of Independence, which were the focus of the activity of the Hebrew Committee for National Liberation. But this endorsement was reluctant, without thoroughgoing discussion and without the development of an overall political approach. To this very day such an overall political approach is still absent in Israel, and its absence is increasingly felt.

Chapter 9 *Zionism and Independence*

Approaching the end of this first — theoretical and historical — part of this book, I will try to demarcate anew the differences of opinion within the Zionist Movement, especially between its Political and Practical streams. This will be a sketch of the radical changes that took place during the half century between the foundation of the Zionist Movement and the establishment of Israel. In particular, the sketch should be detailed enough to refute the current opinion in Israel today concerning the establishment of the state, which is that this was the culmination of Practical Zionism, thereby allegedly proving the truth of Practical Zionist ideas. This is contestable: the fact that Israel's independence was declared by Ben-Gurion and his associates, who were officially the followers of the tradition of Practical Zionism, does not mean their actions were in accord with Practical Zionist ideas: independence was declared outside the mold of Practical Zionism. It was established reluctantly, since, to repeat, Practical Zionist theory is opposed to all political initiative. Why was independence declared nonetheless? Perhaps the leadership was afraid that pressures in favor of independence would bring about a schism in the Zionist Movement and the diminution of control which existing Zionist organizations exercised over the Jewish settlement in Palestine. This criticism is unsatisfactory, since one can answer it with the claim that as long as the leadership acted reluctantly, it acted in accord with the spirit of Practical Zionism, which did not so much oppose political activity as propose its postponement as much as possible. Hence, to refute the Practical Zionist view, a deeper criticism is required. Such a criticism is available; it is deep and comprehensive and bears important implications for the future.

The controversy between the Political and the Practical streams in Zionism cannot be compressed into answers to questions of the form, was this or that political move or practical move correct? For there was, and still is, place for some criticism of any step taken by this or that stream, and the criticism can be both internal and external.

Supporters of the Political stream might admit that every political move that Herzl ever undertook was mistaken and, nevertheless, side with the Political stream, rejecting the Practical stream, whose program was to create the social and economic infrastructure first and wait for the political superstructure to develop later. It is not always possible to indicate a practical difference between the Political stream and the Practical stream in a specific case in which both sides would agree to endorse or reject this or that decision of a foreign government or of the League of Nations. The political move to endorse or reject other parties' political decisions may be an active response or a part of an active response — that is to say, it may be a part of a political initiative. But it may also be a merely passive response of the leadership of a community that caters to its own social and economic needs alone. It follows, thus, that to a large extent the difference between the Political stream and the Practical stream is a general and basic difference that may be reflected in this or that detail, yet is not the sum total of these details, but is their general background.

In the historical case before us, it is easy to see what the general difference was, since it was a difference concerning the most general aims. The Political stream accepted as a short-term goal (or medium-term goal, at most), the solution of a burning political problem: the problem of the sufferings of the Jews. Herzl saw the problem in one way; Jabotinsky in another (because the suffering of East European Jews increased intolerably in the period between the two World Wars), but for both the problem and the solution was a matter of a massive public, of the purchasing of the territory for a state (Herzl) or the establishment of independence (Jabotinsky). Both assumed that immediate action on a large scale was needed. Even if the goal was not practical, the tools required for its implementation (if it could be implemented) are political, and one who aims at it, has to do so by the use of existing political tools: cooperation with governments of existing states which are established and strong and which, due to the justification of the goal or the recognition of a shared interest, could and would agree to harness their efforts to complete the urgent task. Not so with the Practical stream. Its leaders rejected the proposals of Political Zionism as impracticable. They also judged these proposals dangerous and the danger as expressed in the very earliest steps. They argued that it was, therefore, reckless even to try them. In addition, the Practical stream saw political independence as a long-term goal, not a short-term one, and even opposed the use of the term "state" in the statement of the Zionist Movement's goals. This was so until the year 1942! (This was Jabotinsky's reason for his split from the Zionist Movement.) The Practical stream therefore opposed the proposal of mass migration made by the Political stream. The Practical stream reasoned that the only urgent political step was the immediate striking off from the agenda, as soon as possible, the very proposals of the Political stream.

In addition, the leaders of the Practical stream agreed that there was no sense in rushing into a daring attempt to solve the problem of the suffering of the Jews. The reason was despair from the very start: it did not look to the leaders of the Practical stream that they could succeed in easing the sufferings of the Jews significantly with realistic means within a short period of time. This despair of all massive emergency activity explains why the Zionist leaders were not ready when the first news concerning the mass destruction of the Jews of Europe leaked to Palestine and to the countries of the Allies; their immediate response (through panic) was to try to black out the information. In this manner, the whole conceptual system of Practical Zionism collapsed altogether.

From the start, the Practical stream's goal was to found an exemplary, ideal, Jewish society that would live in a suitable way in ideal social conditions (19). It therefore opposed the idea of the Political stream of mass migration (from Eastern Europe). In particular, because the settlement of the land was an act for which the Practical Zionists waved their flags, and because the settlement of the land generally meant agriculture, and since most of agriculture belonged to the settlement movement of the Trade Union Movement, the Practical Zionists took on a socialist color and gave the whole Jewish settlement in Palestine the character of an agricultural — usually Kibbutz or Cooperative — settlement, as well as of a proud, productive workers' society.

One hardly needs to say that this picture has no root in reality. Moreover, I report that the influence of this picture on the youth of the Palestinian settlement was harmful: most of the youth movements preached that young people who did not leave town and join some agricultural settlement betrayed the high ideals of Zionism (of Practical Zionism, of course) — this, despite the fact that the majority of urban youths remained in town. The repeated failure of the education within the youth movements therefore caused defective self-images among its alumni. It is clear that the leadership was (and still is) irresponsible and lacking in concern for the interests of urban youths; its only interest was (and still is) to mobilize as large a number of young urban volunteers as possible for agricultural pioneering activity (or other activity, as the leaders found fit).

Practical Zionism has no exclusive claim on the declaration of independence or the flow of mass immigration that this declaration made possible. For independence was achieved not under the pressure of the accomplished facts caused by the Practical Zionist Movement, but under the pressure of the political facts of the post-World War II period; the flow of mass immigration resulted from the failure of Practical Zionism to deal with the sufferings of the Jews of Europe — which the Zionist leadership had ventured to cover up. (I will discuss at length both these details further on.) Here, the point is a criticism of the Practical Zionist idea, that it is politically best to create accomplished facts. It is dubious philosophically, as it is based on contradictions and confusions characteristic of the nineteenth-century European Chauvinist philosophy that was popular at the time Zionist thought was developed.

Nevertheless, it is proper to ask, how much did the Practical Zionist stream contribute to Israel's independence through social and economic accomplishments? The presence of Jewish settlement in Palestine no doubt contributed to the establishment of Israel as an independent state, and the contribution of the followers of the Practical Zionist stream was a major part of this process. But this is not the place for a full assessment of the contribution of the Practical Zionist stream to the independence of Israel.

A short while after the Balfour Declaration, Britain received mandates over both Iraq and Palestine. Britain might have surrendered the mandate over Palestine when it surrendered the mandate over Iraq, had Political Zionism been stronger and more resourceful and had it been able to direct a wave of mass immigration of, say, tens of thousands of Jews within a few years.

This detail is intentionally and systematically clouded in all books on the history of the Zionist settlement, because their authors assume as a matter of course that mass migration was both impossible and undesirable. Perhaps this is true, but what political consequences follow from this assumption as to the political initiative? It is hardly credible that no initiative could yield any result under any conditions.

This is a general political question. The general obvious political answer that is naturally required is that it is irresponsible to give up general public obligation and political initiative — doing so means the lack of responsibility on the part of a political leadership. This seems significant also in the contexts of the possibility of rescuing the Jews of Europe, the declaration of independence to that end, and in the debate about the future, in the practical matter of the running of the state today, which is, naturally, more important. The present discussion concerning the events that led up to independence, therefore, is only secondary, and was raised here, because those who still advocate the neglect of political initiative prove the value of their recommendation by claiming that the absence of political initiative brought about independence and the mass migration that followed it. The truth is the opposite: independence came about despite the lack of initiative, and the mass migration happened in complete opposition to every political plan of the Zionist leadership, which permitted it only in an attempt to cover up its criminal irresponsibility during World War II, at the time of the destruction of the Jews of Europe (20).

What is left to be done now is to combine the idea of the public responsibility of a political leadership, which is the duty of the leadership to undertake political initiatives, with the idea of the normalization of Israel, which is the guiding idea of this present book. These two ideas can be combined on diverse planes, as will be shown later in this book. But the present part of this book, being theoretical and historical, will conclude with the intellectual and historical combination of these two ideas — the idea of public responsibility and political initiative and of the normalization of Israel.

Hidden behind the present continuing confusion in Israel between the congregational and the political, is more than a mere desire to pay a compliment to the congregational, Practical Zionist stream for having established the State of Israel. This confusion is central in Israeli political life, since it obscures the difference between congregation and nation, and thus perpetuates the myth of the uniqueness of Judaism as a nation-faith. This myth means that the State of Israel is the state of all the Jews, of both the Jews who belong to diverse nations and live in their congregations, and the Jews who are members of the Israeli nation that is not recognized — the nation which the myth presents as another Jewish congregation and no more. The confusion between the congregational and the political is thus a confusion between congregation and nation. This is the myth of the uniqueness of Israel — the myth that says, Israel is not and cannot be a normal state. The opposite of this confusion, the clarification of the difference between congregation and nation, is but the first step in the thesis that normalization is preferable, in the recommendation that Israel should become a Western-style liberal nation-state for all intents and purposes, on the basis of the distinction between nationality and religion, and the separation of state and religious authorities. Only then will the state be the political instrument of the nation, and the religious organization will be the communal instrument of the religious community.

In conclusion, the declaration of the independence of Israel came not by way of application of the idea of Practical Zionism. On the contrary, despite Israel's independence, the Zionist Movement was not updated, and the Practical Zionist stream has not declined and so Israeli governments still refuse to recognize the existence of its nation. They cannot view the state as a means for taking political initiative, as a tool in the service of the nation that lives within its borders.

* None of what was said thus far should obscure the significant fact that the Political Zionist stream failed as well, since the plan for a mass migration as a solution to the sufferings of Jews has failed. The mass migration that began after World War II as the result of the terrible catastrophe, and expanded after Israel's Independence, deviated from all that happened before the catastrophe, since it deviated from anything that could be imagined then: it was a wave of mass migration under conditions previously considered by neither the Political nor the Practical stream of Zionism. The catastrophe also altered Western public opinion about the Jewish settlement in Palestine. Israel displays no awareness of the fact that it initially had no hope of survival but for the recognition it was

accorded by the international community, and that this recognition was born from the catastrophe, in a kind of effort by the international community to atone for the indifference of the Allies at a time when rescue effort was still possible. But the Jewish leadership in the Allied countries (Zionist as well as non-Zionist) was also indifferent, and to date there is no readiness to recognize that fact. Israel emphasizes every year, and rightly so, the heroic struggle of a miserable handful of Jews against a tremendous enemy in the Warsaw Ghetto Uprising, though the situation was dreadfully desperate, but as to the helplessness of the Jewish leadership in the Allied countries, it is said shamelessly that in organizing some feeble escape efforts (mostly against direct orders) (20a) all that could be done was done, and that, in particular, on the political level, there was no room for any activity, since anyway the situation was desperate. The absurdity of this is evident. The indifference and confusion prevented efforts that certainly were more practical than the armed uprising in occupied Europe. This denial, by the leadership and its historians alike, is nothing short of cowardice.

* Whatever the causes of the failure, it is not confined to World War II: attempts at rescue were made by the Zionist Movement from the start, yet they were failures (20b). The little comfort, the survival of the few who did survive to participate in the mass migration and lived to witness Israel's independence, can only partly be considered a success of the Zionist Movement — a success in that it constituted a precedent of sorts, one that was followed by those who showed goodwill after the War (though not exactly by means of Zionist initiative).

* All this is said from a practical perspective. From the political perspective the details of the developments after World War II appear quite different: hostility — from the Jewish leadership in general and from the (Practical) Zionist leadership in particular — contributed much to the failure of the efforts made during the War to create political changes that would lead to rescue. A political effort of this kind was made in the United States of America by an organization that mobilized efforts for rescue and for national liberation. It was a small, unknown organization (now forgotten), that brought the Jewish problem to public attention and awareness. Thus it paved the way to the readiness of the Jewish leadership in Palestine to declare the independence of

Israel as well as the readiness of the international community towards recognition. Of course, Israel's independence created a new venue for the expression of the goodwill, which was too little and came too late. This expression was also vital for the survival of the young besieged state. I will discuss the organization that prepared the political background to this process in the next Part of this book; let me mention now that the declaration of Israel's independence is a pointed example of a political act that brings about much more rescue than the physical act of independent efforts to rescue performed with no help, especially of a weak people. This example explains why, despite the almost complete failure of the Zionist Movement — of the Practical and the Political streams — the stand of the Political stream seems to me more practical than that of the Practical stream in it, even though, of course, the few who were rescued were rescued as the result of the combined efforts of both contending streams, the import of whose contribution to the rescue should be recognized despite the failure of the rescue efforts. This contribution is obscured by the permanent and bitter quarrel between the two streams, which is no cause for national pride. Particularly regrettable is the sabotage that the Practical stream organized against the Political stream. This sabotage will be discussed in Part Two of this book.

* From the practical viewpoint, the most important detail in the whole painful and miserable affair of this sabotage is, to date, the damage that is caused by the aspersions, still cast in the rare moments when mention is made of this small organization that attempted rescue by political means. Those who cast the aspersions charge that it never attempted anything on the practical level. Even were the factual part of this charge true (and it is definitely false), it clearly conveys the view, that even today, practical actions (in the style of Practical Zionism) are preferable to political actions. This is why those who view themselves the followers of Practical Zionism have praised the activities of settlement in Judea, Samaria and the Gaza Strip by chauvinist groups that brag about their preference for settlement over respect for Israeli law. The support that their illegal activities gain from the diverse governments of Israel sanctifies the political helplessness of Israeli governments to date. The total victory of the Practical Zionist stream over the Political one is well expressed in the conduct of the Israeli governments that take pride in their ancestry in Political Zionism, while having fully adopted the ideology of Practical Zionism, despite the fact that Israel's independence greatly facilitates efficient political activity without employing modes of action that are doubtful and illegal if not also harmful. The practically important matter is not which stream has contributed more to Israel's independence, since both have contributed (even though their joint contribution was marginal), but that the Practical ideology should not be used to justify the ongoing lack of initiative on the part of all of Israel's governments. *

Chapter 10

Faith, Nationality And State

This book was written under the shadow of depression and despair that is spreading in Israel, whose situation seems to many of its inhabitants to be deteriorating. This deterioration is both internal and external; it and its causes will be discussed later. Here it will be noted briefly that, internally, the conceptual confusion accepted by the broad public in Israel and the lack of courage to clarify existing positions here, is causing its independence to deteriorate from sovereignty to congregational autonomy and to clericalism. It is disastrous that the want of understanding of the causes of the deterioration imposes inaction on those who wish to act, and this intensifies the despair and the deterioration. The external cause of the deterioration rests on the expectation of the nations of the world that Israel should be a nation-state in the normal Western mold. A generation passed before the situation was clarified sufficiently and the world began to understand and accept that Israel is not a nation like other modern nations, and is still not ready to become one. In concluding this, first part of this book, normalization will be explained again as Hillel Kook proposed it even before the Declaration of Independence of Israel and why it is still significant.

In a normal modern situation, in a liberal society within the framework of the nation-state, what is important is not only the separation of the state and the religious institutions, but also the distinction between nation and state, which requires separation between nationality and faith, or between nation and congregation. It is easy to distinguish nation from state, since the state, but not the nation, is legally definable in a precise and detailed fashion. Moreover, the state is an instrument — and in the modern period, the enlightened state is an instrument in the service of the nation. Furthermore, citizenship is a well-defined characteristic, but in modern liberal society it represents a relation to both the state and the nation. That is to say, by their very citizenship, normal citizens of a state have the duty to obey its laws and the right to its services; moreover, this citizenship is the citizens' nationality, namely, their belonging to the nation to which the state belongs. Options exist other then the normal, such as a bi-national state; alternatively, it is possible to declare some citizens a national minority.

* The gist of the difference between a nation-state that incorporates a national minority and a bi-national state is in the blatant discrimination against the national minority. (Indeed, at times the very word "minority" carries the connotation of discrimination, especially when the minority is not numerical.) This discrimination can be attenuated by the institution of autonomy for the minority. Confusion should be avoided here, since the autonomy for national minorities differs from that for other kinds of minorities — ethnic, cultural or linguistic. A minority is possible, which belongs to the nation without suffering political discrimination. A national minority always suffers discrimination, since it is deprived of political channels. It suffers less discrimination if it is autonomous, and still less if the state is bi-national. It is not clear, whether a bi-national state without discrimination is possible. Nevertheless, if the option of a nation-state is discarded, then the next best option, surely, is a bi-national state. *

In normal situations, as in the United States, there are ethnic, religious and other minorities, but not national minorities. From the viewpoint of both nation and constitution, all citizens are equal. Admittedly, the normal situation is somewhat unclear: originating from one national society and settling down in another, one usually finds it easier to change citizenship than national identity. For, the process of change of citizenship is a clearer and sharper step, than the change of national identity. This is why a national state is unable to absorb a large number of immigrants without changing its national character. Therefore, even liberal countries usually limit immigration. This is in obvious inconsistency with the liberal principle of freedom of migration, but is practiced from lack of choice and in the need to maintain the national character of a society that demands of its state that it limit the freedom of migration.

Here an abnormal or unclear aspect appears, even in normal liberal countries: in principle they side with total freedom of migration, but in practice they limit this freedom. It is customary to hide this behind economic excuses, but when these do not obtain, one has to speak the truth and address the question of national identity. French law states this clearly. But the very concept of national identity, according to liberal political philosophy, is not clear at all; and classical liberal political philosophy makes no room for it at all.

The situation descussed here is clearly described in chapter 4 of the book *Moral Man and Immoral Society* (21), by the famous theologian Reinhold Niebuhr:

> "Nations are territorial societies, the cohesive power of which is supplied by the sentiment of nationality and the authority of the state. The fact that the states frequently incorporate several nationalities indicates that the authority of government is the ultimate force of national cohesion. The fact that the state and nation are roughly synonymous proves that without the sentiment of nationality with its common language and traditions, the authority of government is usually unable to maintain national unity. The unity of Scotland and England within a single British state and the failure to maintain the same unity between England and Ireland, suggests both the possibilities and the limitations of transcending nationality in the formation of states."

The purpose of Niebuhr's chapter where this passage appears is to explain that the duty of politicians to consider the interest and opinions of their people forces them to yield to the selfishness of their nation and that preaching against this selfishness is pointless.

Improving the moral attitude of a state is possible, though its selfishness cannot be entirely abolished. This can be achieved by the improvement of the understanding of citizens that international achievements may bring a general national advantage. And this, of course, is a most significant detail. So much for Reinhold Niebuhr.

Niebuhr's observations do not obtain in Israel the way they do in the normal nations of the world. His starting-point is the normal assumption that the duty of the state is to cater to the welfare and peace of its nation. The lack of normalcy in Israel is precisely in the state's total neglect of the national interest. Israel views itself not as the state of the Israeli nation, but as the state of the Jewish faith-nation, which is scattered among the nations. Almost unanimously, the Israeli public accepts this view without hesitation. It is, therefore, not the top priority of the State of Israel to cater to the welfare and the peace of the Israeli nation, which it does not recognize, and catering to the welfare and peace of the nation is a secondary concern. This does not mean that Israel is less selfish than other states. And so the Israeli experience supports Niebuhr's assertion that the improvement of a state's morality requires the improvement of the understanding of its citizens, not efforts to reduce its selfishness: the indifference of rulers to the welfare of members of their nations only raises the level of their own selfishness — here as in other countries.

Israel is not ready to accept the principle of the separation of nation and congregation as its citizens are not willing to give up the support of Jews of other nations: out of conceptual confusion and for selfish reasons they suppose that this support is conditioned on the identification of members of the Jewish faith with the Israeli nation. This explains why in Israel both observant and non-observant Jews side with this refusal. Non-observant Israeli Jews who want Israel to be more liberal — to exercise less government interference in matters of religion and conscience of its citizens — still prefer, for alleged reasons of national selfishness, to avoid the separation of nationality from religion, so as to fuse the nationality of French, American and other Jews with their own, whether they observe religious practices or not, and this because of a certain conservatism and clinging to a confused past. This refusal constitutes a means of pressure that Israelis exert or try to exert on Jews from Western countries in their demand that they offer Israel political and financial aid. But in principle these Jews can exert the same means of pressure on Israel if and when its policies will appear to them as opposed to their own interest as Jews of Western nations.

If and when Western Jews will consider the very existence of the State of Israel inimical to their own interests, then they will possibly exert pressure on it with the intent to dismantle it. Dr. Nahum Goldmann, the founder and first President of the World Jewish Congress and sometime President of the World Zionist Congress, repeatedly demanded that Israel should be not a normal state but an autonomous unit protected by the United Nations under a guarantee of Western nations.

A similar criticism was expressed by the French philosopher and sociologist Georges Friedmann in his best-selling book *The End of the Jewish People?* (first published in 1965; English translation, 1967). Its first chapter, which studies theocracy and notes the abnormal status of Rabbinical law in Israel, which it explains by reference to both the lack of readiness of the Israeli government to open a conflict over religion for fear it would cause a schism between Israeli and American Jews, and the government's (vain) hope that in time religious leaders will lessen their demands. In the chapter on the distinction between affiliation to the Jewish religion and to the Israeli nation, Friedmann raises again the question of the abnormalcy of the situation, and points to the confusion that born Israelis suffer concerning their national identity, which he (rightly) deems abnormal. A particular cause of the confusion is the government's attempt to raise Jewish religious consciousness rather then Israeli national consciousness, as would be fitting in a normal situation. The upshot of this confusion, which he finds very strange, is the lack of clear distinctions between religion, nationality, and state. As a result, the Jewish religion (whose mission, as he understands it, is to bring peace to the world) changes into a state that has a powerful armed force. Consequently, understanding between Western Jews and born Israelis, he concludes, is impossible. He blames the Zionist leadership, especially Dr. Nahum Goldmann, for the aggravation of the confusion. David Ben-Gurion's demand that all the Jews of the world migrate to Israel (which, Friedmann gathers, will not be accepted; he also notes that migration from Israel to the United States is bigger than migration in the opposite direction) means, that the Jews of the United States face pressure to give up their Jewish identity altogether, especially since the Jewish identity of non-observant Jews outside Israel is doubtful and because assimilation to their local culture becomes increasingly the outcome of their way of life. Friedmann, himself Jewish, though not observant, and a French national, ends his book expressing profound concern.

This supports the opinion that recognition of the Israeli nation and a distinction between a nation and its state are needed in order to separate state and religious institutions — without denying, of course, that the religion governing the sons and daughters of Israel is Judaism, and without denying, of course, that this same Jewish religion governs also congregations of sons and daughters of other nations.

The Zionist contempt for Germans of the Mosaic faith of the last century, which contempt Israeli youths have imbibed with their mother's milk in the Zionist movement, was shockingly justified by the destruction of European Jewry in this century. Israeli youths learn that the conclusion from this is that the American Jews should be wise and see that in their country too what awaits them is hatred and destruction, unless they migrate to Israel. This is the New Zionist Myth that will be taken up in detail in Chapter One of Part Three below. Here it should be noted only, that this claim implies that there is an objectively joint interest between Israel and Jew-haters in the western world. This claim also implies that there are objective conflicts of interests between Western Jews and the State of Israel. Hence, the more Western Jews understand the situation and the meaning of this claim, the more likely they are to turn hostile to the State of Israel. And the more Western governments understand the abnormalcy of Israel, the more likely they will be to be forced to the undesirable position by which they should solve the problems of the Middle East without taking into account the Israeli national interest. This will be dangerous, particularly at any point when the conflict sharpens, and the interest of the Western nations in peace in our region is on the increase. Of course, if the political structure of Israel will undergo changes, then a radical, even rapid, improvement will be possible.

This ends the general discussion on the topic of this book, which has offered a theoretical background to the problem of the Israeli national identity. This discussion, it should be noted, was placed against the general background of the liberal world-view and focused on the problem of national identity in general and of Israeli national identity in particular. Little has been said on the problem from a non-liberal viewpoint, and little has been said about other problems from a liberal viewpoint.

PART TWO

A National Tragedy

According to Hillel Kook, the Israeli nation exists, but is unrecognized and even unawares. That is to say, the existence of the nation is not accompanied by the ordinary degree of national awareness. Every claim of this kind concerns an intermediary stage, an unfinished process. Such a mode of speech, it was explained in the first part of this book, is not conventional and hence not understood. For, according to received theories, a nation is an accomplished fact, or else it does not exist. It is no accident that despite the great simplicity of Kook's idea of normalization, so many find it difficult to understand and see it as the revolutionary innovation that it is.

At the beginning of his political career, Hillel Kook was a young Zionist who accepted the existence of the Jewish nation in the traditional manner, as a self-evident accomplished fact. Thus he considered the Irgun National Military Organization, to which he belonged, a national liberation movement. When he served as the head of a delegation of that organization in the United States, he came across Western liberalism and began to see its decisive influence on the way of life of American Jews. This raised problems for him. In his desire to tackle and solve the problems that this philosophy presented, he found the need to develop a liberal-nationalist point of view for himself. With the help of the members of his delegation, he developed opinions that found expression in their public activities.

All this was almost unknown in Palestine. The political movement founded by Kook in the Western liberal mode was developed across the ocean, at a time when there was no communication between Kook's delegation and the mother Irgun National Military organization after the demise of its commander, David Raziel, early in World War II, and the events that unfolded with a staggering speed because of the war and the mass murder of European Jews. At that time great changes occurred in the Irgun National Military Organization; for a time it almost ceased to exist. Later it reorganized, and Menachem Begin became its commander.

The Irgun National Military Organization published declarations in the names of the Hebrew nation, including the declaration of the need to proclaim political independence and to establish a temporary government. But the revolutionary ideas behind these declarations were not made public, much less explained. The declaration, therefore, remained unclear to the Palestinian Jewish public. The Irgun National Military Organization's command maintained a political position not rooted in a liberal nationalist position. To the extent that it had any philosophical background at all, it was that of the nationalist movements of Eastern Europe in the late nineteenth century.

The background to these movements, as explained in Part One of this book, at best was not systematically identified with liberalism, and at worst it was intentionally identified with the Reactionary Romantic anti-liberal movement. The official Zionist leadership, it is generally admitted, portrayed the Irgun National Military Organization to the Jewish population of Palestine as a part of the Revisionist Zionist movement, which itself was portrayed as Reactionary. I cannot say much about this Reactionary political movement and its connection with the Irgun National Military Organization, nor about the political philosophy of these two movements. I was not among their sympathizers, mainly because I deemed the positions of the Revisionist Zionist Movement, the New Zionist Movement, which I met in my youth, in its youth movement (Betar), anti-liberal and anti-rationalist.

I will not express an opinion as to the connection between the Irgun and the New Zionists, except for what is well known and uncontroversial, since Hillel Kook distinguishes both between the New Zionist Movement, the Revisionist Movement, and the Irgun National Military Organization, as well as between that Organization and its delegation abroad.

A part of the Irgun National Military Organization split off during its lowest ebb and formed a separate group that became known as the Fighters for the Freedom of Israel. During the period following the Declaration of Independence, the new organization exhibited tendencies that were considered left-wing. But during the splitting the Freedom Fighters' commander, Abraham (Yair) Stern (the organization was known also as the Stern Gang), sought help from the enemies of Great Britain (the oppressive enemy). As is well known, the enemies of Great Britain were Nazis and Fascists. This fact strengthened the growing impression (at least among the adolescents) that the Irgun National Military Organization was a body advocating an utterly untenable social and political philosophy. Contributing to the confusion was the fact that the two organizations were presented as having the same political position. (This book offers no discussion of the Fighters for the Freedom of Israel. Even discussion of the Irgun National Military Organization will be limited to details that should help understand the background to Kook's political activity.)

Despite my wish to remain outside the picture presented in this Part, I will add some autobiographical details from that period, which was the period of my adolescence, not as an autobiographical chapter but as evidence of the activities and confusion perpetrated intentionally in Palestine by the official Zionist leadership under the guise of secrecy. The most important detail clearly remembered because of its oppressive character, was the clandestine, underground character of the political processes in the Jewish settlement in Palestine. British censorship and internal national censorship caused deep public ignorance of the political situation. Public political debate had the quality of gossip and of conspiracy. This has caused great damage — persisting to this very day: in Israel, the demarcation remains vague between gossip and conspiracy on the one hand and open and sovereign democratic politics on the other. This vagueness is masked by the claim that it serves some unspecified urgent security needs of the state, even though any critical observer can see through this. The gossipy-conspiratorial atmosphere clouded information on two vital fronts: the inter-relations of the different Hebrew underground movements, and the mass destruction of European Jewry.

Even those who possessed a very strong interest in all political affairs in the region remained ignorant and confused. As to the relations between the underground movements, in my youth I heard repeatedly from diverse sources that during a certain period, called "the [hunting] Season" members of the Haganah Organization (the official Zionist defense movement) tortured members of the Irgun National Military Organization and the Fighters for the

Freedom of Israel and even delivered some of them into the hands of the British police and army. I also heard that there was a period of joint or coordinated activity of the three underground movements. These joint activities became known as "the Resistance Movement": the term designated the three organizations together. Everything else was confused and vague.

The Hebrew public did not know and did not understand the two extreme positions, of hostility and of cooperation, nor the transitions between them. Some historians who study the subject-matter conceal this important public fact. They conceal the even more important fact, that the Zionist leadership kept from the Hebrew public, as much as they could, all information about the mass destruction of European Jewry. The Hebrew settlement in Palestine was fed horrible rumors, about which it received no official responses, thus not knowing how to respond. Personally, I had only a vague awareness of the phenomenon of the mass destruction of the Jews until after the end of the war, when the Hebrew settlement in Palestine was supplied with clear and shocking factual information by the Western mass media. The Jewish and the Zionist media establishment did not supply this information. Even when I had heard, before the end of the war, a public speech by a national leader of the first order, in which he spoke about the relation between the German and the Jewish peoples, I received from it a very harsh picture. That picture bore not the slightest resemblance to the shocking truth. His speech caused such a strong depressive impression that I remember whole sentences from it to this day. Yet the speech does not do him honor: though it was a bitter lament, it expressed his helplessness and meant more to cover up than to reveal.

Hillel Kook is older than me by only one decade or so, but he and his colleagues were then, or saw themselves then, as representatives of the Hebrew national liberation movement during a period of apocalyptic crises. The commander of the Irgun National Military Organization, Vladimir Jabotinsky, described to him the situation of the delegation as that of a unit detached from its mother unit that was then dividing and disintegrating.

Awareness of this brought him to behave like a political leader of the first rank, functioning as the head of a delegation of a military organization, even though the organization itself survived in name only, a name that was used in Palestine by the Revisionist Movement. This book will relate only marginally to the development of the Irgun National Military Organization and will deal very briefly with the development of its delegation to the United States into an independent and innovative ideological movement, the Bergson Group, which, though minute and detached from the motherland, took to itself the honorific title of the Hebrew National Liberation Movement (21a).

Chapter 11 — In The National Military Organization

This chapter is a brief biographical chapter describing the activities of Kook from the day he joined the Haganah Defense Organization as an adolescent to the foundation of the Committee for a Jewish Army in the United States. Its purpose is neither biographical nor historical. Its purpose is to present Kook as a public delegate; Hillel Kook the individual appears in this book only marginally and even then only in a public context.

The Haganah Defense Organization in Jerusalem was split in 1931, by those who opposed the control of the Labor Party over it. Kook joined the splinter group founded and commanded by Abraham Tehomi, a group that became known as the National Military Organization — as it already called itself in duplicated leaflets distributed in 1932. A series of terrorist attacks on Jewish civilians began in 1936, known in Hebrew by the odd diminutive name of "The Events of 1936-1939" and in Arabic by the pretentious name of "The Great Arabic Rebellion". The official response of the Zionist organizations was known as "The Policy of Self-Restraint". The Jewish public in Palestine became restless. The National Military Organization was pressured to undertake reprisals.

As a result, the National Military Organization split in 1937 and most of its members (headed by Tehomi) returned to the Haganah Defense Organization. Very few remained in the National Military Organization, mostly young members and commanders. Thus Kook found himself a member of the general headquarters of the organization, as the finance officer or treasurer. He left his studies at the university and within a short time went to Europe on a mission.

The Irgun National Military Organization under the command of Tehomi appointed to the position of supreme command Vladimir Jabotinsky, who had been the founder of the Jewish units in the British forces during World War I and the founder of the Haganah Defense Organization in Jerusalem immediately afterwards. Though the command was personal, it strengthened the public identification of the Irgun National Military Organization with the political party of Vladimir Jabotinsky, the New Zionist Movement or the Revisionist Party, and particularly with its youth movement (Betar). This confusion discomforted both sides. The public was under the impression, one that is still present, that these two bodies were parts of one body, one part being political and legal and the other military and underground. Hillel Kook still insists on denying this and Vladimir Jabotinsky too insisted on denying it.

At the end of 1937 Kook was sent to Europe to meet Vladimir Jabotinsky to deal with organizational and financial matters. He was appointed the liaison officer between the National Military Organization and its commander and began organizing support for the aims of the organization. The chief activity of the Organization in Europe at that time was arranging the illegal transfer of Jews to Palestine. About 20,000 people managed to migrate illegally to Palestine between 1937 and the beginning of 1940. This activity was performed in cooperation with the youth movement Betar of the New Zionist Movement. Official Zionist reaction to illegal migration was negative, of course: the official institutions of the Zionist movement considered cooperation with the British authorities vital and so they condemned every illegal activity. The Zionist leadership opposed illegal immigration in particular, because they considered this a harmful disruption of selective legal migration.

With the outbreak of World War II, the new commander of the Organization, David Raziel, accepted Vladimir Jabotinsky's opinion that the supreme national goal was the defeat of the common Nazi enemy. This priority brought about a reversal of the Organization's position towards the British authorities, and even to military cooperation with them. Many of the Organization's commanders were released from jail after the Organization published a declaration in the spirit of military cooperation. David Raziel, its commander, died at the beginning of 1941 on a mission organized by the British forces. Subsequently, the Organization ceased its activities and remained an organization in name only. The Revisionist Movement exploited this (21a).

Jabotinsky himself went to the United States to organize a campaign for a Jewish army and Hillel Kook accompanied him.

Before the outbreak of the War, the National Military Organization had delegations in Europe and in the United States. After the outbreak of the War a few of its representatives in Europe were sent to the United States. When Kook arrived there, he met, in addition to the first representative, Isaac Ben-Ami, Arie Ben-Eliezer, Shmuel Merlin, and Dr. Alexander Rafaeli. He accepted the leadership of the delegation at once. Jabotinsky's tour in which he campaigned for a Jewish army was abruptly terminated by his sudden death from a heart attack in 1940. Kook and his colleagues decided to continue the activity that Jabotinsky began and founded a Committee for a Jewish Army. Their activity developed and branched out, and they became known in the United States by the name of the Bergson Group, since, as the authorities in Palestine sought Kook, he adopted the alias Peter Bergson. Later on, the Bergson Group was joined by other activists from the Revisionist leadership who had earlier joined Vladimir Jabotinsky, including Aharon Kopilovicz and Michael Barchin, and later on Aeri Jabotinsky, Vladimir Jabotinsky's son.

Nevertheless, when the Bergson Group was soon attacked by the Zionist and Jewish establishment, the Revisionist leaders actively participated in the attacks (see p. 195). The Bergson Group continued to be active until the Independence of Israel was declared in May 1948. To repeat, this is not the history of the Bergson Group, nor is it a biography of Kook, whose activities are mentioned here only to the extent that this helps understand his contribution to the struggle for the rights of the Hebrew nation.

Chapter 12   *The Bergson Group*

I am not the right person to tell the story of either the delegation of the National Military Organization in the United States, the development of the Bergson Group, or the activities that branched out from it during World War II and immediately afterward. I do not belong to the tradition from which all this developed, nor to any nationalist tradition for that matter. As a philosopher I do not like pictures drawn with strong colors and deeds and actions performed in the limelight. I find it difficult to talk without introducing general and specific qualifications and considerations from diverse viewpoints. Were this a history book, I would happily describe in detail the activities of each member of the delegation (altogether less than ten), particularly the activities of Peter Bergson. The major contribution of researchers, be they historians or philosophers, is the frameworks which they create to suit their topics. Critical writing demands the presentation of competing frameworks to permit the observation of the same facts from different perspectives. Even though various viewpoints warrant mention, in the present case, my own basic feeling from my own viewpoint, is that there must be a radical change in the accepted attitude towards the Bergson affair. Otherwise it will be forgotten within a generation and will remain forgotten until a future historian will find it in a dusty archive, at which time the discovery will have a purely historical value. Of course, it is no disaster if a historical affair is forgotten, except that, as long as it is not forgotten, it may prove of interest and of use, as it may explain to readers why the Bergson Group found it necessary to distinguish between a national and a religious being, that until then had been the same entity, designated with the same label, namely, "the Jews", or "the Jewish people." This fact about the Bergson Group is still significant (22a).

Naturally, every story has different meanings when placed in different frameworks and seen from different viewpoints. So it is with the Bergson affair. First, there is the viewpoint of the official Jewish organizations, Zionist and non-Zionist. The hostility of these organizations to Peter Bergson and his group is no cause for a return of hostility, and certainly no target for the hostility of a philosopher, who prefers the attitude of wonderment over hostility. The question is, why did they see in him a dangerous enemy? Why did they invest so much energy in denouncing him in public with such harsh words? Second, there is the viewpoint of the American political public, particularly the Congress. The question is, why were they ready to help him? Third, there is the viewpoint of those who still remember him, especially Jews. I am no sociologist and I have not questioned Americans concerning Bergson. By accident, his name was mentioned in my presence among elderly or middle-aged American Jews (his name is not mentioned among young people unless as a part of history). Those who remember his name remember him as part of a legend. For American Jews, Bergson was the strange person who spoke about the political independence of the Hebrew nation in real political terms, not in terms of a distant future that lies beyond the horizon. Since I do not like to tell the story of one who is a legend, I shall leave the details of his life to an historian or a biographer. I will discuss here only a few dry facts and present a brief theoretical analysis (22b).

The activities of the Bergson Group focused on five committees (22): the American Committee for Jewish Palestine, which existed before he came to the United States, and four committees that were founded on his initiative: the Committee for the Jewish Army for Stateless and Palestinian Jews; the Emergency Conference and the Emergency Committee to Rescue the Jewish People of Europe; the Hebrew Committee for National Liberation (all three were different bodies for different specific political purposes); and finally, the American League for Free Palestine. These bodies were responsible for impressive achievements alongside with political processes that judicious historians would not overlook. The Committee for the Jewish Army organized a parallel body in Britain. Its supporters in the British Parliament succeeded in forwarding the cause of the creation of the Jewish Brigade in the British Army.

The Committee to Rescue the Jewish People of Europe brought about the foundation by the United States Administration of a very significant body, the War Refugee Board. Despite the failure to name this body "the Board for the Rescue of the Jews" (in accordance with a decision of Congress, which forced the U.S. President to found the Board), it was an important achievement: the Board had an important role at the end of the war and immediately afterward.

This is not the place to study the history and significance of that Board, but let me observe that recently the Board was noticed by the media following renewed interest in the fate of Raoul Wallenberg, the Swede who saved tens of thousands of Hungarian Jews and finally was seized by the Soviet Army, leaving no traces. He had been sent to Hungary by the War Refugee Board. In the estimate of some historians, the Board saved up to 100,000 Jews — an important achievement, although it was too little and too late, says Hillel Kook sadly and without underestimating the value of the few that were saved.

This story is meant not to present Hillel Kook as a partner in the rescue of Jews but to explain and to offer an example of the central difference between the direct rescue activities organized and executed by Jewish bodies (usually underground bodies) and the attempt of the Emergency Committee to Rescue the Jewish People of Europe to act politically. This Committee did not attempt to organize direct rescue missions, except in a few most special cases. It preferred to act politically, in efforts to bring the United States Administration to adopt the rescue of Jews as one of the aims of the war against Nazi Germany. The probing question is, why did the American Jewish leadership, especially the Zionist leadership, declare that Bergson and his associates were not attempting to rescue Jews and that their attempts to act politically were dangerous and undesirable? This question is of particular importance to this book, as it illustrates the vast difference between Practical Zionism, which preferred direct action, and the political attitude of seeking ways to act politically, to make political moves that might substantially alter the situation.

How, then, do political historians consider the significant historical facts concerning the Bergson Group? I do not know. I am no historian, and will not survey the diverse history books and their claims. Later on I will refer to the official history of the Irgun National Military Organization (23), a six-volume book, written by David Niv, which is the most comprehensive and official history of the Organization, publicly declared true by Menachem Begin, its last commander in chief. I will discuss what is said there about the delegation of the Irgun National Military Organization in the United States and its activities. At this stage I am content with one general remark of an important historian, who at least referred (even though briefly) to the Bergson Group, in his book on the history of Zionism. I mean the well-known and respected book by Walter Laqueur (24), which discusses in its penultimate chapter the veil of silence surrounding the destruction of European Jews that even the governments and the mass media accepted voluntarily. When he speaks (p. 551), to use his words, about the bitterness permeating American Jewry on this topic, he quotes from a speech of the chief Zionist leader, Chaim Weizmann, on March 1, 1943, in a giant protest meeting in New York, condemning the Allies for their systematic oversight of the destruction of European Jews. In addition to the anger of Jews and the indifference of non-Jews, he continues, there was also a growing anger against Jewish leaders — he names no names — who refused to talk in public, seemingly for fear that this would throw into doubt their American patriotism. Laqueur also notes that Peter Bergson excelled as a propagandist whose public-relations activities almost eclipsed the official Zionist activities. Nonetheless, he concludes, the results of Bergson's activities were minute (p. 553).

This reference of Laqueur to Peter Bergson is odd. For, his primary activity was political, of course, yet Laqueur presents it as propaganda and public relations. But Peter Bergson has nothing to be ashamed of, since he is in the good company of Theodor Herzl, whom Shlomo Avineri described in the same way (see p. 113). Moreover, no doubt Bergson used propaganda and public relations much more conspicuously than Herzl, both because of the difference in time and place and because the only way to create political pressure during World War II was through dramatic public campaigns, and these required a much more daring attitude than could be found in the official Zionist organizations in the United States. Attention should be directed to the question, where did Bergson acquire the means to devise public relations on such a broad scale? This question suffices to change the picture painted by Laqueur. (The same goes for Avineri.) Generally, public-relations officers are hired by political, economic, or social bodies, whose financial means suffice to mobilize the services of the mass media. How, then, did Bergson succeed in organizing such an impressive public enterprise? It is just as silly to speak about public enterprise as if it were merely a response to public relations, as it is to confuse a propaganda office with the body it represents and promotes (be that body a government or an economic concern). The mass organizations which Bergson formed were political mass organizations, acting for distinct and well-defined political purposes: the rescue of European Jews and the independence of the Hebrew nation in Palestine (24a).

There is no need to explain the assumption that the struggle for political independence is political action. Nevertheless, this assumption is not universally endorsed. On the contrary, it is precisely the root of the disagreement between Practical and Political Zionism (with Spiritual Zionism wavering between them): the Practical Zionists hoped to achieve independence by means of social and economic activity with a minimum of political activity, whereas the Political Zionists acted within the political arena, even without means. How does one act within the political arena without political means? One speaks in the name of a non-existent political body as if it existed, in the hopes of creating it by attracting political allies. The idea of founding a public body and the initiative for founding it precede the founding itself. (This holds for virtually every public body, with the notable exceptions, known in the social sciences as institutions that have emerged, namely, that were not planned in advance.) This is not to say that economic considerations are not linked with the development of a political idea and *vice versa*. But the founding of an army and the declaration of independence are clearly fundamental acts of independence; hence the grounding of organizations as steps in that direction is clearly a political activity as well.

Matters are not so clear concerning the rescue of Jews. This can be an altogether apolitical activity. It can be a humane activity, a religious activity, etc. The Jewish communities in the Diaspora, from Talmudic times to the Age of Reason, were regularly active in the rescue of Jews. These rescue activities were definitely not political. The most straightforward, clear rescue of Jews was their purchase in the slave-market and setting them free immediately and unconditionally. There is much nobility in this activity, but also much shame and helplessness — expressed in the payment of ransom to pirates, thereby creating incentives for them to continue robbing boats of Jews. Another type of rescue was through appeals, including negotiations, accompanied by payments of high taxes to rulers who harassed their Jews. Here, again, is an incentive prompted by Jews, even though unintentionally, to political activities hostile to Jews, such as threats of expulsion, which, it is well known, were repeatedly made in order to squeeze more money out of Jews.

Bergson claimed that since the destruction of the Jews in Europe was a war activity as declared by the German government, it was the duty of the Allies to declare the rescue of Jews in Europe as part of their war aims. He claimed that this would make the war an eminently more just war, which would thus help the war effort more than it would impose an added burden on it. The political aspect of this attitude is clear: accepting such a decision would mobilize for the rescue of Jews a certain part of the resources allotted to the war effort. The War Refugee Board was established to that end and was manned by the U. S. Secretaries of State, Treasury, and War (25).

So much for the political aspect of Bergson's activities. One important point remains: the response to the destruction of about 90 percent of the Jews within Nazi Germany and the territories it occupied, which is still a topic of historical research. Without entering into historical details, which will be explored more critically by competent historians, it is possible to conclude that the Jewish and Zionist leadership in the United States, Britain, and Palestine were shocked by information about the destruction of Jews in Europe, and their immediate response was that of suppression of information and of secrecy. Bergson's response was the very opposite. The day he heard about the mass murder of Jews, he went to an American under-secretary in Washington in order to check this information. That evening, in November 1942, in a meeting organized specifically for that purpose, he spoke of the need to organize an emergency committee to rescue European Jews and began acting towards that end (26).

Chapter 13 *Stateless Jews and the Jews of the United States*

The initial purpose of the delegation of the National Military Organization in the United States was to mobilize help for illegal immigration to Palestine and political and financial support for the Organization. This was at a time when the Zionist leadership opposed illegal immigration to Palestine. That leadership was thus hostile to the delegation, seeing it both as a delegation of a competing organization, and as an organization which implements undesirable activities. Later on the profound difference grew between the Practical Zionists, who initially wanted the migration to Palestine to be selective, comprising pioneers trained to settle Palestine, and the delegation, which tried to rescue Jews as persecuted Jews and nothing more. And, indeed, the last refugee boat to Palestine before the United States entered World War II arrived in February 1940 with 2,400 people on board. A clear expression of this difference is an official letter of five closely typed pages directed to Rabbi Baruch E. Rabinowitz, of B'nei Abraham Congregation in Hagerstown, Maryland, about whose existence I have learned from the manuscript of a book written by Shmuel Merlin of the Bergson Group.

On February 1, 1940, Henry Montor, Executive Vice-Chairman of the United Jewish Appeal in the United States, wrote *ex officio* to explain the refusal of the United Jewish Appeal to support a body called American Friends of Jewish Palestine, instituted by the Bergson delegation. In that letter Montor explains at great length that the immigrants to Palestine must be "young men and women who are trained in Europe for productive purposes either in agriculture or industry and who are in other ways trained for life in Palestine," whereas many of the immigrants for whose transport the Revisionists were "collecting dollars... were old men and women... who were, obviously, not fitted for the hazardous journey..."

This citation of Henry Montor's letter is free of irony, censure, and attempt to restore history in search of lost opportunities. Rather, it is offered as an explanation of the success of the Bergson Group, which comprised a few individuals with neither connections nor money. Neither the American Jewish leadership, nor the American Zionist leadership, gave expression to the misgivings widespread in the Jewish and non-Jewish community, to the response of all those who were sensitive to the Jewish tragedy in Europe.

Neither community was aware of the official Zionist position, nor had they any special interest in it. Herein lies the explanation for events to be described in the utmost brevity in the following pages. The more the Zionist leadership and the American Jewish leadership were aware of the success of the Bergson Group, the more they increased their effort to fight it. The more this effort grew, the more the deep differences between the two approaches became apparent. And then the public tended to increase its support for the Bergson Group, as its position was humane, immediate, and direct, whereas the official Jewish leadership was given to all sorts of considerations of which, in any case, the public had no knowledge, understanding or concern. The American Jewish leadership appealed initially only to a small part of the Jewish public in the United States, and the Bergson Group appealed to the whole American nation.

This explanation does not rest on any assumption that one side or the other is right. The possibility of explaining historical events like that in the previous paragraph rests on the power of the national movement — on the ability of the national movement to present a position that speaks directly to the people in the street. Except that there is a profound difference between the diverse national movements in history and their representatives in the United States, to the extent that such representatives existed at all. For the representative of a national movement in the United States speaks not to members of the nation living in exile, but to members of the American nation who identify with the suffering nation, because a part of the American nation shares ancestry with the sons and daughters of the suffering nation (27).

How much do the Jewish sons and daughters of the American nation identify with the rejuvenating Jewish or Hebrew or Zionist nation? Until World War II, the political sense of Jewish identity in America was insignificant. In the period under discussion here (1940-1948), an unprecedented awakening of political awareness among American Jews occurred. This awakening was caused partly by the events of the time, and partly by the manner they were brought to the attention of the American public — both Jewish and general. The Bergson Group unwittingly fulfilled a role of supremely central import in the development of American Jewish political self-awareness and awareness of the interests of Palestinian and European Jews. The Bergson Group was thus viewed by the local Jewish leadership, including the local Zionist leadership, as a competitor, even though the Group had no interest for which to compete. Despite this lack of interest, the Jewish leadership was amazingly accurate in seeing the Bergson Group as endangering its authority. As an unintended consequence of the activity of the Bergson Group, the political awareness of American Jews radically altered. From a group identified chiefly as a religious group, and one that had refused to act openly within the existing political system, they suddenly turned into an ethnic group, active, and even politically active. But our concern here is the activity of the Bergson Group as political tools for expressing political sympathy by American Jews for the Jewish settlement in Palestine and its struggle for independence. In this the Bergson Group had no following, nor could it have one (as it was a group of aliens with no local interest).

Another political aspect enabled the committees of the Bergson Group to act, especially their mobilization of American Jews to action, and it was the finding of a focus of cooperation in an interest shared by Palestinian and American Jews. American Jews found, in the activities of the Committee for a Jewish Army, a place for expressing their being Jews openly and politically, through the support of a just cause that strongly appealed to them. At this point the interest of American Jews accorded with their readiness to act for Jews across the ocean. Hence the success of the tremendous propaganda campaign mounted by the Committee for a Jewish Army and its ability to mobilize much support of Americans from diverse walks of life and from diverse circles, Jewish and non-Jewish alike. Similarly, it is apparent that already at this early stage (before the beginning of the destruction of the Jews of Europe), the desire to help suffering European Jews immediately and politically was an integral part of the plan to establish a Jewish Army.

This combination of egoism and altruism, which is the secret of cooperation, hints at the fact that two different factors were at play here: the interests of American Jews on the one hand, and of European and Palestinian Jews on the other. This is the origin of the label: "the Committee for a Jewish Army for Stateless and Palestinian Jews". For the Committee had no wish to recruit American Jews. The Committee estimated the desired size of the Army to be 200,000 men, reckoning that the Jewish settlement in Palestine, which counted less than half a million, could not contribute more than 100,000, and that the remainder would come from among the European Jews who would reach Palestine *via* neutral countries. Of course, this approach conflicted with the position of the Zionist leadership, then as now, according to which an optimal number of American Jews should be mobilized to serve the Zionist interest, to contribute money, to volunteer for military service, and to immigrate. To that end, the Zionist movement still demands the maximum of every American Jew in the hope that this demand will increase the actual contribution. Clearly, then, the Zionist Movement and the Israeli governments did not, and still do not, show the slightest interest in what happens to American Jews, or to Jews anywhere else. Their sole interest is, as it was in the past, in possible contributions to the Jewish state, in Jewish contributions to the Jewish settlement in Palestine and its economy.

The readiness of Bergson and his Group to take sincere account of the interests of the American Jews, then, brought to their attention the existence of a nation that comprises Palestinian Jews and other Jews, those who could not or would not belong to other nations, and to their recognition that other Jews share with them a religion but not a nationality. And from this grew a thinking process, whose end product was the idea of the separation of faith and nationality and the political plan of the Hebrew national liberation movement Bergson-style.

Further developments went in two very important, different directions that pertain to the two different human groups. This book relates to the kernel of the principle of national self-determination of the individual, in addition to, and even as the precondition for, the nation's right to self-determination. According to Hillel Kook, the policy of the diverse Israeli Zionist governments still infringes on both the right to self-determination of individual Jews and the interest of non-Israeli Jews.

Chapter 14 *The Wave of Hostility*

This chapter does not tell an entire story but one or two episodes that may explain why the American Jewish leadership and the world Zionist leadership saw in the Bergson Group a dangerous enemy. They spared no effort to frustrate its activity. I should mention that the hostility was both because of discord concerning aims and as an exception to the group's not having integrated itself in any accepted framework and having preferred to act independently. As evidence, I have mentioned in the previous chapter the letter of the Executive Vice-Chairman of the United Jewish Appeal, Henry Montor, who marked, *ex officio*, the differences of opinion and of organization between the Jewish leadership, in this case the Jewish Agency for Palestine, and those who were afterward known to the public by the name of the Bergson Group, the "group of Revisionists", as he called them.

As a bizarre intermezzo, I should mention that the resultant campaign of slander spilled over into a discussion in the United States Senate. It began when the Anglo-American Committee for the discussion regarding the matters of refugees met on March 27, 1943, with President Franklin Roosevelt and Anthony Eden, Cordell Hall, Sumner Wells, Lord Halifax and others. (This meeting was described in some detail by Robert E. Sherwood in his best-selling book, *Roosevelt and Hopkins*.) (28) In this meeting, pressure was put on the British to permit Jews to migrate to Palestine from Bulgaria, then under German occupation. The British refused to yield to the pressure but agreed instead to a conference, which took place in Bermuda at the end of April 1943. The Committee to Rescue the Jewish People of Europe attacked the conclusions of that conference in a full-page advertisement in the *New York Times* on May 4, 1943, sparking on May 6 and May 10 counter-attacks in the Senate from a senator who had represented the United States at the conference. On the first occasion, the senator claimed that the advertisement played into the hands of Hitler; on the second, he claimed that Bergson, a Palestinian citizen protected by a mere visitor's visa, was deceiving diverse public figures, including senators. On February 15, 1944, and, again on March 6 and April 4 of the same year, the United States Under Secretary of State sent secret telegrams to the American Consul in Jerusalem requesting information about the connections of Bergson with the National Military Organization. On August 8, 1945, the British Ambassador in Washington sent a secret telegram to the High Commissioner for Palestine concerning Bergson's request for the renewal of his visa, expressing the strong desire of the American immigration authorities to be rid of him — a desire that seemed to the Ambassador a golden opportunity to be rid of Bergson's presence in the United States. He remained in the United States, where he stayed until May 1948. (My thanks to Shmuel Merlin; end of intermezzo.)

Since this is neither a chronology, a development of a story nor a discussion, but an exemplification, let us glance now at a secret report, American State Department Memorandum 867 N. 01/2347, dated May 19, 1944, which has won a bit of a notoriety, perhaps because, if the topic that it relates to were not so tragic as the mass destruction of the European Jews, it might have seemed a sophisticated joke created by History to prove that the imagination cannot invent a folly greater than Reality does. The document is spread over four closely typed pages and is devoted entirely to a conversation Dr. Nahum Goldmann had on that day with the person in the State Department responsible for the Middle East desk and some of his assistants. (Goldmann was Chairman of the Administrative Committee of the World Jewish Congress.) The topic of conversation was the fact that the Bergson Group had founded "a Hebrew Embassy" and similarly a "Hebrew Committee of National Liberation" (to be discussed in the next chapter). The conversation began with Dr. Goldmann's handing to his host a press release (drawn up by the Zionist leadership as their reaction to the foundation of the "Embassy" and of the Committee), and also expressing great displeasure with the whole affair, and conveying the seriousness with which the Zionist leadership felt concern about the help offered to the Bergson Group by the United States Administration. The whole affair, Dr. Goldmann added, according to that report, was nothing but a big hoax. The activities of Bergson had not brought about the rescue of one single Jew, he said, and now that the War Refugee Board had been established and had absorbed much of the rescue work, Bergson and his friends had developed the "fantastic notion" that they constituted a government-in-exile, representing all the Jews who were stateless and all the Jews of occupied Palestine. Here, to my regret, the description is a bit exaggerated. My own criticism of Bergson is that he did not find a way to take one final step and propose to whomever he could, to cooperate in the act of declaring the establishment of a government-in-exile.

* The only value which the pathetic document under discussion now has, beyond its serving as an illustration, is as an unquestionable testimony that the Zionist leadership was apprehensive lest Bergson should establish a government-in-exile that would gain the support of the United States Government — out of discord with the British, not out of accord with the Bergson Group. Indeed, the attitude of the United States to Britain after World War II explains much of the sympathy towards the Bergson Group during the War, despite the fact that their demand to rescue Jews forthwith was considered an annoyance — by the Administration and even by the President of the United States himself (28a). *

I shall leave this now and continue with the report on the hostility. Dr. Goldmann referred to the position of the Bergson Group as an absolute folly and declared that the Group represented neither the Palestinian Jews nor the Jews in the Diaspora (a claim that Bergson never made, but we will return to this later). Dr. Goldmann further noted the distinction that Bergson was making (another topic to which we will return) between the Hebrew nation and the American Jews or other assimilants (29). Dr. Goldmann observed that this distinction was made in order to acquire financial support from Jews who are not Zionists and from non-Jewish citizens. He further intimated that after lengthy conversations it was concluded that Bergson and his friends were no longer Zionists but mere adventurers. Here Dr. Goldmann was partly right, since he saw the facts quicker than Bergson did. Today Kook (Bergson) agrees that at that stage he was no longer a Zionist. And, indeed, a short while after this incident, he declared himself post-Zionist. This found much sympathy in the United States.

What Dr. Goldmann and the official Jewish organizations of that period (the days at the end of World War II, the height of the mass destruction of the European Jews) found disturbing, the secret report of May 19, 1944, continues to say, was the freedom that Bergson and his friends had, to move about and collect giant sums without reporting them to anyone, while giving the impression that they were performing a broad humanitarian action. Dr. Goldmann mentioned the status of Bergson and his friends, who were staying in the United States on the basis of temporary visas, temporarily released from the draft. He could not understand, he added, why they were neither deported nor enlisted.

According to the document at hand, Dr. Goldmann testified that he and other Zionists often discussed the matter with certain members of the Senate and the Congress. The intended result was not delayed, for, the document reports, almost all of them broke their ties with Bergson. This of course is more than a little bragging, and it is difficult to estimate the degree of success of this propaganda campaign (30). Despite all the energy invested in the campaign, more than two hundred members of the Congress and the Senate remained in the committees that Bergson had established. What is so strange about all this is that in the middle of the period of the mass destruction of the European Jews, Dr. Goldmann invested much time and effort in intensive propaganda in the American Congress against a group of people who had organized a committee for their rescue (31). In addition to those who backed Bergson, a new and strong organization supported him, namely the War Refugee Board, that was a government organization. This body was founded on the instruction of the President of the United States after the American legislature had passed a decision demanding that the President create a body for the specific purpose of saving European Jews. This activity was effected, as is well known, under the influence of the Bergson Group, which collected funds and instead of using them to save Jews directly spent them on gigantic advertisements in the newspapers, and on gigantic mass meetings, and so on. In the continuation of his discussion, after many libelous remarks, Dr. Goldmann came to the heart of the matter. He declared to the person in charge of the Middle East Desk in the

State Department that the general director of the War Refugee Board saw in Bergson the person responsible for the establishment of that Board. The Jewish leadership did not consider this a minor matter. This report says that Dr. Goldmann also reported then about the position of Rabbi Stephan Wise, the head of the American Jewish Congregations and a leading American Zionist at the time. In one of his meetings with the executive director of the War Refugee Board, Rabbi Wise went so far as to say that he considered Bergson an enemy of the Jews equal to Hitler. This was because Bergson's activities could only increase hostility towards Jews. Dr. Goldmann added that the previous day he had met that director and had informed him that if the War Refugee Board did not stop supporting Bergson, the World Jewish Congress would have to denounce the Board publicly. According to Dr. Goldmann, the director agreed to break his ties with Bergson. Nevertheless (this deserves some attention), Dr. Goldmann added, if the ties were not broken, the Zionists would find it difficult to continue putting pressure on it because of the clear Zionist interest in the activities of the Board. In other words, here is the focus of the meeting, according to the report: Dr. Goldmann admitted that the Zionist leadership had no intention of executing their threat. And because the threat against one senior government official was thus feeble, the busybody went to another senior government official in the State Department, and complained about him.

I shall skip the further discussion about finances and about Dr. Goldmann's regret that Bergson was successful in mobilizing funds from the public. I should mention that the honorable Doctor explained the activities of the Bergson Group as manifestations of personal ambition of an irresponsible group of members of the National Military Organization, fugitives from the British authorities in Palestine.

The senior official in whose office this conversation took place pledged not to recognize the Bergson Group. The pledge, of course, did not calm the spirits. The pressure on that senior official continued. In a letter from that senior official to an Assistant Secretary of State of June 2, about three weeks later, he expressed anger about the pressure exerted by certain Jews on the State Department in order to have Bergson deported. Deportation, he submits, is a matter not for the State Department, but for the Department of Justice. Moreover, he recommended that pressure be put on the local draft board where

Bergson was registered. Added to the letter was another report, in three single-spaced typed pages, of June 1, this time from the senior official to the Assistant Secretary. It described further pressure on the War Refugee Board to end cooperation with Bergson. The cooperation is going to cease, said the letter echoing the earlier report. The cooperation did not cease.

This chapter is concerned not with the cooperation between the Bergson Group and the War Refugee Board but with the wave of hostility; not the hostility of one senior American official in charge of the Middle East Desk, that is none of our concern, nor in the competition between various government officials in Washington: what is a quarrel between senior government officials to us? Nor does this chapter mean to complain about the hostility showed by Rabbi Wise or Dr. Goldmann towards the Bergson Group. Rather, this chapter raises the question: why so much hostility? The answer is, as Rabbi Wise observed, the fear that Bergson was encouraging the awakening of anti-Semitism. And why did that worthy Rabbi fear that Bergson was arousing anti-Semitism? Because, in his opinion, the distinction between the American Jews and the Hebrew nation is dangerous, since it raises the question of the status of Jews, and according to the Jewish leadership this matter is taboo. In addition, the Zionist leaderships saw the Bergson Group as competition, due not to personal considerations, but to competing priorities: the Zionists saw migration to Palestine as a first priority, and therefore they considered treasonable the very proposal to rescue Jews without directly linking this rescue to the opening of the gates of Palestine to them. Bergson and his friends saw the first priority as the rescue of European Jews doomed to extinction, regardless of the question where might they find refuge.

Chapter 15

For the Rescue of European Jews

The aim of this chapter is not to describe the mass destruction of the Jews in Europe, the response of the Zionist leadership, or the response of the Bergson Group and its American Committee for the Rescue of the Jewish People of Europe, which prompted the establishment of the American Government's War Refugee Board. However, I find it impossible to continue with our agenda without mentioning a few details pertaining to the helplessness of the American Jewish leadership, particularly the Zionists among them, since it is hard to believe that they would oppose actions for the sake of the European Jews, that they would even sabotage the efforts of others for their sake. Clearly, without accepting this fact, the confusion they perpetrated between religious and national identity is barely comprehensible.

On this matter let me offer a brief extract from a paper by Sarah E. Peck, "The Campaign for an American Response to the Nazi Holocaust, 1943-1945", published in a respectable and well-known learned periodical, *The Journal of Contemporary History* (32). It describes this campaign and the American Jewish leadership's response to the mass destruction of the Jews.

In addition to her sharp criticism of the American Jewish leaders because in their effort to look patriotic they did not contribute to the rescue of Europe's Jews, Ms. Peck reports that the Jewish voice was first heard forcefully in the struggle of Bergson's Committee to Rescue the Jewish People of Europe. Relying on a letter of a Jewish Senator to President Roosevelt (see footnote 6 in her paper), she observes that the fear that impeded the rescue activities was that of the American Jewish Committee (a non-Zionist body, of course). This fear was that if Jewish refugees were allowed entry into the United States, they would arouse a wave of anti-Semitism there. The Zionist establishment, she adds, including the American Jewish Congress, showed more sympathy towards the European Jews, but less efficiency, especially because the President of the American Jewish Congress, Rabbi Dr. Stephen Wise, was in an embarrassing situation: although he was depressed by the condition of European Jews, he tried to maintain friendly relations with President Roosevelt and act only through official channels; in particular, he refused to demand of the President Jewish immigration to the United States. The Administration was more indifferent, as it considered the rescue of Jews a great burden on the war effort and feared that allowing them entry into the United States would put the country in danger of infiltration by spies and enemy agents. The fear of hostile Arab responses also had a negative influence, since it reduced the prospect of putting pressure on Britain to permit Jews entry to Palestine. Nevertheless, public pressure demanding help for European Jews increased and brought about the Bermuda Conference. The Committee to Rescue the Jewish People of Europe placed in the *New York Times* an impressive advertisement critical of that conference. This is not the place to describe the debates on the establishment of the Committee, its activities and its programs. Nor is this the place to discuss the sabotage directed against it by diverse xenophobic American officials, or the details of the assistance which these officials received from Rabbi Wise and from Dr. Goldmann, an assistance described in footnotes beginning with footnote 34 of Peck's paper and in the literature that she cites. One detail, however, may be mentioned: the Zionist leadership attempted to neutralize the activity of the Bergson Group in every possible way. These attempts were increased as the group became more successful. In Peck's opinion, the cause of the group's success was the fact that Bergson and his colleagues were not integrated into the established system — Jewish or Zionist.

At the August 1943 conference in which the American Jewish Committee was established (a conference which the anti-Zionists did not attend and some of the non-Zionists left), Peck reports, the chief Zionist leader, Rabbi Wise, claimed, "We are first and foremost always Americans, and our chief task is to win the War together with the other citizens of our beloved country." As for

Jewish refugees, he added, the demand should be not merely for their rescue, but also for the opening to them of the gates of Palestine. The other Zionist leader, Rabbi Dr. Abba Hillel Silver, expressed opposition to the demand to rescue European Jews, even without tagging to it the demand that they should be permitted to migrate to Palestine. These are historical facts, reported in official documents of the Zionist Movement. Peck explains this brutal attitude of the Zionist Movement in the United States in a sympathetic manner: Rabbis Wise and Silver wanted to use the suffering of the Jews as a lever to achieve support for the idea of a Jewish national home (p. 384). In order to maintain some sense of proportion, let me mention here in passing the very famous book by the Israeli writer and journalist, Amos Eilon, concerning the Joel Brandt affair: the conduct of the Zionist leadership in Britain and in Palestine was no different (33). Admittedly, Eilon suggested that Moshe Sharett was exceptional in that he lived with enormous remorse over the Zionist Movement's abandonment of the European Jews. But there is no reason to assume that the conscience of other leaders did not bother them; quite possibly they all suffered remorse (33a).

Sarah Peck describes the establishment of the War Refugee Board which was delayed because of the opposition of the Jewish leadership. The success of the operation, despite opposition, rested on cooperation with the Bergson Group, especially by some high officials in the Treasury, including the Secretary of the Treasury himself, Henry Morgenthau Jr. (34). It is perhaps advisable to skip Peck's description of the activities of the Committee for the Rescue of the Jews of Europe and of the War Refugee Board, of their frustration, and of the visits which Rabbi Wise and Dr. Goldmann paid to high government officials for the purpose of slandering Bergson. To the point itself, the Zionists opposed all activity aimed at the rescue of Jews unless intended to transport them to Palestine. The anti-Zionists, including some American diplomats, opposed, of course, all activity aimed at the rescue of Jews intended to transport them to Palestine. But nobody prevented the Zionists from organizing further slander campaigns against Bergson and his group after they founded the Committee for National Liberation. Peck ends with a very sad picture. Her final paragraph quotes Rabbi Dr. Stephen Wise: in his memoirs he accused the State Department of neglect through bureaucratic confusion and want of personal interest, a neglect that prevented the rescue of thousands of Jews and the lessening of the disaster. The author does not counter his accusation, but she does lay a more severe blame on his shoulders — on the shoulders of the Jewish leadership or, as she calls it, organized American Jewry. It was party to the disaster, she says, because it did not do what it could, since it was both divided and excessively cautious, moved by long-range considerations alone in times of emergency (34a).

This ends the presentation of the hatred of the Committee for the Rescue of the Jews of Europe. The next chapter discusses the hostility towards another committee — the Hebrew Committee for National Liberation.

Chapter 16

National Self-Determination

The story of the encounter between Dr. Nahum Goldmann, one of the leaders of the World Jewish Congress, and high government officials in the United States, raises many difficult questions. First and foremost among them is, how could a person in his position and with his status not devote at least one minute to the demand that the government should do something for the rescue of European Jews? Peter Bergson's first assumption was that Zionist organizations showed very little practical interest in the rescue of European Jews. His second assumption was that he was considered as evil not because he demanded the rescue of European Jews but, as his opponents said, because he seemed to them to be agitating anti-Semitism. Why? Why did Peter Bergson, who was trying to rescue European Jews, seem to them an instigator of anti-Semitism? How did a person who advocated a Hebrew national army and Hebrew national independence seem to be arousing the hatred of Jews? Why did they oppose him so?

The first claim against Peter Bergson was that he was not elected by any public body and that he therefore had no right to represent anybody. This is not a serious claim. Generally, leaders of national liberation movements are not elected precisely because of the absence of a technical possibility of attaining official mandate from the people; it is precisely because of this obstacle that people tend to sympathize with them too strongly. Of one thing there is not the slightest doubt: all the Jews of occupied Europe who suffered intolerable and indescribable torment and had no knowledge of the existence of Peter Bergson would have been ready to support him with what little remained of their power, wholeheartedly and with no qualification, had they only been in the position to hear of him and express an opinion. No doubt the situation would have been different had the activities of the Bergson Group been known in the Jewish settlement in Palestine, where there was considerable hostility to the National Military Organization and its activities. It is impossible to know why there was such a great effort in Palestine to obscure information about these activities both during the years 1940-1948, and since then. What did it — and what does it — matter to the leadership of the American Jews or to the leadership of the World Jewish Congress whether Bergson represented or did not represent those in whose name he spoke? They were not against him because of, or in the name of, the European Jews who desperately needed the help Bergson tried to procure for them. Nor were they opposed to him in order to protect their good names against him. The matter was just this: they opposed him because leaders of American Jews, British Jews, and similar Jews who were living in countries where there was no anti-Semitism, were afraid of an outburst of anti-Semitism in their countries. This is pathetic. In Central Europe, Jews were being murdered *en masse*; in the United States Jews faced no real danger. If it had been otherwise, it would have been impossible for Bergson to obtain — as he did — the official support of 200 out of 600 members of the United States Congress, dozens of presidents of American universities, and thousands of other public figures.

The problem, therefore, was not whether Bergson did or did not represent this or that person or this or that group. Those who do not agree that the problem was not the problem of representation have to come up with a new and stronger argument. In particular, they will be unable to justify this denial by claiming that Bergson was or is a rogue, liar, or con man. It is very well known that one can simultaneously be a representative, a rogue and a liar. Yet Bergson was not elected. But neither were Rabbis Wise and Silver, nor Dr. Goldmann; at most they were elected by minute bodies that did not represent much, bodies that were notoriously undemocratic and that never suffered from excessive democratic public control. I do not mean to say that these gentlemen simply competed with Bergson for positions of power. Bergson himself, at least, rejects this claim without reservation not only as false but, more deeply, as a claim that is not to the point; for such a claim is personal, whereas the question at hand is political. The question is not whether the Jewish public in the United States is represented by Tom, Dick, or Harry, nor is it whether these are honest or dishonest, but what is the political platforms for which they stand. The platforms are more important than the persons who lend them their names.

The distinction made by the Bergson Group between Hebrews and American Jews, to repeat, angered Dr. Goldmann very much and seemed to him a tool for extracting money from non-Zionists. What did it matter to Dr. Goldmann which funds came out of the pockets of the non-Zionists? What did it matter to him that a distinction was made between American Jews and other Jews? Generally, he was not against distinctions. He never opposed distinctions *per se*. Distinctions were made on countless occasions. Within the United States, for example, Jews were initially organized according to their countries of origin — as they were in Israel. But there is a very important difference here between the two. In Israel, organization according to country of origin was always very weak and the political parties were from the start very strong. In the United States, in contrast, prior to World War II and to the activities of the committees organized by Bergson, organization according to country of origin was strong and the Jews had participated hardly at all in organized party-political activities, not even in the Zionist movement. American Jews had not been active in a concentrated fashion in American internal politics — particularly not as an ethnic group. Until Bergson appeared and mobilized the support of so many public figures and statesmen, American Jews did not act as a politically weighty ethnic group, as they regularly do nowadays (34a). When one examines what is socially common to American Jews, one should note that the determining concept at the time for Americans — including Jews — had been not the cultural autonomy of the ethnic groups but the theory of the melting pot. This was the recommendation that immigrants assimilate as fast as possible — nationally, socially, and culturally (thought not religiously). In this spirit, immigration was legislatively limited according to country of origin. This limitation, enacted in 1925, was abolished only in the seventies by the United States Supreme Court, which declared it unconstitutional. The purpose of limiting immigration was to facilitate the national assimilation of immigrants.

Hence, Jewish leaders lied when they spoke as if their objection to Bergson was on the grounds that he distinguished between American Jews and the Hebrew nation and thus raised the specter of anti-Semitism. What angered them was that he described this distinction as between the Jewish faith and Hebrew nationality, or, to be more precise, the Jewish nationality, whose name he proposed to alter in order to emphasize the existence of two separate entities.

The public nature of Bergson's activities was the target of hostility; secrecy seemed right to the Jewish leadership — both in the United States and elsewhere. The Jewish leadership in Britain, for example, appealed in secret to the British Government for the establishment of a Jewish brigade in the British forces. By contrast, Bergson shouted from every street corner, appealing for the right to mobilize a Jewish Army, even though it would not enlist American or British Jews. Here he threw a wedge, and openly so, into national unity. In the Zionist view, then, national unity requires silence. The Zionist leaders strove for quiet diplomatic activity through an authorized unified representation. They did not want modern political activity, noisy and apparent on every street corner, complete with internal disagreements and a diversity of political opinions (34b). We shall see later on that Ben-Gurion publicly declared that clandestine activities are always preferable to activity in the limelight. The heart of the disagreement is in the answer to the question, why does national unity require secrecy? Why does publicity put national unity at risk? Why does the national interest always demand quiet activity, and why does the limelight harm it?

It is worth noting that this question has changed its character with Israel's attainment of independence, for the independence of Israel as a country to which Jews of different nations can migrate has changed their status even if they do not wish to migrate — as the fathers of the Zionist movement had predicted. We will return to this important detail in the discussion of the present situation and the current relations between Israel and Jews of other nations. For now, in this historical discussion, let us stay with the question, why did the leaders of the Practical Zionist Movement prefer clandestine activity to activity in the limelight before Independence? Why did they view the limelight as undesirable? It is immediately apparent why the Political Zionists and the

Hebrew Committee for National Liberation preferred the limelight and why the Practical Zionists had no use for it. But why did the Practical Zionists prefer secrecy? Why did they consider publicity harmful to the national interest?

Bergson's conclusion: the moment the persecution of the Jews appears as an official policy in one country, a political conflict of interest occurs between the Jews of that country and those of its neighbor. For the continuation of the persecution threatens Jews of the neighboring country. Thus it was assumed to be in the interests of the Jews of the United States, Britain, or any other country, who were not victims of persecution but who saw themselves as vulnerable, not to arouse the attention of the non-Jewish local population to the fact that they also could freely persecute Jews. For according to their own views, they could not respond forcefully when the hatred of Jews was aroused. Jews in the Diaspora were therefore silent when the Nazis began harming Jews in Germany (as early as 1933). It is no mere hindsight that justifies asking the question, why did the Jewish leadership do nothing for the rescue of the European Jews in the thirties? It was already then clear to any observer that the ground was burning under the feet of the Jews of the European Continent (20b). It is clear that the same religious leadership that ignored the political situation systematically and traditionally also ignored all political questions. The silence of Zionist leaders and their inaction cannot be justified on the grounds of ignorance. They were not ignorant. Possibly they tried to collaborate with the British authorities because they considered migration to Palestine as primarily a pioneering activity and therefore it had to be selective and not massive. This is why they attacked Jabotinsky when he renewed Max Nordau's idea concerning the massive transfer of Jews from Europe to Palestine. Jabotinsky's concern resulted from his political perception of the deteriorating situation of European Jews, even though he did not come close to grasping the enormous dimensions it would reach. In the forties the Zionist leaders not only did nothing to rescue Jews in a manner commensurate with the magnitude of their disaster, but they also suppressed information. Afterwards, their excuse was that the information was so shocking that it might have dangerously demoralized Jews elsewhere. Clearly, this excuse was senseless. Even today it is surprising that such an excuse was at all possible; perhaps there is truth in Kook's claim that the Zionist leaders lost their bearings in their fear that American propaganda for the rescue of the European Jews might harm American Jews without helping European Jews (34c). But even if this were so, why was the information kept secret in Palestine too? Hillel Kook tries to answer this question generally by saying that there is not — and cannot be — any national unity of the Jewish people; the leaders of the Jewish settlement in Palestine, like the American Jewish leaders, catered first and foremost to their local communities and thus did not grant sufficient priority to the desperate situation of Jews in Europe.

In the national wars in which Jews participated, the interests of Jews in one country conflicted with those of Jews in the enemy country. In World War I, Jews participated in the war on both sides of the front and even shot at each other. But they did not do this as Jews; as Jews they had no interest in either side of the front. Jabotinsky's proposal at that time, that Jews as a nation should consider Britain their ally, created a new situation. And, indeed, Max Nordau hesitated over Jabotinsky's proposal, both because he did not know which side would win and because Jews fought in the armies of both sides and he was concerned about their fate and wished to avoid harming them. It was a very difficult political decision, requiring great political courage, and one for which diverse historians of Zionism praise Jabotinsky unanimously (35). Nevertheless, as long as there was no Jewish Army, there was no clear national Jewish interest. This is not so in the case of the hatred of the Jews, since the political interest of every Jewish community was to prevent the spread of the hatred of Jews to the country where it was settled. A clear conflict of interest would arise, however, if one country's mobilization of public opinion against the hatred of the Jews in another country might hurt its own Jewish community.

Then as now, the hard question is, when and under what conditions is it necessary for political conflicts of interest to arise between different Jewish communities? As long as Jews were protected by local rulers in the style of medieval Europe, nothing could be done to prevent such conflicts. Nor was it intelligent to overlook them, even with the sure knowledge of the self-sacrifice called for when a Jewish community in one land tries to help one in another land. Some Jews nobly rushed to the aid of other Jews despite conflicts of interest. Today, however, solutions of this kind to such questions are not possible at all. In the modern world, Jews are members of the nations in which they live; they are not ruled as Jews but as citizens. Therefore, a more radical solution must be sought — one that permits the abolition of the conflicts of interest at their very root, since in Israel the Jews are not merely members of a religious community; they are also members of an independent nation, and they are the greatest majority and the decisive majority in the political life of that nation. Clearly, the interests of an independent nation cannot always be consistent with the interests of all the Jewish communities of all other nations, especially when the modern world is split into blocs. Hence, there is a political and constitutional need to maintain the rights of these Jewish communities not to depend on the daily interests of Israel. The solution is a separation of nationality and faith, and the recognition of the fact that today the Jewish faith is the faith of members of many nations, including Israel, of course. Therefore, Judaism should be purged of all political content.

This is the context in which Bergson-Kook put forward the principle of the national self-determination of the individual: the right of the individual to self-determination is the root of the right of the nation to self-determination. This is also the right of Jews to declare themselves members of the Hebrew nation; only because the Jews of Palestine and Europe had not had the proper opportunity to express such a will, did he found the Hebrew Committee for National Liberation in order to speak in their name on the supposition that they desired liberation and national liberation at that. This assumption did not apply to American Jews, for they had the right and freedom to define themselves as members of the Hebrew nation or as members of the American nation.

Too little written material exists as yet about the growth of the idea of national self-determination, even though this idea seems today to be well-known and plainly understood, as if it were a corollary to some social contract that invites no discussion. The nationalist idea became of moment with the rise of the Romantic Movement, which saw the collective, not the individual, as the bearer of the right to self-determination. Individuals who are unluckily not linked to the collectives in which they grew up, said Romantic thinkers, are rootless and alienated from their people and have no place in any human society, unless they are geniuses who have outstanding inner spiritual resources. Some students of politics suggested a compromise solution. The collective, especially if it is a nation, is a central part of public affairs, they said, but individuals have the right to contribute voluntarily to the development of collectives. After World

War I, the idea of national self-determination gained popularity, especially as a tool for dismembering multinational empires, the Austrian, the Russian, and the Ottoman. During World War II this idea became even more popular, especially for dismantling empires that ruled over backward countries, and as a motive for the newer idea of nation building.

There was still no substitute for the philosophies of the Enlightenment and Romantic Movements. The idea of national self-determination, as it developed in the political arena, remained then without a proper philosophical theoretical foundation and therefore it is still unclear. Ever so often those who support this idea are forced by its weak theoretical grounding to borrow ideas and fragments of ideas from conflicting philosophies in order to strengthen it. This causes much confusion, which bears a high price, as a few historians have observed. Now, it is possible to formulate the principle of national self-determination in a liberal and symmetrical way: that is to say, the right to self-determination should be declared both national and individual. Moreover, there is no need to discuss the question, which collective, which collection of individuals is, as a matter of principle, a nation; suffice it to consider the desire of this or that public to be identified as a nation.

There was never any doubt about the desire of the Jews of Palestine and Europe to be identified as a nation. Most of the Jews of the United States had no wish to join this nation: they openly wished to remain members of the American nation. This may be exemplified by the speech the American Zionist leader, Abba Hillel Silver, delivered during the Twenty-Second Zionist Congress in December 1946. He stated there explicitly that American Jews had no intention of accepting the challenge of Golda Meir and David Ben-Gurion to migrate to Palestine. Despite this declaration, and despite Ben-Gurion's agreement in principle with Silver at that Congress, that the Jewish state should not deem the Jews of the United States its subjects, the official Zionist doctrine, then and more so now, denied and still denies Jewish individuals the right to choose their nationality; moreover, it attempts to oblige the Jews of the United States and of other Western countries to abandon their present nationalities, regard themselves members of the Jewish nation, and actively join the Jewish nation that dwells in Zion (36). The present discussion takes as given the hate of the Jews in Europe during the war (and by extension one can include the hate of the

Jews in the Soviet Union). Also taken as given here is the desire of Jews of the Western countries to remain citizens of the countries in which they dwell. It airs neither the question of a possible spread of the hate for the Jews, nor the question of what the position of Israel should be concerning such a possible spread. This matter will be discussed in some detail in Part Three of this book. At the moment the discussion still centers on the period prior to the foundation of Israel. As a result of what was discussed here, Bergson declared himself a post-Zionist — because he declared himself already a member of the Hebrew nation — and his approach was welcomed in the United States. These facts point at the possibility of establishing new relations between Israel and the Jews of the United States, different from what they are today. To repeat, Bergson did not intend to accelerate the establishment of public Jewish bodies within the United States that might express opinions different from those of the Zionist establishment there, questions that pertain mainly to the American Jewish community. This is so, despite the success of American Jews in finding an expression as a patriotic American group with no fear of asserting its Jewish uniqueness and even its identification with a foreign people with which it shares origin, culture, and religion. The opinion of the celebrated historian Walter Laqueur should be mentioned again. His hypothesis about the Jewish leaders in the United States is that they were silent about the destruction of the European Jews for fear it would throw into doubt their American patriotism. Clearly, today the picture is radically different.

    This is not the whole list of confusions concerning nationality. There is a reactionary confusion and there is an ethnic confusion (the ones just discussed), but on top of all this there is the liberal confusion. One of the greatest students of the national problem in the twentieth century was Professor Hans Kohn. He was a German Jew, one of the earliest followers of Martin Buber, and a refugee, a disappointed Zionist who chose to live in the United States, where he stayed until his death. He was hostile towards reactionary nationalism, seeing in it the roots of fascism. In his important books he opposed all nationalism, as he was a liberal who saw no possibility of a stable liberal nationalism. As a result, he was not interested in or familiar with the activities and ideas of the Bergson Group. Nevertheless, after reading a newspaper article about the cooperation between the American Secretary of the

Treasury, Henry Morgenthau, and Peter Bergson, he wrote a letter about it to the New York Times, on August 4, 1944, which is partly quoted by Shmuel Merlin. He described there the members of the Bergson Group as fascists.

Chapter 17   *Peter Bergson to Chaim*
              Weizmann, April 2, 1945

Bergson's letter to Dr. Chaim Weizmann is a document of fourteen printed pages in the form of an open letter from the Chairman of the Hebrew Committee for National Liberation to the President of the Jewish Agency for Palestine. (The original letter, written in English, is in the Weizmann Archives.) In this letter, Bergson presents the platform of his Committee to the Zionist leadership, together with a recommendation that the leadership accept it (37). The significance of such a move is mainly declarative. What, then, does Bergson declare in April 1945?

He says that the destruction of the European Jews differs from any other disasters in Jewish history (not only because of its extent and cruelty). There is, therefore, a need to clarify positions anew, while trying to organize the migration of one-and-a-half million Jews to Palestine within a year and a half. Since the opposition of the British Mandatory Government is the major obstacle to this, Bergson proposes to fight British policy in the open with the help of friendly countries, especially the United States. It deserves notice that the major problem with organizing mass migration within a short time is solved here in one short paragraph that says, the Hebrew nation has to declare its plan, insist on it, and mobilize international public opinion in its support. The claim is that world public opinion rejected Britain's position before World War II, and it will be even less popular at the end of the war.

This raises the problems of the document at hand: the question of the position of Western Jews and of the relation between the Jewish religion and the

Jewish Commonwealth. * (The term, "Commonwealth", like *"Res Publica"* or "Republic", means the common interest or the common good. It was used in the United States in this sense and adopted by the Zionist leadership in a convention gathered at the Biltmore Hotel in New York City in 1942, where it was resolved that the purpose of the Zionist movement was the creation of a "Jewish Commonwealth".) Had this decision been accepted but a few years earlier, Jabotinsky would not have split the Zionist movement and then perhaps there would be no need for Bergson's letter to Dr. Weizmann. Despite the great import of the resolution that determines the aim of the Zionist movement, the name of this resolution, "the Biltmore Plan", is clearly inadequate, as it included no operative plan at all, due to the excessive dependence of the Zionist leadership on the British Government (to be described in some detail in the next chapter) (37a). *

At the center of the plan for the establishment of a Jewish republic are two problems — the problem of the relation of the nation to the Jews of the West and the relation of the nation to the Jewish faith. These problems are one and the same, for, in the same sense in which the Jews of Western democratic countries are not members of the Hebrew nation, nationality and religion are not identical, despite the fact that the Jewish nation is also Jewish in its religion. This is analogous to the fact that the Italian nation is Catholic but Catholic Americans are not Italian nationals — even if they are Italian by origin. So far Bergson. Clearly, he grasped a principle whose significance grew particularly under his influence: what happened to the American Jews happened also to other groups. American Jews tend to be not only Americans of the Jewish faith but also, as a result of the disaster of the European Jews, and under the influence of the Committee to Rescue the Jewish People of Europe, they were perceived both as Jews and as an interest group. They were therefore accepted in the United States immediately after the war as an ethnic group. The American Italians, who in addition to being Americans in their nationality and Catholic in their religion, were also perceived as an ethnic group. In the language of Bergson's letter to Dr. Weizmann, they were a public of Americans of Italian origin. Not only the Italians and the Poles in the United States are different from each other, despite the fact that members of these two groups are both American and Catholic; in addition, there are many Americans who are more

American-Italian than they are Catholic Americans, because their Catholicism may be less a matter of faith than of ethnic and cultural origin.

I am stressing the ethnic aspect more than Bergson did in his letter, even though the main principle is, as Bergson insists, the distinction between nationality and religion. I do this because it is easier to distinguish between the two, nationality and religion, in light of the third, ethnicity (country of origin), and also because the ethnic aspect has become more conspicuous since the war. Similarly, the identification of ethnicity and country of origin renders American Jews, especially the non-observant among them, Americans of Hebrew origin. The significance of the distinction between faith and nationality according to Bergson, as he stressed, is the claim that the nation — he calls it the Hebrew nation — already exists. Conflation of the nation and the religious community implies that all Western Jews belong to that nation. Consequently the existence of the Hebrew nation will be not a political fact similar to the fact of the existence of the American nation but a mere potentiality. In other words, to recognize Palestinian Jews and Jewish refugees in Europe as belonging to an existent nation, American Jews must be recognized as not the same in this respect.

To stress this distinction, Bergson asks Dr. Weizmann the following questions. (He intentionally worded the expressions in these questions — quoted here in part — in the language of the Zionist leadership, not in the language of the Hebrew Committee for National Liberation.)

1. "Does every Jew in the world automatically become a citizen of the Jewish Commonwealth? And if not, which Jews do and which do not?"
2. "What would be the status of Moslems and Christians who will reside in the Jewish Commonwealth, or who might wish to enter the country? Would their nationality be Jewish?"
3. "Who would be the diplomatic representatives of the Jewish Commonwealth?" Today [at the end of World War II] Palestine is represented by the World Zionist Organization whose representative in the United States is Rabbi Wise, an American citizen, not qualified to represent the Commonwealth.

4. "What will become of the Jewish Agency [for Palestine] which was intended to represent the interests of the Jews of the world in Palestine?"

Here Bergson contrasts the interests of all Jews with those of the Jews of Palestine.

5. "What will become of the World Zionist Organization? Will it continue to exist as a sectarian international Jewish organization, or will the fact of the establishment of the Jewish Commonwealth call for some changes in its structure?"
6. "Finally, what will become of the World Jewish Congress? Will this, too, continue its existence as an international Jewish body and attempt to speak for the 'Jews of the World' on political questions…?"

Hillel Kook claims rightly that to the present day answers to these questions are wanting, that the required structural changes were not made since the establishment of Israel. This causes confusion, and "confusion is the enemy." It was less important for Bergson what answers were given to these questions, since the mere recognition of them would impose on one who recognizes them the distinction between nation and religious community (37b). But the failure to recognize the questions prevents the possibility of mobilizing goodwill in the general public because of the confusion. In order to overcome the confusion, the open declaration is required that, in contrast to the Hebrew nation (or the Israeli nation), the Jewish people has ceased to be a political entity. Judaism is in essence a religion and politically a religion is not an active entity, for a faith has no government and no army, and so on. Also, it is impossible to invite all participants in the Jewish religion or the Jewish people as a sovereign to take part in the United Nations Organization. It would be impossible for Rabbi Wise to represent the Jewish people, because he is an American citizen. The same was true of Dr. Weizmann, a British subject. Even were it possible to represent American Jews as a part of the Hebrew nation, this would not be agreeable to them, because it would differentiate them from the other American citizens and arouse hatred of Jews there, on the old excuse that they constituted an alien element. Similarly, it would not suit the needs of the nation as it would turn the nation into an international entity and thus devoid of the quality of a nation proper.

The existence of the World Jewish Congress and similar international Jewish bodies prevents friendly governments from relating to the Hebrew nation in a desirable manner, without their being able to protest against the presence of these bodies and against this confusion, since these are internal Jewish affairs. Demanding the recognition of the Jewish nation as well as of loyal Jewish subjects of the countries of their residence, was and may still be the cause of a national disaster.

"The Jews must decide," continued Bergson, "*what* they are." Every Jew has the right and the duty of national self-determination, to use another wording. Things will be different when an "ideal world will be established when it will make no difference whether one has a country or a nation or a territory or a border or an army." But in our present world, in order to prevent a new disaster, there is need for a decision. Bergson states as a principle his own preference for a world in which "all human beings can live under God in true freedom and equality." He adds, "I believe that such a world will eventually come to be, but if we let the Jewish situation remain as it is, there is no doubt in my mind that hardly any Jew will survive to live in that era."

The central error, according to Bergson, was an extremism expressed in the desire of the assimilants to have every Jew assimilate, and in the demand of the Zionists to have all Jews migrate to Palestine. Here is the basis of Bergson's pluralism — if the use of a term developed later on is allowed — and the only democratic, practical outlook that he considered available.

Two principles emerge, then. First, Jews have the right and duty to define themselves as members of the Hebrew nation or of the nations in which they dwell. Second, the nation already exists, whose members are Jews, inhabitants of Palestine and refugees in Europe. The nation in Palestine demands "a free state" so as to be able to tell the American Jews who belong to the American nation, including the non-Zionists and anti-Zionists among them, not to interfere in its internal affairs. This way the nation will cease to live in inner conflict.

And so to the socio-political aspect of Peter Bergson's letter to Dr. Chaim Weizmann. The aim is still declared in the traditional Zionist terminology: "All that we want, as I very well know all you and your fellow Zionists want, is to bring an end to the scandal of the territorial homelessness for a great and ancient nation."

The program is this: a declaration of independence, planned in a simple pattern:

1. There should be the State of Palestine, whatever its name might be, as "the national territory of the Hebrew nation," of a few million citizens of different religions, mostly, but not all, members of the Jewish faith or of Jewish origin, and without Judaism being a state religion.
2. Jewish religious communities should be there, but they will be "purely religious communities," with no political or national designation. In addition, just as there are Americans of Italian or of Irish origins, so there will be Americans of Hebrew origins. The Hebrew Committee for National Liberation, adds Bergson, was founded in order to perpetrate the recognition of the difference between Hebrew or Palestinian Jews and American or British Jews, with the aim of demanding the recognition of the Hebrew nation by the United Nations Organization. Attempts of the Committee in that direction proved how easy it was for the public to accept the distinction between faith and nationality.

Here, in order to avoid redundancy, I skip a part of Bergson's letter describing the Bergson Group and its work. Let me come, then, to the heart of the letter:

"We therefore propose that the Jewish Agency for Palestine, augmented" by representatives of the Jewish settlement in Palestine, "should constitute itself and become a representative national authority to speak for the Hebrew Nation temporarily, until such time as, in due democratic process, a more representative provisional government may be established." In brief, what is required now is a transitional government-in-exile.

"I wish therefore to inform you most solemnly and publicly that if the essence of our proposal is accepted and a Hebrew national authority is established, we [the Hebrew Committee for National Liberation] will hasten to recognize the authority of the newly formed government or committee." If "the Jewish Agency ... deem it advisable to launch now the establishment of a Hebrew government-in-exile, they should take over the title of Hebrew Committee for National Liberation, since such pattern has been successfully established by other nations.... The very minimum ... would be simply to reconstitute the Jewish Agency into a Hebrew agency...."

On the assumption that the plan would be accepted, Bergson recommends that the temporary government-in-exile should seek recognition from all governments and from all possible international organizations, that it should recognize the naturalization of Jews in the still-non-existent state in accord with emergency regulations; organize mass immigration in the open, with publicity, and in opposition to the laws of the British mandatory government which the temporary government should ignore on the supposition that this will be met with enormous sympathy from other nations; try to open direct negotiations with neighboring countries to establish understanding and friendly relations; strive for international arbitration with the government of Great Britain; and seek international loans of enormous sums.

So much for the extract from Bergson's letter, which presents a program based on understanding, daring, and initiative. What the likelihood of its realization was cannot be assessed now. Likely to remain controversial for a long time is the question of what influence the Hebrew Committee for National Liberation had on the establishment of the State of Israel (38). It is hard to deny, however, that the declaration of Israel's independence and the establishment of a temporary government in May 1948 constitute a unilateral political activity in accord with the proposal of the Committee for National Liberation. It is quite possible that the broad political activity organized by this Committee over the previous four years or so helped to create the required political background and world public opinion in its favor. All these factors surely played a vital role then. Similarly, it is not disputed that the Irgun National Military Organization had declared repeatedly that if the Zionist establishment did not declare independence then that Organization would do so. According to Kook, the very existence of a plan of the Hebrew Committee for National Liberation from the year 1944, according to which independence should be declared, influenced and contributed to the Declaration of Independence. Regrettably, however, the independence declared was not the independence of a nation distinct from the people with whom it shares religion and tradition. Hence it was not a declaration of genuinely national independence, but the foundation of a strange and unique administrative entity. Therefore, the vital need remains of declaring real national independence as a part of the normalization of Israel, in an attempt to overcome the present ongoing national crisis.

* The above discussion centered on the problem of normalization, and thus on the inner logic of Peter Bergson's letter to Dr. Chaim Weizmann and the need, still not dated, to answer the questions it presents, as Hillel Kook stresses ceaselessly. I have neglected the aspect that has meanwhile been resolved, the need for declaring independence and the way to establish it — by declarations plus the mobilization of world public opinion that should bring democratic nations to support the new nation.

* This neglect of mine was an error on my part. Just as the clear questions that were posed in it were not answered to date (and also not asked by the Israeli public to date), so the message as to the matter of attaining independence through one-sided initiative was unclear to the Zionist leadership as it was unclear to Dr. Weizmann (who, a year prior to the establishment of Israel's independence, saw in that independence a distant dream; see below), and is still unclear in Israel, where an official version is popular of the story of the achievement of independence. According to that version, independence was achieved because the United Nations Organization ensured its success. The historical fact is different: as is on record, that Organization was busy preparing an alternative plan to the original plan of independence for the Jewish settlement in Palestine, thereby making Moshe Sharett, who was then representing the Jewish settlement in Palestine there, demand of David Ben-Gurion that he avoid declaring independence, at least temporarily. Another (semi-official) version presents as the condition for independence the one-sided liquidation of the British mandatory government and the departure of the British forces from Palestine. The historical fact is different: as is on record, the departing British authorities deemed their departure a threat to the very survival of the Jewish settlement in Palestine, and they departed in the expectation that the Jewish representative would request that they return.

* Perhaps this discussion is redundant. Perhaps it is all too clear that, under any conditions, without the ability to decide, there is no independence. Perhaps the very need for this discussion testifies to the Israeli inability to make political decisions and to the absence of an Israeli awareness of this inability. This absence is here explained as rooted in Israel's abnormal situation. *

Chapter 18

In the Zionist Establishment

Before World War II, the Zionist movement blossomed in Eastern Europe and received a significant expression in Western Europe, especially in Britain. Offshoots of the movement also began growing in the Arabic-speaking world, as much as was possible, and had modest beginnings in the United States and in Canada. As is well known, the North American branch of the Zionist movement was small and unwelcome. Anti-Zionist and non-Zionist Jewish organizations had decisive weight in the United States (so much so that Bergson referred to this fact in his letter to Weizmann). In addition to this, before independence there was in Palestine the Jewish settlement of about one-half million people. This settlement was considered in the Zionist movement exemplary and it was run by Zionist organizations such as the National Committee and the Jewish Agency for Palestine. The Russian Revolution struck Russia off the Zionist map and during World War II the whole of the European Continent dropped out of the picture. This increased the relative importance of the Jews of English-speaking countries and of Palestine. Only after World War II did French Jews and those of Arabic-speaking countries enter the picture. Upon the outbreak of the War the Jews of the United States appeared on the Zionist map as a significant factor whose significance was and still is on the increase. It should be noted that the majority of the leaders of the Zionist Movement came from Eastern Europe, notably Dr. Chaim Weizmann, Dr. Nahum Goldmann, and David Ben-Gurion. These were in the first line of the leadership of the movement, to be joined later by two Zionist leaders from the United States. The reaction of the Zionist establishment may be examined against this background. One who prefers not to dig in archives and undertake comprehensive research, such as the author of these pages, might very well rely on existing trustworthy summaries. I will use here one document of a character completely opposed to everything said here, since it is a significant official document of the Zionist establishment itself: the minutes [in Hebrew; translation mine] of the first Zionist Congress after World War II and the last before independence, a congress that stood at the crossroads between the destruction of European Jewry and the realization of the dream of independence. It was the Twenty-Second Zionist Congress that took place in Basel, Switzerland, in December 1946, after seven years of war and national disaster, during which even the Executive Committee did not meet as often as required (see the minutes of the Congress, Ben-Gurion's summary, pp. 332ff.). The Zionist Congress was a kind of parliament that met once every two years for a few days, and in this case after seven years of great changes and a national disaster. This Twenty-Second meeting, the last Congress before independence, thus stands out as a major and representative event. Though many ceremonial details are omitted from the stenographic minutes, these contain more than 600 pages. Only 300 of them, however, are political, and even these include much empty verbiage. Even the little that does matter is understood better when the texts it contains are compared with the comments on them. The whole of the significant political material covers only a few pages. In addition, the minutes devote a few pages to decisions (39).

The most conspicuous thing about this Congress was its structure. The total number of delegates was less than 400: only a few delegates from Eastern Europe appeared — 16 from Germany, 14 from Romania, 10 from Hungary, 5 from Czechoslovakia, and 5 from Transylvania; by contrast, the number of delegates from the United States was the largest — 121, as opposed to 79 from Palestine, 10 from Britain, 7 from South Africa, 7 from Argentina, and 6 from France. All other countries had less than 5 each, and usually only 1. The appearance of the large body of American delegates was a major change in the character of the Congress. The delegates from Palestine, especially Golda Meir and David Ben-Gurion, had demanded that American Jewry send a significant number of immigrants to settle in Palestine; instead, the American delegates offered financial aid (the aid from the United States covered most of the budget; see pages 349 and 360) and propaganda; they expressed the hope that their influence on the United States administration might be important and bring useful political change. This last point can be examined in the light of the debates in the Congress. For a tool cannot be used without political aim or task.

The debates in the Twenty-Second Zionist Congress, were centered on 1. Goals; 2. Recruitment of allies; 3. Modes of action; and 4. Enemies from within.

1. What was the goal of Zionism? A Jewish state, of course. Says Weizmann, "We are confident that our aim is before our eyes and we will achieve it — if not in our generation, in my generation, then it will be in the next generation"! (p. 23). Ben-Gurion speaks about "the Establishment of the Jewish State in the near future" (p. 59). He also adds that "the Hebrew State turned from a final goal to an actual demand" (p. 61).

2. What is the meaning of "actual demand"? From whom is it demanded? From the British Government. Admittedly, confesses Rabbi Stephen Wise, "It was difficult to believe" that the British Government would be as cruel as it was (in preventing Jews from migrating to Palestine as they were being murdered *en masse*). Nonetheless, he declares, "I am confident that the British Government... would not wish to play the role of a traitor to Zionism" (p. 21). Well, then, despite everything, the British Government it is. How does one demand anything from the British Government? By negotiations, particularly while organizing agricultural settlements, explains Ben-Gurion (p. 62). In response, Jacob Hazan ridicules Ben-Gurion's analysis by which just those evil Gentiles "who would not execute the mandate", would willingly "give us a Jewish state" (p. 105). Dr. Brodetsky sees no choice: either a government-in-exile, he says, which is impossible, as in no country can such a government sit; or efforts to continue "to try and influence the English Government" (p. 190). In concluding the debate, Zerubavel says that they all want to "accept a state", and even "immediately", but things are not so simple. Possibly, of course, the problem is one of finding allies,

but there is almost nothing about this in the minutes. The Left wants the Soviet Union as an ally, the Americans want the United States, and Dr. Chaim Weizmann wants Britain. But it was all talk. There was no program as to how to recruit any ally or how to mobilize public opinion for support for the Zionist aim "to obtain a state".

3. How, then, is it possible to advance negotiations with Britain? Perhaps by putting pressure on it through international forums, perhaps to cancel the British mandate over Palestine, perhaps even through the heir to the League of Nations, the initiator of that mandate, namely, the United Nations Organization. But should the United Nations Organization declare independence for Palestine while the majority of the population there is Arab, then, by the rules of that organization, Palestine would be an Arab state! (Goldmann, p. 146) This difficulty has to be surmounted by means of mass immigration. Almost all members of the Congress enthusiastically support this idea, barring a very small opposition, which opposes it as illegal, since the British Mandatory Government has enacted laws limiting Jewish immigration to Palestine. Ben-Gurion mentions the alternative solution of the transfer of Arabs to another country and ridicules it as the Revisionist solution. The establishment of a bi-national state is no immediate practical solution due to the Palestinian Arabs' refused to cooperate. Even delegates of the Hashomer Hatzair Party, who advocate this program, have no practical solution other than the partition of Palestine into two states. But even this program does not seem to the members of the Congress an immediate practical solution. "An agreement with England — in 1947 — concerning a Jewish state in Palestine is unavoidable.... The Congress should declare today that it wants a partition... not that it should permit [the Executive Committee] to sign anything — merely to negotiate and to require the results — should there be any — be brought..." to an additional discussion at another congress (Goldmann, pp. 149-150). Even the partition plan calls for prolonged negotiation.

What advantage is there to prolonged negotiation? That in the meantime Jewish immigration and Jewish settlement in Palestine would continue. But, to repeat, such activities are illegal and a minority in the

Congress opposes breaking the law. The majority was for it, but in secrecy. But then what should be done if violators are caught? Moshe Sneh, commander of the Haganah Defense Organization, recommends the use of force in such cases. Ytzhak Gruenbaum recommends the use of force even in additional cases, on the assumption that the British Government can "overcome the terror" only "by the suppression of the whole Jewish settlement" (p. 207). Guerrilla warfare should impose on the Government some willingness to negotiate (still p. 207). But Dr. Weizmann opposes guerrilla warfare as it ruins the chances of the negotiation to succeed, as this depended on the goodwill of Britain (p. 340). Moshe Sharett also shows that negotiation may be useful, since, he claims, as a result of negotiation he, Sharett, had been freed from Latrun jail and permitted to leave the country in order to participate in the Congress (p. 164) (13). Moreover, according to Sharett, anti-British guerrilla war would provoke internal terror (p. 163). This discussion begins to look a little more practical and to the point, until one notices two significant items: not the dissident organizations attacked by Sharett, but his own Haganah Defense Organization practices internal terror; and a short while before the Congress, all three organizations together were busy in anti-British guerrilla war, known at the time as the Resistance Movement. All participants in the Congress knew this as the question before the Congress was, what is the political value of the guerrilla activities of the Resistance Movement? Except for Ytzhak Gruenbaum, a member of the Zionist Executive Committee, no one discussed that question openly, perhaps because the central speech in the Congress, by Ben-Gurion, had clearly shown that the activities of the Resistance Movement were politically valueless. The chief question on the agenda was, how is a state acquired? Ben-Gurion answered it. By settlement activities in the tradition of Practical Zionism, and by negotiation, but decidedly not by combat. In particular, everything must be done "quietly, carefully, silently, without drawing the attention of the general public" (p. 26). Why, then, did he ever give his blessing to the activities of the Resistance Movement? This question was answered by the two Revisionists who participated in the Congress even though the

Revisionist Party had left the Zionist Movement in the mid-thirties (founding the New Zionist Movement, headed by Jabotinsky). Meir Grossman demanded that they should "create a government of our own" (p. 103). And William Ziff of the United States, a supporter of the Bergson Group, offered his own wording of Bergson's proposal. He said, there is a need for an intervention by the United States in the Middle East (p. 246) in order to arrange for international action, as well as for activism, namely in favor of anti-British guerrilla war of the Irgun National Military Organization. But in order to facilitate this intervention, "a temporary Jewish government" should be established (p. 248), and the Zionist Congress must "decide here and now on its support" for such a government that should be "at once and due to this fact alone the representation of the whole Jewish settlement and of all the refugees" (p. 249), meaning the Jewish refugees in Europe (40).

Ziff's proposal met with no response. The Congress voted for a Jewish state, not when, not how, even in a refusal to endorse any practical move, a refusal expressed in the decisions to boycott the London Conference, whose agenda was the partition of Palestine, and to reject any alternative mandate.

4. The denunciation of dissident underground military organizations and of the Hebrew Committee for National Liberation in the last Zionist Congress before the Declaration of Independence. The purpose of this denunciation was national unity, not dissension. As to the dissident underground organizations, as long as the Zionist Organization did not denounce the Resistance Movement, nor the opinion of Moshe Sneh, the Haganah chief commander, clearly, the grounds for the denunciation was their rejection of the authority of the national institutions, not of this or that view. The same goes for the Committee for National Liberation. Admittedly, their ideology was attacked in the Congress by the claim that "the distinction between Jews and Hebrews" is "misleading and baseless" (p. 484 and p. 579). But the aim of this attack was to provide the impression that there was a consensus among the delegates to the Congress, which the Committee for National Liberation allegedly deviated from. It is easy to refute this impression by evidence included in

the minutes of the Congress, and even in a respectable position there, namely, in the keynote speech by Ben-Gurion, where he stressed his just opposition both to a state specifically for the Jews, which he labeled "theocracy", and to a state which would have "all Jews of the world as citizens" (p. 59). Jews of other nations should not be citizens of the Hebrew state, he said, "just as the Frenchmen and the Englishmen in America are American citizens even though there is France and there is England," and "the [American] Irishman... who is linked to the tradition of his people and wishes well to the country of his origin" (pp. 59-60). Moreover, according to Ben-Gurion himself, though "the idea of the Jewish state is... certainly not new" (p. 61), as Herzl had presented it, even if as a mere distant ideal [this is untrue], today "the Hebrew State has turned from a final end to an actual demand." The criticism of the views of the Committee for National Liberation, then, is not serious; there remains only the complaint against the Committee's rejection of the authority of the Zionist leadership. In the debates no argument against the Committee's views was voiced. In one question from the floor the American Revisionists were identified with "the Bergson Group in all of its metamorphoses", and their "corrupting activities" were denounced as activities which "violate the honor of the Zionist Movement". Worst of all was their "collection of funds assigned, according to their own announcements, to help the terrorist dissident military groups which constitutes a great danger for the Jewish settlement in Palestine and for Zionism" (p. 166). To repeat, the danger here referred to is not from terror as such, but from the rejection of the national leadership.

Elsewhere in this book I have expressed my profound astonishment at my not having heard about the Committee for National Liberation, at that time or later, except from Hillel Kook himself. There is no better evidence of the concealment of facts from the Jewish population in Palestine than in the minutes of this Zionist Congress, the last before Independence. Nevertheless, the Congress could not entirely overlook the existence of this Committee, and found a way to condemn it, even though in transparent deceit. And there is no need for better evidence of the success of the Committee in the United States, than in the interest shown it by the many delegates to that Congress from the United States and Canada. The reader interested in additional historical material should compare the material cited in the article by Sarah Peck in Chapter Fifteen above (see note 32) both with the speech of Ytzhak Gruenbaum, who accused the Allies of indifference, explaining it by the claim that they "were apprehensive, apparently... lest their Allies be tempted to believe that this was a Jewish war, as the Nazi propaganda machine tried to describe it", and with the complaint of Rabbi Abba Hillel Silver, who claimed that among the Jewish leaders there were some who made great efforts to frustrate the Zionists: "Some Zionist leaders showed impatience to our regret... and supported the government in its effort to prevent" the passing of a pro-Zionist resolution in the United States Congress (p. 49). The whole story of the attitude of the Zionist establishment towards the massacre of European Jewry in the years 1942-45 appears in the minutes of the Congress in a most nebulous and outlandish way. No one among the delegates to the Zionist Congress protested or criticized; if some of them did protest or criticize, the official minutes include no hint of what they said. This is the disgrace of that Congress.

Perhaps there is no need for accusations; perhaps the whole story is too pathetic. It is sad that not being able to close historical books permits the continuation of confusion and injustice, especially so in a state in which the distribution of funds to political parties today is made in accord with agreements signed in 1946 in that last Zionist Congress before the Declaration of the Independence of Israel, a Congress in which the majority of the delegates did not think it possible to establish a Jewish state within a few years. Fourteen months after this confused, pathetic, and faltering debate, David Ben-Gurion declared independence.

The cause of this *volte face* Hillel Kook sees as the struggle of the three underground organizations against the British as a foreign occupation force, and in the great support that this struggle won both in the Jewish settlement in Palestine and in the American public at large, including its legislative bodies, and in the support offered by the political activity of the Hebrew liberation movement, that spoke in the name of the existing Hebrew nation and demanded the immediate establishment of a government. The combination of these activities, Hillel Kook claims to this day, is what created a political situation in the world at large permitting the undertaking of a political initiative and bringing Ben-Gurion to do just that.

* Historians employed by the national institutions and in the institutions of the Zionist Movement continue to publish biased historical researches, official and semi-official. Public pressure should be exerted by interested citizens so as to make them critical of the last Zionist Congress before Israel's independence, and especially to examine the condemnatory resolutions in it. In Israel past questions were reopened, including the question of the justice of the verdict in the case of the murder of Arlosoroff, and certainly to reexamine the condemnations made by the Twenty-Second Zionist Congress is much more simple, relevant and significant. *

Chapter 19

The Hebrew Committee for National Liberation and the Irgun National Military Organization

The Hebrew Committee for National Liberation grew out of the delegation of the National Military Organization to the United States. This is not to make light of the difference between these two bodies, since it amounts to the change in Kook himself from being a young chauvinist to holding the revolutionary ideas of liberal nationalism and developing the idea of the separation between faith and nationality, which radically altered his political struggle for national independence. The question remains, what was the attitude of the Bergson Group, with its new ideas, towards the mother group, with its old ideas? History sometimes leads astray and cruelly or perhaps generously curtails a logical development. The National Military Organization ceased to exist and the problem of their differences fell off the agenda. The Organization ceased to exist because World War II brought a radical change in its attitude towards British rule. The Organization split; its commander, David Raziel, was killed in an action in cooperation with the British forces; and its supreme commander, Vladimir Jabotinsky, died suddenly.

This is not the end of the story. The Bergson Group accepted Jabotinsky's advice to call off the military struggle against the British and cooperate with them against the common Nazi enemy. In the light of the destruction of the Jews of Europe and Britain's persistent refusal to admit Jewish refugees into Palestine, Bergson and his companions agreed that an emergency situation had emerged, so that in addition to the war against Germany, a war against the British Government should be declared as part of the political struggle for the rescue of the Jews of Europe. The Group sent to Palestine one of them, Arie Ben-Eliezer, to help restore the Irgun National Military Organization in light of the Group's new view, and to start the military struggle against the British authorities in Palestine as a part of the effort to rescue the Jews of Europe — both as individuals and as a nation. Menachem Begin was appointed the Organization's chief commander and Ben-Eliezer used his connections with the Committee for the Rescue of the Jewish People of Europe to get him released from his service in the Polish Army. At the beginning of 1944, the Organization declared war against Britain and demanded the immediate establishment of a Hebrew government.

This is the place to offer a response to the pamphlet of the Irgun National Military Organization. I remember well that the impression that the pamphlet made on me as an adolescent in the Jewish settlement in Palestine was most baffling. It was difficult for me even to imagine that the small Jewish settlement could seriously declare war on Great Britain. Of course, the idea seemed to me fascinating and even daring, but also hopeless from the very start. The establishment of a Hebrew government seemed to me even more fascinating, but it was proposed in the pamphlet as the final stage of the struggle, yet the likelihood of the struggle to succeed to that extent seemed nil. The pamphlet proposed that the Hebrew government should negotiate with the government of Great Britain in the expectation of achieving a friendship treaty, but, of course, this seemed even less realistic. Thus the pamphlet looked most baffling, and I did not find one person in the Jewish settlement in Palestine who could explain it to me. As for the Hebrew Committee for National Liberation, I knew nothing about it then. The plan of this Committee was not for a vigorous struggle to bring independence expressed as the establishment of a government. Their plan was of the kind of which I had never heard until I met Kook himself; it was to establish a transitional government as part of the struggle for independence, and its role should be to mobilize world public opinion while supporting the armed struggle in Palestine, combined with the transfer of

Jewish refugees on a large scale — repatriation — to their old-new motherland in reliance on world public opinion whose sympathy was aroused by news of the disaster of the destruction of the Jews of Europe.

The Irgun National Military Organization had no clear political program. True, within two years it managed to compel the Haganah Defense Organization and the official Zionist political organizations to join its guerrilla war activities — joint activities that went under the name of the Resistance Movement. But the absence of a political plan obstructed the continuation of the collaboration and blocked the ability to consolidate achievements.

Begin's autobiography hardly refers to Bergson or to the Bergson Group. I shall therefore refer again to David Niv's book on the history of the Irgun National Military Organization, an account which Begin has given his blessings to and which notes that the Irgun National Military Organization sympathized with or at least did not object to the political moves of the Hebrew Committee for National Liberation, including Bergson's letter to Dr. Weizmann, quoted at length above. That book also praises the activities of the Committee and its success, pointing out that there was no point in the guerrilla warfare were it not accompanied by propaganda abroad so as to mobilize public opinion to accept its claims and exert pressures for a negotiation for independence. But this opinion obtains only if the Irgun National Military Organization is viewed as a national organization and not as a military arm of one political party. Yet the violation of this condition is implied in the story of the concord made between the Irgun National Military Organization and the Revisionist Party (volume 2, pp. 184-189). But, Niv reports, when Begin accepted the command of the National Military Organization, the command disconnected all ties with the Revisionist Party (volume 5, p. 208) (41). The definition of the nation and the distinction between Hebrew nationality and the Jewish faith appear in the early volumes, but the critical discussion of this point appears only in the fifth volume and begins, after a long and sympathetic report, on page 205, where it is narrated that the headquarters in Palestine sent a special envoy to the United States early in 1946, demanding its representatives abroad "to relinquish their ideological teaching", especially concerning the plan for "the establishment of the Hebrew government-in-exile" (p. 207). Begin opposed this, as he claimed after a year and a half of futile debate, in a letter to Kook dated June 6, 1947, that "an early establishment of the government will add nothing to the real struggle, it will only weaken — there is no shadow of doubt about this — the external struggle" (p. 207) (41). Within less than a year Ben-Gurion declared independence. It is clear, then, that Begin missed an opportunity. His claims make some sense, though: after all, the Twenty-Second Zionist Congress had denounced the dissident underground movements as well as the Bergson Group, and had even forced the Revisionists to dismantle the New Zionist movement and return to the World Zionist Organization. In addition, tells Niv (volume 5, p. 209), the Revisionists themselves endorsed the Zionist Congress' condemnation of the Bergson Group. Begin always represented the Irgun National Military Organization as permanently a part of the Revisionist Movement, and Kook denies this sharply; put together, these two facts clarify the picture in retrospect (42).

What was Begin's error when he so wrongly estimated the situation that he did not see the opportunity for immediate independence? To repeat, the British Government blocked the possibility of Jews to becoming the majority in Palestine. In his speech to the British Labour Party Convention in June 1946, the British Foreign Secretary Ernest Bevin threatened to grant independence to Palestine. That independence would have been to a state that would be Arabic and Moslem in character, since its establishment by the Jewish minority would be racist. As Dr. Goldmann mentioned in the Zionist Congress at the end of 1946, the United Nations Organization stood for principles that corroborated Bevin's position (p. 189). The situation looked impossible to all concerned. And this was so despite the fact that the platform of the Committee for National Liberation overcame this difficulty with its proposal to separate faith from nationality, while including in the nation the Jewish refugees in Europe, and combining it with the further proposal to declare both immediate independence and a plan for the transfer of a million-and-a-half members of the nation to Palestine — as stated in Bergson's letter to Dr. Weizmann. It is impossible to estimate in retrospect the chances of realizing this plan, and, of course, it was difficult to do so at the time. But certainly, it was a daring and possible plan. Begin's hesitation is therefore understandable and somewhat justifiable. For the plan was daring, and therefore not without risk, so that the option of rejecting it was open. Yet Begin erred when he claimed that this plan would necessarily sharpen the inner struggle, since he was thereby overlooking the desperate situation of the Zionist Organization which had no political plan whatsoever. Similarly, Begin erred when he overlooked the force of the public political activity of the committees of the Bergson Group in the United States and their ability to whip up enthusiasm in both Palestine and the United States. This ability not only was left unused, but was not even properly examined. Begin's hesitation caused him to lose a great opportunity; the enthusiasm whipped up by those Committees was reaped by Ben-Gurion in his stead, in his unilateral Declaration of Independence.

The facts are important, as they give rise to the problem of authority. The problem of the division of authority between the National Military Organization and the Committee for National Liberation was not simple and it matters because of the ideological conflict between them. The fact that Begin praised in his autobiography the delegation of his Organization in the United States is insignificant in the present connection, because he did not mention the political aspect of the situation. He neither endorsed nor rejected the principles of the Hebrew Committee for National Liberation. Niv presents the problem of the division of authority as unsolved (pp. 205-206), since it is "beyond any doubt that the Committee tried to see itself as the political command of the Organization, since it saw in the Organization the military arm, namely, a division of functions reminiscent of the Jewish Agency and the Haganah" (p. 206). Since Begin expressed agreement with Niv's book, it is possible to conclude that either he preferred to leave the problem unsolved, or that he is altogether unaware of it, since possibly he had no interest in matters of principle. But to a large extent this book examines questions of principle, and when necessary also historical questions. So it is right to observe here that although in David Niv's remark there is a compliment to Bergson, his account does not get at the true ideological issues and, according to Kook, nor at the historical truth. According to Kook the mission of the Irgun National Military Organization became a political body that assumed authority in view of the national emergency. This did not apply to Palestine after the mission agreed to the appointment of a new command for the National Military Organization — this command represented a part of the nation whose support it won and was in no need for legitimization from the outside. The mission and Committee for

National Liberation that it established, thus strove to coordinate with the Organization and supported its activities, while maintaining political independence.

One important ideological detail Niv does notice clearly, though only incidentally, apropos of a discussion concerning the demand of the Organization that the Committee should transfer more funds. He quotes a letter from Eliahu Lankin, the Commander of the European branch of the Organization, who wrote to his commander Menachem Begin, two weeks after Begin had rejected Bergson's plan for the establishment of a government in exile. Apropos of discussions of complaints about the transfer of funds and about the Hebrew Committee for National Liberation, the letter says, "In my opinion they are the sole political body which responds to every event in a sovereign manner" (43).

Chapter 20   *Then and Now*

The purpose of the second part of this book is to offer a presentation, albeit very fragmented, of the evolution of the idea of separation between faith and nationality within the framework of the Hebrew Committee for National Liberation. Unlike the Zionist establishment, the Committee disbanded after independence, but the Israeli Declaration of Independence serves to this very day as the basis of the absence of this separation in Israel and the lack of normalcy here. This, then, is the end of my story. Let me, nonetheless, add a few details concerning Kook, so as to update my story.

The end of the story presented here in a mere brief outline is the declaration of Israel's independence with no readiness to examine basic questions and a possible normalcy in Israel. The declaration of independence was made after a lengthy discussion between Bergson and Ben-Gurion on the possibility of declaring independence unilaterally, and through Ben-Gurion's and the national leadership's recognition of the Irgun National Military Organization's ability to declare independence on its own first, and that such a declaration would have far-reaching political consequences.

In a legend the hero has to leave the stage at the end of the last act. Not so in our story, and this calls for an explanation. The explanation concerns an event that began shortly before the Israeli Declaration of Independence and continued afterwards in a complex manner. It is the tragic case of the weapons-carrying boat "Altalena".

Historically, there is a place for a retrospective criticism. It is possible to criticize the founders of the young state, chiefly David Ben-Gurion, for flawed political responsibility, for not having clarified sufficiently what sovereignty is. Such criticism, however, should be attenuated by an understanding of the difficult conditions that prevailed during the early weeks and months of the independence of Israel. It is easy to show this: the political system was intended to facilitate political debate, yet the web of lies that surrounded it blocked (and is still blocking) mutual trust, understanding, and collaboration between political opponents concerning significant political problems, as expected in a normal democracy.

The lack of clarity concerning authority erupted onto the political stage of the young state in the tragic case of the weapons-carrying boat "Altalena," procured by members of the Committee for National Liberation and brought to Israel under the auspices of the Irgun National Military Organization, first with the Government's consent; finally it was bombarded by the direct order of Premier David Ben-Gurion. The problems were not only due to a lack of mutual trust, though certainly this played a significant role. Both Menachem Begin and David Ben-Gurion negotiated concerning a national matter in efforts to achieve party-political gains. They thus showed the inadequacy of their political understanding. At that point, Hillel Kook was not affiliated with any political party and had no authority. He came to the shore at Kfar Vitkin to welcome the boat. After the unloading of weapons began and some one thousand passengers disembarked, a dispute erupted between Begin and Ben-Gurion. Kook disowned Begin's attitude, left the scene, and tried to get in touch with Ben-Gurion, but was arrested.

In the meantime, Ben-Gurion issued an order to attack the boat. It was a civil war on a small scale. Soldiers on both sides were killed and some Irgun National Military Organization commanders were detained. The boat itself was bombarded and went up in flames. Begin himself was allowed to go free, though he was one of the two commanders responsible for the tragedy.

The militarism and the narrow party-political concern of Israeli party politics began not with a civil war in the period prior to the Declaration of Independence, since that was a different era, nor in the small civil war over the "Altalena" — that was a tragic error on both sides — but when Ben-Gurion introduced into Israeli political terminology the terrible concept which is entirely alien to the spirit of the Jewish tradition — "the sacred cannon", as he called the howitzer that had been used to bombard the boat.

Released from jail, Hillel Kook found himself a private citizen; he did not belong to the political party that Begin created after the Declaration of the Independence of Israel. After his release from jail he had to go and dissolve his diverse committees. Before he left the country, he was invited to join the list of candidates of Begin's party to the Constituent Assembly. He consented, in order to partake in the decisions on the content of the constitution that the Constituent Assembly was intended to shape, to try to influence its political principles in the spirit of the ideas of the Committee for National Liberation. The Constituent Assembly was turned at its first meeting into the first Israeli Parliament, the first Knesset, despite the protest launched by Kook, who called this move "a putsch", a petty rebellion. For about one year, he and Aeri Jabotinsky (who was also a member of the Constituent Assembly) tried to convince members of Begin's political party to join them; they then left the party.

Hillel Kook was in despair and decided to wait for the next generation, in the hope that it would be freer from the ghetto limitations that characterized the founders of the Jewish state. As is obvious in retrospect, this was a serious error, since the next generation would remain limited if it could not be critical, and it could not be critical without proper public debate. In retrospect Kook himself considers this a very serious error. His other activities consisted of the mere keeping of the flame alive. In 1957 he and Shmuel Merlin founded in New York a political research institute, the Institute for Mediterranean Affairs. In 1957 that Institute published a proposal for the solution of the problem of the Palestinian refugees. In the same year Shmuel Merlin and Hillel Kook published a full-page announcement in leading Israeli dailies with the heading "A Proposal for National Debate". The proposal was a failure. I met both Kook and Merlin as a result of this announcement, in a meeting that was arranged for them at the headquarters of the Citizens Rights Movement, where they discussed their proposal. Their audience was not impressed and did not see in it any plan for radical change.

Nevertheless, this led to more meetings between Hillel Kook and myself and to the writing of this book.

PART THREE

An Updated Program for the Israeli Nation

Part three presents a proposal for the realization of the concept of normalization: the general idea of the establishment of Israel as a republic, as a liberal nation-state on the Western pattern. The discussion of the realization involves technical details and relates to the state of affairs that obtains as these pages are written. This creates a number of layers in the wording of the detailed proposal. Parts of the proposal are fairly stable, such as the concept of liberal nationalism and the Western concept of liberal representative democracy. Other parts are given to alteration within the medium range of time span. For example, when Hillel Kook conceived the idea of normalization, he presented the possibility of including the whole of the population of mandatory Palestine in his plan for the establishment of the Hebrew Republic of Palestine. In his opinion, it was necessary to offer to the non-Jewish inhabitants of Palestine the choice of joining the Hebrew nation and becoming Hebrews for all intents and purposes — with equal rights and duties. Today he sees a need to recognize the Palestinian nation and admit the partition between the two nations of mandatory Palestine on both banks of the River Jordan as an accomplished fact, so that the entrenched, interminable, deep hostility may be rendered into a boundary conflict that can be resolved by direct negotiation towards a peace settlement. Common to both plans is the idea that a normal state strives for peace with its neighbors. But this idea is abstract and demands some practical expression. This expression was changed and is likely to change again. This is why the present part of this book is not made of one cloth. Its chief aim is to show how normalizing Israel is possible under the present conditions, how the transition can be effected to normal relations with the neighbors in the region, with Jews of other nations, and with the nations of the world. Moreover, even if this or that proposal is implemented without success (regardless of whether it originates in Kook's proposal or in an alternative to it, as long as it is implemented), then it will constitute an enormous advancement over Israel's current absence of all political initiative, which harms it and forces its sons and daughters to live without normalcy, particularly in the protracted state of war. The purpose of the proposal for normalization is to update the existence of Israel in the modern age and to enable it to struggle with its problems democratically.

* The second edition of this book includes this part as it was in the first edition (with only minor changes, mainly stylistic) plus additional passages marked with asterisks (as elsewhere in this edition) so as to enable the readers to judge how much normalization is required under different conditions. For since the first edition appeared Israel underwent far-reaching changes, including the intensification of the terror, faltering peace talks conducted with no guarantees for the cessation of the terror, and a polarization of the map of Israeli political parties. Despite the intensified feeling of the strong need for peace, regrettably the peace talks are hopeless. At first glance it seems that the absence of the chances for peace is rooted in the absence of a language common to both sides, or even in the refusal of the current Israeli Government to consider peace the top item on the national agenda (and in the absence of hope for a significant change in the Government's position on this matter). There will always be spokespeople who will contend that Israel must make considerable concessions in order to ensure the success of the peace talks. But the causes for the feeble likelihood of the success of the peace talks is not only the positions of the different parties, since on this matter the question should be asked how peace can be imposed on the parties that refuse to establish peace in our region. Similarly, the failing is not in the attitudes of the various Israeli governments towards peace, since these have to be ironed out around the negotiation table, where peace talks are to be conducted, and so these need not be stumbling blocks. The cause of the failing is also not the stubbornness of this or the other party concerning minor details that delay the possibility of a solution, since these too are to be dealt with in the peace talks. But this stubbornness is damaging because it is caused by the absence of a constructive position,

especially in the absence of an Israeli position on basics, of course — as to the main components of the national question in our region.

1. Israel refuses to recognize the national minority in its midst and to consider it problematic.
2. Israel does not recognize the national aspirations of the Palestinians and it refuses to discuss them.
3. Israel disregards the reasonable demand from the Hashemite Kingdom of Jordan to find a way to arrange for a proper representation of the Palestinians in the peace talks.

On the contrary, the root of the Israeli support for that Kingdom (which support is vital for that Kingdom) is that it thereby justifies its refusal to recognize Palestinian national aspirations.

These three factors are rooted in Israel's refusal to examine its own basic problems, to examine publicly the option of establishing itself as a normal republic. For if it refusal to recognize the national aspirations of the Palestinians makes any sense, then it has no need (nor possibility) to hide behind the Hashemite Kingdom. Peace-loving Israelis, who are concerned with the future of the nation, owe it to themselves to examine the contention that the abnormalcy of Israel prevents it from taking a political initiative to make peace.

* [These paragraphs were written before the dramatic change and the partial establishment of the Palestinian autonomy and the success of the peace process with the Hashemite Kingdom. I have not foreseen the active United States participation that has dramatically changed the situation, but my apprehensions are still not weakened, for reasons that will be clarified later. Still, the changes prove me mistaken on one basic issue: the global situation has altered so much as to permit the introduction of radical changes in small steps. This is not to say that such processes are preferable to clear, bold implementation of sane policies and of the conscious development of means for political initiative. Still, all may go well despite all apprehensions, no matter how justified: a slow and unclear development obviously beats stagnation, even though it is not the best.] *

Chapter 21 *Decades of Internal Exile*

On May 14, 1948, David Ben-Gurion took an unprecedented step in the history of Zionism. Taking advantage of the fact that the mandatory British Government had pulled out of Palestine, he undertook a revolutionary political initiative and prevented the creation of a new mandate by declaring independence and political autonomy and establishing a transitional government. Historians will decide whether there is justice in Kook's claim that Ben-Gurion in this way was following the theory of unilateral initiative, which the Hebrew Committee for National Liberation proposed in 1944 and which Menachem Begin, to repeat, refused to undertake even in the year 1947, for fear that it would instigate a civil war within the Jewish settlement in Palestine. Clearly, Begin made a mistake on a matter of principle; generally, the undertaking of political initiative only inspires activity and joint activity prompts the search for unity. Thus, in the Declaration of Independence, Ben-Gurion bridged the gap between his people who opposed independence and the members of the Irgun National Military Organization who had threatened that if the Zionist leadership would not declare independence and create a transitional government at once, it would do so by itself. Nevertheless, this very military organization, which agreed to cooperate in underground activity with the Zionist-run Haganah Defense Organization, surprisingly did not seek negotiations to coordinate political activity with the same leadership. It failed to do this even in the final days before the Declaration of Independence. Had there been such a search, the tragedy of the "Altalena" weapons-boat would have been averted.

Without diminishing the significance of the Declaration of Independence and of Ben-Gurion's contribution to Israel's independence, the wording of the Declaration as given in the original document should be criticized. A declaration of independence has to be done in the name of a nation that declares its autonomy, including the right of the nation over the national territory. In other words, the autonomy of a nation — of the Israeli nation — is what creates and justifies the existence of its state as its tool for self-rule.

The Declaration of Independence does begin with a reference to the Jewish people and their historic rights to the land, but it includes no declaration of the independence of the Jewish nation (for a good and clear reason): Ben-Gurion was cognizant of the fact that Jews have the right to be members of different nations, while keeping an affinity to and friendship with their country of origin (44). Therefore, the Declaration of Independence should have included a declaration of the independence of the Israeli nation as the political heir of the Jewish nation. This has not been done to this day. The matter has not even been opened for general discussion as yet.

It should be noted that Ben-Gurion was aware of the distortion he had caused and that he tried to rectify it. In the early 'fifties he tried to split the Zionist organization into two bodies — the Organization of Friends of Israel and an organization for those who intended to migrate to Israel within a reasonably short time to join the Israeli nation. He demanded that only the second body should be allowed to use the title "Zionist". He expected that turning all Zionists into Israelis would constitute the victory of the Zionist movement. But he was attacked by his colleagues in the Zionist establishment as a Bergsonist and he quickly withdrew. As a result, he legitimized the concept of Zionism-in-quotation-marks (a concept that was widespread in the fifties and sixties), which developed into a New Zionist Myth. One should not ridicule Ben-Gurion because of his failure — not only because his failure was accompanied by brilliant victories, but also because the matter itself is fundamental and very complicated (45).

The need to determine long-range political ends was expressed in the promise within the Declaration of Independence that within a reasonable period an constituent assembly would be elected to draw up a constitution. As Professor Amnon Rubinstein notes, the Constituent Assembly, that is to say the first Knesset, "violated the duty which was bestowed on it to compose a constitution" (46). He adds, "As long as this duty is not canceled in an explicit law, this duty applies to each and every Knesset" (p. 23). In other words, according to Rubinstein, every Knesset since the establishment of the first Knesset is guilty of neglecting its duty to devise an Israeli constitution.

The first Constituent Assembly was abolished in the very alteration of its name from Constituent Assembly to First Knesset. Today the meaning of this is clear. As Professor Rubinstein presents it, "Formally, this is no… essential change. But this change indicated the tendency to empty the content of the duty of the Constituent Assembly to devise a constitution for the state" (p. 21). Here again, Kook was conspicuous in having been the only person present who noticed at once what was happening. He called from the floor that it was putsch, gave a speech on the spot, and demanded a legal opinion from the Minister of Justice, claiming that this step was not legal. (Kook's speech was omitted from the Knesset minutes.) In Professor Rubinstein's opinion cited above, the step was and still is illegal. Hence, it was and still is an act of deception of the nation, for which the nation continues to pay a high price.

To repeat, the situation is problematic. According to Hillel Kook, the Jewish people have to undergo a transition from nation-religion, an abnormal situation as a nation-religion that persisted for generations, to an autonomous existence of a part of the people that turn into a nation-state. This is a prolonged process that requires thinking, planning, and a transition period. The transition, which is called by the ideologists "the Zionist Revolution", has not materialized. On the contrary, the abnormal existence of the nation-religion has today become more abnormal, in that a state has been added to this unique combination. Decades have passed with no planning; the transition has not been realized. Time has passed and opportunities were wasted. The enormous physical achievements of Israel have only sharpened the problem by increasing the conflict between a shaky foundation and a huge political system that rests heavily on that foundation.

The weakness of the present situation is in the fact that the "Zionist vision" or, more precisely, the vision of auto-emancipation, was not realized and, in the present situation, is not even possible. The liberation of the Jewish individual is the fundamental principle of auto-emancipation, which includes the principle of the simultaneous national self-determination of the individual and of the collective. According to this principle, it is required that all Jews could become Israelis if they want and they can refrain from being ones. This principle amounts to the recognition that Jews who do not want to be Israeli have the right to continue to belong to nations to which they belong. Contrary to this, traditional Zionist idea, a new and very dangerous Zionist chauvinist myth was developed. This myth denies the very existence of an Israeli nation. It sees the state as belonging not to its nation, not to its citizens, but to the scattered Jewish people. According to this dangerous myth, even if national affiliation normally is a right, for Jews quite abnormally it is a duty. There is, therefore, no right to national self-determination for American Jews, for example, according to this dangerous myth, since it disregards the fact that they belong to the American nation, by imposing on them the Jewish national identity, namely the fact of their being members of the Jewish people, despite the fact that this is not a political national identity. It follows from this myth, that the right to national identity is also denied the Israeli Jew. Thus Jews have no right to be members of the Israeli nation (whose home country is Israel), since the myth does not recognize the nation as long as there are Jews who live outside Israel's borders. Not only the recognition of the right of American Jews to separation from the Israeli nation is denied but also, and to the same measure, the recognition of the right of an Israeli to belong to the Israeli nation willingly. For, belonging there voluntarily is what independence amounts to. To admit this, what is needed is the recognition of the existence of the Israeli nation, as a political entity separate from the Jewish religion, and the right to belong to it. According to the New Zionist Myth, to belong to the Jewish people is a political duty (the foundation of which is possibly the Jewish faith and possibly Zionism), not a right. In the current situation, holding a public debate on this myth is taboo. There is, therefore, no such debate.

Israeli Jews are thus not members of an independent nation. In this sense, they are also not citizens, since their nation is not recognized by their own state. They remain members of the Jewish people and perhaps even of "the Jewish nation", which is a historical entity devoid of political national identity. Therefore, they are devoid of a legitimate national identity. Israeli nationality is a mere administrative matter, akin to the Israeli citizenship of its Moslems or

Christians, whom Israel considers members of the Arab nation, which also does not exist as a political entity. Thus the citizenship of Israeli Jews and that of Israeli Arabs are on the same plane, yet according to their identity cards they are members of the Jewish nation and of the Arab nation respectively (47).

This situation of abnormalcy is covered up with lies. First, there is a catch here concerning the relations between Israeli Jews and Israelis non-Jews. Second, a deception — and an unhealthy one — is perpetuated concerning the relations between the Jews of Israel and the Jews of Western countries. Third, Israel becomes a theocracy in its character and laws. The evil is all the sharper because Israel is a theocracy founded by people devoid of religion. The reference to Israel as a Jewish state only obscures the fact that the founders themselves did not attend to the great historical weight that religion had as a component in the history of the Jews. For generations of Diaspora, Judaism was sustained despite difficulties only because the Jews clung to their religion. Therefore, despite the fact that Israel exhibits mannerisms of independence, its structure is still that of a ghetto, except that it has military power, vast property, and a relatively high standard of living. But its advantages over the traditional Jewish ghetto do not protect it from having a ghetto mentality. On the contrary, they strengthen it. This ghetto mentality is the target of attack of this chapter. It creates a form of existence that keeps Israel separate.

This separateness is rooted in Israel's character as a Jewish ghetto. The fact that the community of this ghetto is also a state and a religion in one entity does not weaken but rather intensifies the ghetto characteristics of Israel. The conflation of these two forms in one system is intolerable. Twenty percent of the citizens of the State of Israel belong to other religions, and are therefore declared not members of the nation. In the deceptiveness customary in Israel, they are at one and the same time both Israeli citizens possessing equal rights and, members of the "Arab people" (living in a state which is the enemy of this people).

* (Indeed, the absence of normalcy in Israel is reflected in a grotesque manner in which the myth that governs Israel draws the image of the peace with Egypt. According to it, the peace accord with Egypt does not cancel the state of war with it, since it is one of the states of the Arab nation which is still in a state of war with Israel.) *

Israel overlooked the fact that it denied its Arabs the right to accept or reject belonging to Israel when they were forced to have Israeli citizenship in the very middle of the War of Independence. Israel thus created a large national minority that demands equal rights for itself; being a religious state, it is neither ready nor able to demand from them the fulfillment of citizens' duties (such as the duty of national military service). The state-ghetto sees every Jew as a citizen — potentially if not actually. The percentage of Israelis who migrate to the United States is twenty times larger than the percentage of American Jews who migrate to Israel. Nevertheless, the New Zionist Myth views the state as belonging to Jews of other nations as well. This view causes Israelis to lose their autonomy while the Jews of other nations derive no political benefit from this supposed citizenship. (It might possibly cause them political harm.) An example of this absurd situation is given in verdicts of the Israeli Supreme Court that have determined that the terms "Jew," "Hebrew," and "Israeli" are synonymous (48). From this it follows that Jews everywhere on earth, without consideration of political status, are Israeli citizens, even if they are not practicing Jews or belong to a trend within Judaism that Israel refuses to recognize, whereas all others are not — not even the non-Jewish members of the Knesset, of Israel's Parliament. And this could not be more clearly untrue. The absurd conclusion that Israeli Arabs are both Jews and non-Jews follows from these verdicts of the Israeli Supreme Court. The view that a contradiction within the law is not a source of political harm is self-deception. This is no gain for Jewish citizens of Western countries from Israel's view of them as Israelis. But there is loss for Israeli Jews, since their independence is necessarily distorted due to their relations with Israelis who are not Jews and with Jews who are not Israelis.

A modern liberal state cannot function normally unless it serves a modern, normal nation. The distinction between faith and nationality and its formal expression as the separation of state and religious institutions, comprise a necessary condition for the normal, egalitarian and cultural life of a modern progressive society. In Israel this is very much more important, particularly because of the need to bring an end to internal hostilities. As long as Israelis who are not Jews are not able to have equal rights and duties, as long as the non-Jewish citizens of Israel do not have the full right of integration and equality, there is little hope that Israel will achieve stable relations with the surrounding people, who are largely Moslem and Arabic-speaking. The theocracy current in Israel, which many Israelis consider but a concession to the religious political parties and no more, is the consequence of the absence of national identity that perpetuates a conventional lie, which in turn perpetuates the confusion and prevents the development of normal proper neighborly relations. The absence of separation of religion and nationality is one of the causes for the state of war that has engaged Israel for the duration of its existence. This constant state of war perpetuates Israel's ghetto character, and this ghetto character perpetuates Israel's abnormalcy.

Chapter 22 — The Root of the Evil

The state of affairs in Israel is so nebulous, that it is difficult even to describe it. It is easy to show, however, that this nebulous situation is convenient for the diverse Israeli governments and the Israeli political leadership in general, because it means the postponement of attending to difficult problems — both of relationships with the non-Jewish minorities in Israel, and of the possibility of large-scale Jewish migration to Israel, and some consequences to all this. This nebulous situation is convenient precisely because it facilitates escape from planning. Short-range planning keeps shrinking, since the situation leaves Israel in its nebulous situation concerning the non-Jewish minorities, who are Israeli, allegedly possessing equal rights but not membership in the nation, concerning the Jews of other nations, and concerning Israel's neighbors.

The lack of clarity is the allegedly positive aspect of the situation, as it permits ignoring the very existence of the non-Jewish Israeli citizens and viewing all the Jews of the world as Israeli citizens; or, as is customary to say, to see the uniqueness of Israel in it belonging not to the people who dwell within its borders, but to the Jewish people as a whole — whether citizens of Israel or of other countries. This, of course, is a full admission, even though implicit, that the traditional Zionist vision has failed or abated, that the people gave it up completely (49).

For, the vision was of the auto-emancipation of the Jews and thus of normalization of the Jewish people. Today the abnormalcy of the scattered Jewish people remains, but by now it has acquired theoretical and political justification from the State of Israel, since this is a state whose uniqueness lies in it being the center of the abnormalcy, at least according to the official version of the World Zionist Organization and according to different Israeli governments one after the other. Israel, as a state that claims for itself the status of the center of the Jewish people, claims to be the center of the continuing abnormal situation. Recently a proposal was put forth that the Jewish abnormalcy of Israel should be established and perpetuated under the title of normalcy, as if a fig leaf of a respectable title justifies a shameful situation (50).

Some people find this situation appealing — those who favor the lack of normalcy of the Jewish nation-religion, of a people without a homeland, and who view Israel, a small homeland of a part of the nation, as a mere beauty spot in the present situation. Some people still deceive themselves, saying that Israel is a refuge for all Jews, who can escape from the countries in which they dwell if they have to, and be welcomed in accord with the Israeli Law of Return.

This is not the case. The country which opens its gates to persecuted Jews need not forever be a state held in a reserve state for Jews who belong to free nations even if they might one day be persecuted. Between the duty to those who suffer and the duty to those who possibly may suffer there one day, is a fundamental difference. For whether we readily endorse the idea of Israel as an abnormal state of a nation-religion scattered in the world, or whether we view this as a distorted idea — a hybrid between a medieval and a modern state of affairs — we should know that in the modern world a reserve state is not viable for very long. In an attempt to understand this point, let us assume that all the Jewish citizens of Israel are in agreement that the abnormal situation of a reserve state is desirable. We see immediately, that such a situation will be considered intolerable by all other connected parties, namely, the non-Jewish citizens of Israel, its neighbors, the Jewish members of other nations, the Western nations, and more. This is an important claim: even on the assumption that the abnormal situation of Israel as the reserve state for all the Jews is desirable for Israeli Jews — which is extremely dubious — it is still definitely not desirable to other parties. If we succeed in showing that this claim is true, we will thereby succeed in showing that the current state of affairs cannot remain as it is for long, since this means that Israel will put itself in a very tenuous situation, losing the support of the Western nations and of the Jews of other nations and increasing the hostility of its neighbors and of a large national minority that dwells within its midst. There is no need to explain that a small, separate, and isolated state surrounded by enemies cannot sustain itself for long. In Israel everybody knows that it is impossible (in any respect) to continue to stand against hostile neighbors without continuing international support. The attempt to conceal this well-known fact only increases the frustration and despair. The phenomenon known as the Masada complex is widespread in Israel to a worrying degree. [Masada, it may be remembered, was the last independent Jewish fortress after the fall of Jerusalem, where warriors held on for three years under siege and then committed mass-suicide.] What is worrying is not that a free nation prefers physical annihilation to the loss of national liberty, or even that in the view of the same nation it is isolated and surrounded by enemies. What is worrying is that the Masada complex is rooted in the emotional inability to separate oneself from the past, to update oneself and one's society to meet a new situation and endorse national sovereignty in a modern, liberal sense. The official attitude of Israel towards the Jews of the world is an expression of this sense of dependence. For, despite their support for Israel, Israel views itself as a Masada, isolated and on the verge of suicide. The dependence on Jews outside Israel constitutes the past and the inability to adjust to what should be admitted as the political sovereignty of Israel. This is the source of the desire for isolation, since the isolation prevents the possibility of normalization and therefore prevents the possibility of access to normal, adequate relations with neighbors and to a stable existence.

Unfortunately, the Masada complex that engulfs Israel is obscured by the idea of the ingathering of the exiles, since the former suffers from excessive despair rooted in an inability to adjust and the latter from wishful thinking that there is no need to adjust. It is impossible to build a realistic political plan on the hope that all the Jews of all the nations will migrate to Israel in the near future. But the usual answer to this argument is that the ingathering of the exiles will happen despite everything simply because the whole world is opposed to Israel, namely, to the Jewish People. In this way the despair of the Masada complex and the wishful thinking about the ingathering of the exiles do merge. Yet in the age of nuclear weapons, the gathering of the whole Jewish people in one place is nothing short of the invitation for a nuclear Masada.

It is easy to show that even if abnormalcy is desirable to Israeli Jews, it is undesirable to others. The national minority in Israel, known as the Israeli Arabs, that is to say, the Arabic-speaking, non-Jewish Israeli citizens who are Moslems or Christians, increasingly view themselves as Palestinians, both because they were never given the right to define themselves and declare whether they wanted to be Israelis (since, instead, they had Israeli citizenship imposed on them), and because they do not possess the equal rights that are theirs according to the laws of the State of Israel that are conflict-ridden. There is no way, therefore, for Israel to fulfill the promises for equal rights to its religious minorities that it has made in its Declaration of Independence, especially because the frustration of non-Jewish Israelis is rooted in the want of a plan for a way out of the present maze. Israel cannot reduce the suffering of its non-Jewish citizens as long as it does not recognize the Israeli nation, namely, as long as it views itself as belonging to the Jewish people, which makes it a Jewish theocracy. As it cannot reduce the suffering of its non-Jewish citizens, so it cannot reduce the suffering of other members of the Israeli nation, who suffer inner strife, though in a fog, over the question of their identity and their national affiliation. This inner strife receives many expressions in the daily affairs of the nation and causes a general malaise, the feelings of no escape and despair that are increasing and deepening in the Israeli public, which are responsible to a large extent for the high rate of emigration to the West.

* The isolation of Israel strengthens the sense of dependence that Israeli Jews feel towards non-Israeli Jews, thereby strengthening their feeling of isolation even from their own people: Israeli Jews often envy non-Israelis Jew — not only because of the economic hardship in Israel, but also because of the sense of dependence that troubles them because of a sense of inferiority (rooted in the absence of a clear Israeli national identity, even though this absence is denied in Israel repeatedly and with an exaggerated emphasis). Therefore, there is the feeling in Israel that justice dictates rotation, the right of every Israeli to stay abroad for a while. This feeling strengthens the common-yet-unexpressed sense that, to realize this right, justice requires that every Jew should return to Israel, at least temporarily, and perform some obligatory service here. Hence there is little sense in the official Israeli propaganda against emigration as long as it is coupled with the official Israeli propaganda for obligatory service of

non-Israeli Jews here. And this is so despite the absurdity of the idea of rotation. The idea is absurd as leaving Israel does not generate a sense of national identity. This absence is the root of the problem. (Israelis living in affluent countries suffer a sense of separation; some of them seek relief in local Jewish communities, but in vain, since the members of these communities have their own national identities.) The feeling that justice prescribes rotation and obligatory service in Israel is an integral part of the illusion that the Israeli abnormalcy is a sacrifice Israelis make for Jews of the other nations. *

The difference between a national minority and an ethnic group is crucial. The Irish Catholics in Britain, for example, are a national discriminated minority, whereas the Irish in the United States are an ethnic group of citizens to all intents and purposes, sharing equal rights. (They express none of the complaints characteristic of a national minority because they are not.) This is not a matter of wording. We may call a national minority an ethnic unit and *vice versa*. What matters is the distinction between political status and the status of national and cultural origin or religious affiliation. For the national minority is of a different political status, which is the source of discrimination against them; the case of members of an ethnic group is different. American Jews have a political status equal to that of others in the United States, just like the Irish there; but this is not the case regarding the status of the Jews of the Soviet Union, since they have a recognized political status of a national minority, and hence they are discriminated against. * (Moreover, the discrimination was not abolished in the Commonwealth of Independent States that has inherited the Soviet Union, and it is unrealistic to expect a radical change there in dealing with the national problem in general and the Jewish problem in particular.) * Yet Israel insists on equating the political status of the Jews of the Soviet Union and of the United States regardless of their being a national minority or equal citizens.

Israel can diminish the suffering of the Jews of the Soviet Union by viewing them as potential citizens. Seeing all Jews who are not its citizens in this way, it overlooks the difference between those who wish to have the protection of the State of Israel and those who refuse it, preferring to stay out or to emigrate. Such preference is in Israel a target for ridicule and contempt, and proof of the correctness of Zionism. Israel thus limits the right of choice of the Jews of the

Soviet Union [and the Commonwealth of Independent States] considering their migration to Israel a duty and not a right, and since it even tries to narrow their options without considering their suffering and their human rights, including the right to try to migrate wherever they wish, and the right to self-determination, which they acquire as they are set free of the Soviet tyranny.

Similarly, Israel cannot maintain adequate relations with the Jews of the West, particularly those of the United States. Of course, the Judaism of Jews there is considered a matter both of religion and of ethnic origin. Of course, the State of Israel views them as members of the Jewish nation and citizens of the United States; it views them as members of the Jewish nation-faith, over which it claims ownership, and in whose name it speaks. It is even difficult to say when it explicitly says so and when and to what extent it refrains from saying so. But it is clear enough that there exists a conflict between the conception according to which the American Jews are potential Israeli citizens, namely, the principle that renders Israel the state of all the Jews, and its short-term interest, expressed as the constant and even noisy exploitation of the American Jews as members of the American nation. This conflict is dangerous in the long run, both for Israel and for the Jewish communities in the United States. The same holds for other Western countries, though to a lesser extent. Additionally, in Israel the opinion is popular that Western Jews have no right to voice their own opinions publicly about Israeli affairs, especially regarding relations between Israel and Western countries; in particular they allegedly have no right to voice criticism of Israel to the non-Jewish public. Democracy affirms as a principle that every citizen has the right to express any opinion about any topic; Israel is an unjusttifiable exception.

The situation becomes embarrassing, and seems increasingly abnormal and dangerous, when one enters into a detailed discussion. Since Israel is not a normal state but a theocracy, it cannot recognize the religion of the members of the Jewish communities in the affluent societies whose religion is not precisely the same as it recognizes at home. Israel is the State of the nation-religion and, therefore, has to grant exclusive recognition to the Orthodox trend in the Jewish religion, which is the unofficial state religion, and to overlook the choice of most of the members of the Jewish faith who are organized in Reform communities, Conservative communities, and others. Worse still, Israel is a theocracy founded by secular leaders who have used and still use religion as a political instrument. This has given rise to a new attitude in diverse circles in Israel, of contempt and disregard towards the traditional religion as a faith, as a relation between individuals and their creator. This disregard did not disturb the endorsement of the abnormal situation of Israel as the state whose members share a religion, and therefore those Israeli Jews who are not religiously observant support of necessity their having a status inferior to that of the Israeli Jews who are religiously observant. The contempt for religion then turns into self-contempt. Thus an absurd situation obtains in which the majority of the population in Israel, the religiously non-observant, hostile towards the Israeli clerical establishment, are also hostile to the Jewish Reform and Conservative congregations only because the Israeli clerical establishment is so.

* The Israeli clerical establishment relies not on the law of the land and not even always on regulations, but on customs that emerge on grounds specific to Israel, and the citizen is not aware of the details of the procedures involved. Even after investing some effort, information may remain deficient. For example, even the advisers of the educational television network are not familiar with the fact that despite its enjoying the status of a national organization, it cannot broadcast geological programs or standard biological programs on evolution, not to mention sex education — allegedly for fear of offending some unspecified fundamentalist circles. It is much harder to acquire information as to blacklists kept by different clerical bodies. But even without detailed knowledge, it is clear that some specific difficulties await the Israeli citizen who might clash with the Israeli clerical establishment: its *de facto* authority makes it harder to deal with it, than were its authority *de jure*, since the law facilitates awareness of the situation and thus some degree of public control.

* Above all, it is the Israeli woman who suffers humiliation despite her being a citizen of a liberal egalitarian state. In practice there is no way to realize the rights of women, despite the law that grants them equal status — and there is no way to protest against this vile procedure because of the pretext that the State of Israel has to impose the Jewish faith in its orthodox version on all its Jewish citizens in matters relating to laws of matrimony. This pretext constitutes a colossal inducement for government officials in charge of matters clerical to

seek ever newer ways to impose the religious laws on ever increasing aspects of civil life, private and public, by linking them to matters matrimonial, to which religious law already applies, and in total disregard of the basic democratic right of religious freedom.

* There is no limit to the nastiness of Israeli clerics towards streams in Judaism that are not orthodox, including the practices of Jewish communities that did not undergo the process of polarization into reform versus orthodoxy that the Jews of Central and Eastern Europe underwent in the early nineteenth century, including the Italian Jews and the Jewish communities of Arab origin which had little contact with European Jews before they reached Israel. To some extent but not sufficiently, these communities are protected by the institution of a Sephardi chief rabbinate (according to the nasty Israeli fiction that there are only two Jewish traditions, the [Yiddish speaking] Ashkenazi and the [Ladino speaking] Sephardi, and none other, in the face of the fact that many Jewish communities are neither). All this is well known.

* These details sum up in a sketch the situation specific to Israel. Most Israelis are not religiously observant. The politicians who are seen as the spokespeople for the non-religious, demand of a time-honored religious system that it regroup as a political system, with the task of instituting a Jewish character in the country. A considerable portion of Israeli Jews and of their political leaders declare openly that the religious establishment in Israel prevents religious freedom here despite the fact that this establishment is a body authorized and financed by the state. Hillel Kook rightly says that the very existence of Israel already constitutes a radical reform in the Jewish religion: Israeli Jews differ from those of the affluent part of the world in that they are citizens of a clerical state rather than of a liberal one; as Gershon Weiler notes, contrary to Jewish tradition, the Israeli religious leaders are political activists, devoid of qualifications and of responsibilities. The question is not, should Israel revolutionize the Jewish religion? Rather, it is, what kind of revolution should it be? In particular, is it possible to prevent the revolution from being obscurantist, under the rule of an establishment that pretends to support religion and democracy while violating the freedom of religion and conscience? (50a) *

Distinguishing nationality from religion enables the separation of state and religious organizations. Then the two systems — the political and the religious — are free of each other. This way Israel can become the center of the Jewish religion without any discord (51). Israel could try to be what the founders of the Emancipation Movement had hoped for — the revival and updating of an ancient nation that returns to its land.

The root of the evil is the confusion between a nation organized for political ends and a community organized for religious ends. Confusion about this isolates the State of Israel from the Western world and from the Jews of other nations, as well as from its neighbors in the region, and from its national minorities. As a result, the situation even brings about the isolation of the State of Israel from its own citizens; for the clouding of the situation now current in the State of Israel leaves no room for recognizing the Israeli nation nor for the Israeli national identity becoming of its citizens. The need for the existence of a nation and a national identity is the need for the endorsement as a national goal of the creation of a regime that caters to the peace of the nation and the welfare of its members. This goal should replace the mystic, new Zionist goal, a doubtful and unclear goal towards which Israel is thought to serve as a bridgehead.

A democratic regime is open to the participation of people in the regular running of public daily affairs for purposes that they deem significant. But Israel's abnormalcy empties democracy of its content; what remains is merely the empty shell of democracy since elections once every four years constitute a choice between groups of activists from a very small, established pool using fuzzy verbiage in their efforts to hold on to key positions (52). This is the reason that the current immediate need for normalization, for offering citizens the possibility of a genuine and continuing influence on the growth of the way of life in their country; in this way, normalization would facilitate the election of a political leadership well integrated in the public that it should represent.

Chapter 23

Is Israel Today a Nation-State?

What is the situation in Israel today? Does an Israeli nation exist, the nation that has fought a war of independence, which independence it lost on the day the Constituent Assembly gathered and, instead of fulfilling the task for which it was elected (the establishment of a constitution for the people and the state), turned into the first Knesset? Or is Israel, perhaps, the state of a nation-religion in a blind alley?

This question is not academic. If Israel is a nation-state, then the cloak of bureaucracy that obscures this should be removed. If it is a religion-nation living in theocracy, then it must wake up and change radically. Perhaps the situation is a mixture of the two, so that the two descriptions are partially correct, to this or that extent. Here is a key question that is left open, as an inseparable part of the obfuscation that is the cause of the abnormalcy of Israel today. This is why intermediary stages were presented as significant in the first, theoretical part of this book, contrary to current philosophical-political theories, in an attempt to examine the question, to what extent there is an Israeli nation here and now. Let us assume for a moment that Israel really is the state of the abnormal Jewish people which is a religion and a nation and thereby unique, as the supporters of the thesis of abnormalcy in Israel claim. Then there would be no need to obfuscate the present situation. The sincere supporters of the idea of abnormalcy, who sincerely consider Israel the state of the Jewish people, will not dispute this and will rest their case on the claim that there is no obfuscation here. They will claim that it is a clear fact, both the declared and the desired situation.

This response merits a serious rejoinder, despite the cynicism with which so many Israelis pay mere lip service to the idea that Israel belongs to the Jewish people. Indeed, in order to revalidate their claims they repeat old Zionist slogans the meanings of which they themselves forgot long ago. This is so well known that the word "Zionism" has become a buzzword. And when they wish on occasion to communicate that they use the word sincerely and not as a buzzword, they use expressions, such as, "Zionism-without-quotation-marks" and "genuine Zionism". There is something noble in the idea that Israel belongs to the whole Jewish people and that in this it is unique. This is so despite the fact that so many Israelis consider the myth according to which Israel belongs to the whole Jewish people as resulting in a rental contract for a state as a reserve home or as a summer home for which the people have to pay rent to the Jews who dwell in Zion. The noble idea that Israel belongs to the whole Jewish people merits examination in all the seriousness that it deserves. In some distinct sense this idea is even true, namely in the historical sense, as there is continuity between the Jewish people and the Israeli nation, and also in the continued religious sense, since Israel is a Jewish country as an undeniable fact even though not as a political fact.

Let me, then, comment on the view that there is no clouding here, that the lack of normalcy is both a fact and an openly declared situation. With the respect due to an ideological opponent who claims that Israel belongs to the Jewish international religion-nation, let us distinguish very sharply between opponents committed to faith in the Jewish religion with all their heart and the not religious ones, those dubbed "secular". Among the religious opponents who observe the Law are those who also observe the secular law of the state, and those who refuse to recognize it. Among the non-religious opponents are those hostile to religion and those indifferent to it, even those who themselves partly observe religious law or at least respect it.

As to observant Jews, the difference is merely secondary between those who consider Israel as the state of all the Jews of the world and endorse its laws, and those who do not endorse them. Both share the conviction that Divine Law is superior to human law, namely, state law, and that of necessity the former are eternal and solid and the latter are temporary and shaky. This is the effect of Israel having no constitution, as the Constituent Assembly was canceled and turned into the Knesset, which soon passed the whole system of matrimonial laws over to a religious judiciary system. The rest of the laws have remained in one confused state, since the Knesset is both a secular national institution and a Jewish one; therefore, against its will — because of the absence of distinction between faith and nationality — it is also a religious institution (53). As a result, conflict prevails between the secular laws of the State of Israel and the Divine Law according to the Jewish faith — in many ways and in many places, sometimes with no prior intention or expectation. So in Israel a special status has developed for Gush Emunim [a radical extremist nationalist group] which relies rightly or wrongly on religious edicts — since the state demands of the citizens to follow the Jewish Law in matters of marriage and divorce, and since there is an understandable demand to broaden the domain of the applicability of this demand. And so diverse political bodies came to openly violate the laws of the State of Israel and overlook direct instructions from its government. In their defense they base their claim on the Jewish faith and exhibit an ideological and moral preference for faith over national policy as a whole, including this or that law, government edict, or government decision. Admittedly, not all those who violate Israeli law in the name of religion are honestly religious people moved by religious outlook. But, as usual, it is preferable to appeal to the best in every circle, and to the best by the judgment of that very circle. Therefore, when speaking of the abnormalcy of Israel as a state of a unique nation-religion, it is preferable to relate first to the religious adherents to this opinion. Moreover, since the religious leadership in Israel prefers religious law over civil law, the burden of the political responsibility that they undertake this way is too heavy and lies beyond their competence. This means that theocracy in Israel may cause harm to Israel and to the religion of Israel and, in particular, to the Jews of other nations. This becomes particularly conspicuous upon examination of matters of security and territoriality, which are beyond the professional or the institutional competence of the religious leadership. This way the adjudication of religious leaders becomes a supreme military or political adjudication that has priority over the official adjudication of military or political experts.

We started with the question, are the Jews of Israel an Israeli nation? And we reached a deliberation concerning relations between state and religious institutions, between government and rabbinate. The idea current in the West, of the separation of religious and political authority, of church and state, called in Israel the separation of faith and state, is the recognition of the need to separate the authorities of religious and of political institutions, not between religion and politics. The separation of faith and nationality is expressed politically and legally by the separation of religious and political institutions.

As for the Israelis who are not religiously observant, it is difficult to understand how they take seriously their opinion that Israel belongs to the dispersed Jewish people, which is a nation-religion whose uniqueness is essentially religious. It is hard to understand how they manage to endorse such a significant opinion, the significance of which is based on religious arguments alone, and yet without themselves being honestly and sincerely religious. Since they are not religious they underestimate the significance of the Jewish faith, both in the life of the historical Jewish people and in the life of the Jewish communities of other nations; and this way they overlook the fact that Judaism was and still is a faith. And still they endorse the abnormalcy of Israel, and the integration of religion and nationality here, without being troubled by the absence of a separation between the religious and secular authorities. Most of them are then fully aware of their own admission of the superiority of religious Jews over secular Jews. Without the separation between faith and nationality, religious inferiority is also national inferiority. So they are surprised when they discover that, even as Israeli nationals, they view themselves as inferior even to those who refuse to recognize the nation.

But perhaps the intention of the secularists is presented here with insufficient precision. Perhaps their intention is different from the one presented here. If they intend to say that once Israel was a nation-religion and is now a nation-state, then there is justice in what they say. But perhaps they mean to say that since Israel once was a religion-nation, even today it remains a scattered nation, despite religion being a non-political component in the life of every modern society. If so, then they should explain how it is possible that Jews in Western countries may hold high political offices, including membership in cabinets of their countries, and nevertheless also be citizens of Israel, members of the nation of the State of Israel. How can they overlook, then, the fact that the separation of the Jewish faith and the local nation is endorsed by the Jews of Western countries? For it is clear to the Jews of the West that they do not belong to the Israeli nation, that they are Jews only in the religious or the ethnic sense, but not in the political sense. The secularists who endorse the abnormalcy of Israel should likewise explain, how it is possible that so many Jews who can come to Israel without much effort relinquish the right to naturalize here and prefer to keep and develop Jewish centers in Western countries. For this position towards Israel, shared by religious and secularist Jews, assumes that the present situation of dispersion is a permanent, desired state of affairs. The official plan of the Zionist Movement today — The Jerusalem Plan — declares with great pride the centrality of Israel in the life of the scattered Jewish people. This helps cloud the fact of the defeat of the historical Zionist hope for normalization. It may be remembered that as Israel was declared independent, it was deemed the state of the whole Jewish people on the assumption that the Jews of the Diaspora would all return to Israel. But this is not the case. How long will it take before the Zionist leadership will recognize the fact that many Jews prefer not to migrate to Israel? How long will the Israelis have to wait before the Zionist Movement recognizes the State of Israel as an independent nation-state? How long will the nation of Israel remain unrecognized by its own state and its own elected institutions?

And perhaps it is not the intention of the secularist Israelis who claim that Israel is the state of the scattered Jewish people, to say that the Israelis are still a nation-religion. Perhaps they mean (as they seem to) that the Jews of the whole world are potential citizens of Israel. If this is the case, then all they mean to do is justify the idea of the ingathering of the exiles as a political idea. This is an abnormal idea that has to be abandoned, since it makes Israel the bridgehead of a nation that does not exist today within its borders. The decisive question remains: Is there today an Israeli nation, or is Israel only a part of the scattered Jewish world, or is it an independent Jewish community with armed forces? For a Jewish community with armed forces not only lacks national identity but is also necessarily in a continuous state of war with the neighbors: in not being a nation-state but rather a part of a process that continues for generations, Israel loses its present right to exist.

Perhaps Israel is a potential nation or an occupied nation. For, the presence of a nation is conditioned by the presence of either national independence or a national liberation movement, whereas the independence of the State of Israel today, unlike the independence of the desired normal Israeli republic, is not the independence of the Israeli nation. It is not clear what this independence is, except that it is a complex system of relations of Israel with the Jewish people that is scattered all over the world. And just because of that, it is impossible that the revolution will occur the way revolutions of occupied nations usually do. Israel is not occupied by a foreign oppressor. It is captive in the chain of the confusion of its own conception (54). In conclusion we could say that a component of the Israeli national awareness is missing because of confusion; the completion of the Israeli nation will occur, then, when the national self-awareness clarifies and develops. This completion will not be bestowed from the outside; it has to emerge from self-liberation, from that auto-emancipation which the fathers of the Jewish national movement longed for, the process of development of the Israeli national identity in the desired Israeli Republic. This is not an abstract political-philosophical claim, but a key political proposal, whose aim is a radical and revolutionary change of the structure and character of Israeli society in diverse areas of life, one that will permit it to join the enlightened Western world. Israel cannot survive for long within an intermediary, cloudy situation.

Chapter 24   *The Purpose of the Change*

On the assumption that Israel is an independent ghetto state and that the root of the evil is in its abnormal situation, normalization should be presented as a primary urgent target. The defects and helplessness that characterize the Diaspora ghetto and that have stuck to Israel, did not lessen with the introduction of the Israeli components of sovereignty (currency, police, and armed forces), but increased and even sharpened. The root of the evil is in the abnormal situation of Israel, which is not a nation-state like all Western nation-states but is the state of a religion-nation scattered in the world, whose members are members of diverse nations, with Israel's Jewish citizens being only a small part of the people to which Israel belongs. Simultaneously, the status of the non-Jewish Israeli citizens rests on logical inconsistency and in a cloudy and implausible state of a citizenship that is no citizenship and of equality within the law that the law, the nation and the government refuse to honor in practice. This abnormalcy prevents Israel's progress away from its state of belligerence with its immediate neighbors.

To repeat, the purpose of the proposed change is to normalize Israel's national situation, to turning it from the state of a Jewish religion-nation into the nation-state of Israel on a normal pattern, the pattern of the normal democratic nation-state that belongs to its citizens, to the members of its nation — a state whose government has to do all it can to fulfill its declared purpose, which is the furthering of the peace, welfare, happiness, and quality of the material, spiritual, and cultural life of its own citizens. It is clear that the plan for change offered here will solve only those specific problems of Israel that are anchored in its unique status. But these specific problems are basic problems of Israel, and their solution is a necessary condition for a free approach to its other problems, for then they can be attacked in a normal way, as is customary in diverse normal countries. As a normal state, Israel will be secular, but as a normal state it would not be lacking in a religious character; of course that religious character will be Jewish, but on the basis of the separation of religious and political institutions.

The most important and basic change is the turning of Israel into a land able to undertake political initiative. The inability to do this has characterized Israel ever since its establishment. This is not the inability to take initiative as such; the diverse Israeli governments did undertake military, settlement, and even economic initiatives (55). The absence of political initiative is a characteristic typical of the ghetto, which, in the view of Gershon Weiler, has deep roots in the Diaspora Jewish tradition, as he describes in his excellent *Jewish Theocracy* (56). It is not easy to liberate oneself of many generations on end of a tradition of absence of all political initiative. In the bitter moments after the Yom Kippur War, the Israeli public felt a strong need to undertake political initiative, but despite all the strong feeling, despite all the goodwill, even the beginning of real political initiative was not to be found. It is no accident that the initiative that was mobilized sought its expression within the accepted Israeli party-political framework. Consequently, there was no possibility that it would proceed beyond the stage of public protest, of opposition to the government's line, and at most to the demand that the government resign. (When the demand that the Israeli Government resign was met, the public lost its ability to demand from its new government additional improvements.) This basic absence of political initiative is the cause of the fact that from the very start of its independence Israel lacked all public expression of properly designed political initiative (57).

What is the cause of the permanent Israeli inability to take political initiative?

One need not seek the cause of this inability in this or that particular historical obstacle, nor in the tradition of the absence of political initiative, since it is always possible to expect that someone would stand up and demand a change in the tradition and the updating of the situation after the Declaration of Independence. Such a person did stand up in Israel, and his name is Hillel Kook.

But he found no listening ear, nor even a readiness to open a public debate. Kook's proposal was that the ghetto mentality in Israel be viewed as the obstacle that causes the constant lack of political initiative. His proposal for the surmounting of this obstacle includes three steps. First, public recognition of the very problem. Second, the description of the desired normal state in Israel. Third, the outline of a way to achieve normalcy. And the picture that should emerge must be no utopia, not a vision for the end of days, of a society free of all daily problems, not of an ideal society in any respect. It is a picture of Israel on the political pattern of a common, Western, democratic country (57a).

On the agenda here is the pattern of a common Western democratic country, more precisely the political qualities of this pattern. Other qualities of this pattern — economic, social, and cultural — will not be discussed here. No doubt, the pattern of a normal Western country from an economic point of view includes a developed economy, with an industrial sector, with organized labor, and with a considerable part of the nation having the benefits of vocational education. The discussion about them will be skipped here, since the place for it is in the platforms of political parties of a normal state, and the plan for normalization proposed here is non-partisan. Other, more politically relevant economic points, will be overlooked here, as, for instance, the need to reduce the economic gulf between rich and poor, the need for social security and comprehensive medical insurance; partisan political controversies arise over these issues, and therefore they have no place in a discussion of a non-partisan proposal. Social issues and the problems of improving the quality of life will also not be discussed here, and so also the significance of a rich and broad national and religious culture and of a broad system of popular education of high quality. The remainder of this book will discuss only the non-partisan political domain, describing the normal state desired for Israel not as an ideal, but as the next necessary step: the political structure that would facilitate and even contribute to a reasonable treatment of the nation's problems. The immediate purpose of this book is to arouse a comprehensive public debate that would be intensive and deep and that within a short while might turn Israel unambiguously into a modern nation-state, which would then permit both citizens and their government to undertake political initiatives as required. This plan, therefore, is for the medium-range, on the assumption that the time at our disposal within which to execute it is very short. For according to Kook, the Israeli nation exists in fact but is only partially aware of its very existence, not being recognized by the Israeli ruling party-political establishment, this because of the power that the New Zionist Myth has over the Israeli establishment. In brief, in Kook's opinion, the Israeli nation exists, but does not function properly for want of political self-awareness.

According to the image presented here, Israel will turn within a short while into a nation-state, and a clear national identity will be given to all members of the Israeli people. The Israeli people will be recognized as the political heirs of the Jewish people as a whole, and thus the fact that the Jewish people is no longer a political entity today will gain official recognition. Since Israel lives in the modern age, the central item in its constitution should express the principle of the distinction between the Israeli nationality and the Jewish religion, so as to anchor within this material principle the formal principle of the separation of state and religious institutions, between secular and religious authority. The continuity of the existence of the Jewish people, as a historical entity that has preceded the Israeli people, will not be violated, and will receive the diverse expressions that fit the new situation that would stem from the establishment of the autonomy of Israel as a nation-state. The Jews of other nations would thereby be free to develop their Judaism as religion and culture, and would be able to improve their relations with Israel, and will even be able to continue activities in aid of Jews without homelands (such as the Jews of the Soviet Union and its heirs). This will permit the normalization of Israel as the only nation in the world in which Jews make up the majority of the people, but as a people renewed and updated. It is clear that once the wheel of history should turn fully, and then under certain conditions (as is done in every Western democracy) Israel will enable those who want to become naturalized to become members of the Israeli nation without any consideration of their religion or country of origin. This will legitimize the existence of those Israelis who are not Jews but members of different religions (even though the majority of the members of the nation will belong to the Jewish religion). In this sense Israel will be frankly Jewish (just as France is frankly Roman Catholic).

In the image presented here, the status of citizens of the State of Israel who, according to the current identity cards, are not members of the Jewish nation, will also change: they will have the opportunity to choose whether to remain in Israel as alien residents, or as Israelis with full citizens' rights and duties, considering themselves Israeli members of the Moslem or the Christian faith, as Israelis of Palestinian or other origin (similar to the Americans who are members of the Catholic faith or of the Jewish faith and Americans of Irish or Israeli origin). They could thus develop their religion and ethnic culture undisturbed, perhaps even with the aid of government funds, as is customary in some democratic countries, and be proud that the contribution they make to their ethnic culture is at the same time a contribution to the general Israeli culture (just as the contribution of an American Jew is considered in the United States a contribution both to American culture and to Jewish culture and perhaps at times even to Jewish religious culture). Of course, the non-Jews who choose to join the Israeli nation would have to turn Israeli both in the content of their national identity and formally in accord with naturalization legislation that should render this possible.

Thus would emerge a normal Israel with no national minority as a political entity — even though it would have religious, cultural, and ethnic minorities. There is no disagreement concerning the fact that the presence of national minorities within Israel is a persisting evil, though some prefer not to take any political initiative, but learn to live with this persisting evil in the hope that the problem will solve itself. It is no accident, therefore, that the other initiative proposed — currently merely alluded to or hinted at in the Israeli public — would solve the problem by abolition of the national minority in Israel in a non-political manner. A non-political initiative for the abolition of the national minority means expulsion. Admittedly, this plan is not broadly endorsed in Israel and it raises public opposition, as it prefers the continuation of the present confused and inconsistent situation. But this admission, though true, is not to the point. Taking comfort in the fact that the demand for expulsion is a minority opinion is living in a fool's paradise, for when there is a need for a decision concerning political matters, and only one proposed initiative exists in the field, then that initiative wins, even if it is a minority opinion (58). Those who repudiate this particular initiative must develop an alternative to it. To that end they should envisage a possible alternative situation (whether the one mentioned above or any other). Those who suppose that it is possible to implore the members of the national minority to leave, or even to bribe them to leave, are also living in a fool's paradise. There is no political initiative in this position, for it does not include a consideration of the question, what should be done if the members of the national minority refuse to leave? And, indeed, they do refuse to leave, and the current confused situation drives them to organize in order to realize their legal position as a national minority and turn Israel into an openly bi-national state.

In conclusion, the current situation of an increasingly large national minority in Israel may become as disastrous as is predicted by most of the students of the problem of the Israeli Arabs within the diverse political movements and parties. The other logical alternative is the one presented here: the abolition of the status of the national minority by which, according to the right of personal self-determination, part of the minority would become a proper part of the nation and the other part would be recognized as alien residents. It is self-evident that the more decent and attractive the proposal that they join the nation, the more it will improve the situation for both the minority and the majority. As a result, with one blow Israel could improve its relations with the Israeli Palestinians and with the Palestinians on the other side of the border.

Here is the place to clarify the status of a resident alien (59). The position of resident aliens is not the same in all countries. Generally, they have no citizens' rights but rather the rights of residence according to the legal definition of residence, and this differs from country to country. What is important is that in a normal country the status of the citizen and of the resident alien are clear, making it easy to maintain and respect the law, and the equality of rights is actual and genuine, just as the inequality of rights is actual and genuine. In Israel the situation is deceitful, and therefore the demand for new legislation for the sake of normalization must include legislation on this matter.

The idea presented here is, intentionally, rather simple and devoid of all sophistication: the distinction in content between nation and religion and the separation in form of state and religious institutions, between secular and religious authority, would permit the establishment of an Israeli republic that as a nation-state would recognize the right of Jews of other nations to view themselves not as citizens or potential citizens of one country while being loyal citizens of another country. As a result, what today is impossible by definition would be possible: the Israeli nation would have Moslems and Christian as full members. This would bring about the abolition of national minorities, though there would still be groups of citizens of this or that national origin, or religious or ethnic minorities. In addition, as the Israeli republic would represent the Israeli nation alone, and not the Jews of all nations, the republic would be able to concentrate on a new order of priorities, that would express the wishes of its citizens, and cater to their peace and welfare according to the pattern accepted in free countries.

Normalization is no solution to any problems; it only opens the possibility of solutions. One might hope that after the enactment of the normalization proposed here, Israel would be able to handle its problems in a normal manner. That is to say, that Israel would be able to handle its problems in future much more efficiently than at present.

* Reading certain passages in this chapter filled me with nostalgia: when this chapter was written, not long ago, the option of expulsion seemed so distant that there was need for caution and a reminder that it was not as distant as it seemed. In the meantime, much precious time was wasted, and the option became too close, and the Israeli Parliament has a seasoned political party that preaches this option openly. Admittedly, the members of this party restrict their dangerous proposal to the expulsion of the erstwhile citizens of Jordan from the west of the River Jordan to the east of it, but it is doubtful that great efforts will be made to prevent a last-minute-addition of the Israeli non-Jews to the ranks of those condemned to expulsion. There is a precedent to this, which surprisingly has not raised any protest: the Israeli General Security Service decreed that their suspicion that a non-Jewish Israeli has collaborated with a terror organization deprives that person of the status of a citizen, for, in 1992 Mustafa 'Acawi, a Jerusalem resident, was brought before an Israeli military court outside the Israeli civil jurisdiction, though he had been arrested in his home, charged by the Israeli General Security Service with the suspicion of terrorist activity, and the judge rejected his request to be returned to Israeli territory and be judged there, basing the decision on the claim of the Israeli General Security Service that he was suspected of terrorist activity. The judge added that, since he had been tortured in jail, he had earned the right to medical examination. He was

taken to hospital and died there. This event raised protest in Israel and in the West because of its humanist aspect rather than its legal aspect, since, after all, according to the New Zionist Myth current in Israel, citizenship is an insignificant matter and only nationality counts. The claims of the political party siding with expulsion should be understood accordingly: when they pacify the Israeli citizens with the claim that their intent is not to expel those recognized as Israeli Arabs, they say that they will not be expelled as anyway they do not exist. And after the expulsion the only inhabitants of Israel will be those recognized as Jews — except for those few who will be allowed to stay by special permits. Then, it may be assumed, those Palestinians who today visit Israel in daytime only from Judea, Samaria and the Gaza Strip, will still come, also in daytime only, but from the east of the Jordan River (till the next expulsion).

It is no comfort that the expulsion party is advocated by irresponsible activists who have not weighed the meaning of the endorsement of the expulsion option as a national policy. For the very existence of this party points to the despair that engulfs Israel, despair originating from the absence of choice. This absence of choice originates from the absence of a person (except for Hillel Kook) seeking an alternative outside the national consensus, in search of an alternative to it. The Israeli consensus is crumbling, but the consensus as to the New Israeli Myth is stable, and the more the Israeli consensus crumbles, the more tenaciously the Israeli leadership clings to this myth, on the supposition that it is the ultimate instrument for the prevention of a collapse of the Israeli consensus, despite it being the very source of the absence of an alternative to the expulsion, an absence that spells despair and despair that spells the danger of a total disintegration.

Apprehension is repeatedly voiced that the proposal for normalization endangers the Jewish identity of Israel discussed in this chapter. For even if in the process of normalization Israel would be declared the heir to the political aspirations of the Jewish national movement, it could later on, as a normal sovereign state, renounce this inheritance. Indeed, as in all steps, this has its dangers. The question is, however, is the present state of affairs not more dangerous? The present state of affairs encourages hostility to the Jewish faith, and so, unless normalization is established soon, in principle it is possible that the majority of Israelis will reject the proposal that the Jewish faith will be the ruling religion in Israel, regardless of the preference of normalization or of its absence. Clearly, the absence of normalization in Israel is more dangerous to the Jewish character of Israel, particularly since this Jewish character fades as the absence of normalization causes corruption and inhumanity to non-Jews and even to non-observant Jews — contrary to Jewish tradition. Initially, Orthodox circles in Israel tried to overlook its very existence, even as they benefited from it. For years this is no longer so: the absence of the recognition of the State of Israel on the part of the Israeli religious leadership was received by most of the Israeli public, observant and non-observant alike, as an expression of its abnormal situation; of its being a religious community rather than a nation, even though most of the members of the community are non-observant — perhaps, particularly, because of the fact that they are non-observant. In other words, the apprehension that normalization will hurt the Jewish character of Israel is rooted in the confusion between community and nation: the nation has to be secular and the community sacred, and the distinction between the sacred and the profane that is recommended in this book fits religious tradition better than the intervention of the religious leadership in secular matters. The normalization recommended in this book should relieve the religious and the secular leadership from unrealistic, heavy, and redundant obligations. *

Chapter 25: The Alternative Plan

The previous chapter discussed the desired situation of national normalcy. The presentation of this was accompanied with the general outline of a plan. This chapter will discuss the plan in more detail.

A plan for practical action has to outline activity from the present situation to the first step and from the first step to the second and perhaps to the third. It is not desirable for a plan of action to be so detailed that everything is decided ahead of time. Such a plan might be defective, since the planner has to describe in detail the second step as a response to the first step of the second party, and if the second party has a few options, then a few plans are required for the second step. If the concern is with a comprehensive plan, then the third step becomes even more complex. Hence, either the plan is not detailed enough or it is too complex. Even a chess game suffers from this problem; it is an insoluble problem in chess, and political life is much more complex and rich than chess. Chess players present strategies in general outlines, while leaving decisions about details for their users. But without a general strategy, even one step cannot be planned, for it is strategy that gives meaning even to that first step.

The initial purpose of the strategy proposed in this book is to arouse public debate. Its initial supposition is that the present situation is grave, that there is a public awareness both of the gravity of the situation and of the fact that the solution of the problem is not going to come by replacing the government or changing of an official governmental attitude to this or that detail from among those on the national agenda. The assumption is that a considerable number of Israelis feel a sufficient sense of responsibility to start a public debate concerning the proposals presented in this book (whether in defense of these proposals or against them or in proposing alternatives to them). First, I will show the plausibility of a discussion as a result of this book, as it has something to offer to those who are willing to participate in the debate, and that it is, indeed, desirable for the debate to develop along the expected lines.

There are those who view the very debate of the proposal presented in this book as a national risk. They would propose to minimize the debate, with the result that it would die down for want of interest. Possibly, they will present this national risk as the risk of splitting the nation, as a risk for religion, and so on. Indeed, it is broadly agreed that such claims have succeeded in the past to silence similar debates that might have originated among the Israeli public. But we should remember that the blocking of public debate has repeatedly permitted the perpetration of open lies in Israel, and this perpetuated the abnormalcy here since independence, forcing it to remain in a blind alley.

Therefore, it is hoped that those who claim that the political debate proposed here is dangerous, will be countered with the observation that the silencing of a political debate is even more dangerous. This step would depend on answering the question, What is the point in having a public debate of the kind proposed here, as opposed to the current public debates executed to no end? We shall come to this in a moment. But, assuming that there would be some people who will value the debate, they could say to the critics that blocking debates has not brought about national unity, has not brought about normalization, has not brought about a normal situation, and has not prevented deterioration. Quite generally, one could say of every society in the world, that when severe criticism is heard in it, some people in it would say that washing dirty linen in public is objectionable. Yet washing dirty linen in public is precisely the character of democracy. Admittedly, there is some damage in washing dirty linen in public, since, in principle, there is damage in every action whatsoever. But it is clear that the benefit is far superior to the damage, and in general one could say that blind trust in the government or in the people who hold the reins of government results in damage to ruler and ruled together, whereas public criticism raises the levels of the seriousness and responsibility of the ruler and the government and its efficiency. These things seem paradoxical, but habits of democratic thinking make them self-understood. It is no accident that in Israel it is still customary to think that washing dirty linen in public is prohibited; there is no sufficient democratic tradition in Israel, since most Israelis stem from non-democratic countries. Israeli democracy seems to many sufficiently normal and even sufficiently liberal, simply because they lack direct information about proper liberal regimes, Western style. Moreover, the tragic and grotesque situation in Israel is that it is allowed there to display dirty linen in public, but not to wash it; in particular, it is prohibited to touch basic issues of the nation.

There are also those who would see in the present proposal danger, but who nevertheless would agree to discuss it publicly. It is reasonable to assume that they will attack this proposal, seeing it as a sabotage of national unity, an attack on the Jewish faith, and a discussion that will prove divisive between the Jews of Israel and the Jews of the rest of the world. Those who are interested in critical debate on these details should ask, why the proposal for the separation of religious and political institutions is an attack on faith. For the nation-religion is the non-normal and the nation-state is the normal, and there is no contradiction between the acceptance of the secular nation-state and the recognition of the fact that the religion broadly sanctioned in the Israeli nation is the Jewish faith, just as the Roman Catholic faith is in France, Anglicanism is in Britain, or as Christianity — which is not a religion but a collection of diverse religions — is in the United States. One could say the same things against the criticism that the proposal creates a separation between Israel and the Jews of other nations. But this is not so. Today Israel receives from them only financial support and perhaps also a little immigration (even though the migration from Israel to the West is larger than the migration in the opposite direction). The Jews of other nations who support Israel today, even in a politically active manner, do so without any frustration or conflict between their national affiliation to their own countries and their being Jewish precisely because they endorsed the separation and they act precisely as Jews and members of other nations. That is to say, the separation proposed here exists in the relation of the Jews of the Western world towards Israel in fact but not in theory. The plan proposed here, therefore, is to stop the received lie and turn the situation accepted in practice to a situation accepted in theory too. This will enable its application in the desired measure to all areas of the nation's life, and to prevent difficulties caused by Israel's refusal to recognize this present situation. Israel's refusal presents difficulties today already and it may spark complications that would threaten the Jews of other nations in the near future.

The most dangerous response to the ideas presented here is that of a general agreement combined with practical indifference. One who views the nation-religion as an abnormal phenomenon and the State of Israel as deteriorating, is not necessarily inclined to seek any connection between these two facts, because of a fear that discussion in this direction may be hostile to Jewish religion and traditional values. Possibly things would look different if the separation between nation and religion could be shown as a way, not only to save the nation from a very difficult political situation, but also to save the Jewish religion from disgrace and destruction. Of course, an increasing number of religious Jews view the placing of Judaism in the service of the interest of Israel as an insult to their faith, but most of them live outside Israel. Israeli religious Jews not familiar with the nationalist idea, have no interest in the whole matter, even if they casually endorse nationalism. Theirs is not a realistic attitude. Even so, there are those who claim that this attitude is predominant in Israel. As a result of this unrealistic attitude, the principles of normalization may be accepted casually and without drawing any practical political application. Indeed, some Israelis are aware of the need for normalization but do not view it as a political lever. As to those who accept the religious nationalist idea received in Israel, obviously this idea is the polar opposite to the idea of normalization. Before speaking against these two groups, one should speak against those who tend towards normalization without viewing it as a political lever. They overlook the decisive significance both of normalization and of the possibility of its application. They, thereby, overlook their own power, rooted as it is in their being a majority in Israel: their overlooking of the political potential of normalization is rooted in their being captives of the ideology of Practical Zionism which prevents them from engaging in political initiative.

If the passivity of the majority will be reduced and a political debate concerning normalization will take place, and if this debate will bring about awareness and awakening, then it will be possible to undertake the steps described below. This awareness is the very lever that might bring this awakening, and therefore it may be vital. One must stress, in addition, that this awareness might come about in recognition of the possibility that the changes proposed here might force the governments of Israel to cater on a short-term basis to the welfare of the nation that dwells in its boundaries, and desist from trying to represent an amorphous, scattered people that may or may not gather after the time span of generations, that only a small part of whom dwells within its boundaries today, and whose government permits itself to overlook its daily problems and caters for the distant future only. To that end, Israel should rest not on received lies that relieve the government of its responsibility to its citizens, but on an open agreement between the government and the nation. The received lies should cease and Israel will no longer be described as the refuge for potential refugees who are not coming, and who, perhaps, will never come, and it will cease to be viewed as relatively normal and simultaneously as unique in catering for a unique nation-religion, so that it alone, among other nations, is both secular and theocratic. All this is untenable. Also the lie should cease that Israelis sacrifice themselves for the sake of their brethren, the potential refugees, while accepting from them alms and donations. With these lies put to rest, the whole structure of Israel may alter. The question is, how can the development herein described be accomplished?

Here, in brief, are the basics of the plan. As a result of a broad public comprehensive political debate, in the political parties, in the legislature, and in other institutions, a public juridical committee should be established to work out the details of the declarations and the constitutional laws to be brought for the approval of the Knesset; the transition should be marked by the enactment of constitutional laws. These should be the rudiments of the constitution. As a result, two declarations should be made in the Knesset in revising past mistakes, and with all the solemnity of a repetition of the Declaration of Independence. First of all, Israel should be declared a republic and the state of the Israeli nation (without this nation losing its affinity to the world's Jewish people and while retaining the position of the Israeli republic as a possible refuge for refugees persecuted as Jews). Secondly, a full distinction between nation and religion should be declared, that is to say, a separation of state and religious institutions. This should be done, while fully recognizing the centrality of the Jewish faith both in the life of the Jewish people from antiquity to modern times, and in the movement of the Jewish national revival and its contribution to Israeli and world culture, and while recognizing the Jewish faith as the faith widespread in the Israeli nation.

The citizens of the Israeli republic should be given new Israeli identity cards which designate neither religion nor nationality. They would be given to members of the nation alone, that is to say, to citizens only (and the same should hold for Israeli passports, of course). Israeli citizens will be, first and foremost, those Israeli citizens who are already represented in Israel today as members of the Jewish nation, except for those among them who prefer to remain resident aliens. These should be provided with resident-alien papers. The same should be said about the other resident aliens in Israel. Similarly, the citizens of the State of Israel who are today considered as retaining non-Jewish nationality, including those whose identity cards say that they are members of the Arab nation, should be allowed to decide either to join the nation and become members of the nation for all intents and purposes — while retaining their religious freedom and the freedom of developing their ethnic culture and accepting all the duties of a citizen to nation and country — or to stay in Israel as aliens (as aliens with rights and duties in accordance with that status). Those who undertake to join the Israeli nation will be Israelis, members of the Israeli nation for all intents and purposes. In addition to that, they might view themselves, of course, as Israeli Moslems, Druzes, Christians, or members of any other denomination, and as of Arab Palestinian origin or of any other origin, and develop their religion and their culture as they wish.

Thus, the current situation in which the terms "Jewish" and "Israeli" are used in confusion and in deceit will change. The situation will be clear and the concept "Israeli" would apply to all members of the Israeli nation who would be as matter of course, citizens of the Israeli republic without religious discrimination.

A constitutional law should determine, in principle, conditions suitable for immigration and for naturalization. In addition, Israeli governments of the future should determine numerical limitations on immigration as required, without discriminating against members of other religions or nations or races. In the framework of this constitutional law a substitute for the Israeli Law of Return should be enacted that would secure an open door for all those who seek refuge in Israel because they are persecuted as Jews in their own lands, in order that they be permanent residents who would have the right to naturalize as any other permanent residents. Naturally, the declaration of the republic must also include a declaration concerning the national territory.

Chapter 26   *Concerning National Minorities*

Since antiquity there has been a sense of conflict between the love of one's people and motherland and the love of all humans as humans. This feeling was expressed in the Old Testament ("Your father is the Amorite, your mother is Hittite") and in the writings of Plato ("I consider you all my relatives and friends and compatriots, of course not according to convention but according to nature"). The nationalist movements encouraged the love of nation and of motherland on the basis of the claim that we are unable to practice the love of all humans as humans. "The universal man," said the German philosopher Hegel, "that is to say, the dead man...." As opposed to the Romantic Chauvinist movement, the liberal movement, daughter of the Enlightenment movement, required complete equality between members of the nation and aliens. Hence it found little political value in the love of motherland. In this way, the contrast between the love of humans and the love of compatriots took root. The liberals viewed the love of motherland as nothing but a psychological limitation, even though a limitation that might be politically exploited. This exploitation was accepted even in the Marxist movements, despite the fact that official Marxist philosophy claimed the existence of only two nations, the rich and the poor (60). Marxist leaders and ideologists found nothing wrong in the mobilization of the love of motherland for the purpose of a war against the enemy, which was both an alien nation and, allegedly, the representative of the international imperialist bourgeoisie (Hitler as the representative of the Rothschilds, no less!). The celebrated comedian Charlie Chaplin claimed in his autobiography that the love of motherland is linked emotionally with a beautiful childhood, and that since he had a difficult childhood, he had no love for his motherland. The celebrated scientist Albert Einstein found it difficult to accept any affinity to any specific human grouping, yet he became a Zionist for practical reasons.

But national identity is something of a completely different kind. It is a thing that has a personal component, a private, emotional, and even intellectual one; but it also has a political component. In the name of liberalism, an attempt was made to recognize the personal component and ignore the political component. This attempt is likely to bring about the demand that every state should recognize every national minority that it has. For example, the Jewish national minority in Poland in its period of blossoming managed to attain recognition both when for a couple of centuries it had a certain degree of autonomy and in the period of before World War II, between the foundation of modern Poland and its joint occupation, and its partition between Germany and the Soviet Union. The earlier period will not be discussed here, since this is the period prior to the formation of the nationalist movements, when the system was very different as its roots were in the Middle Ages, in which the right to self-determination, together with the right to a certain degree of autonomy, was granted to diverse classes and in diverse manners. Similarly, at that period there were no national currencies and no national armies (61). In modern times, the aim of the state regarding the national minority was to provide for the personal needs of the members of that minority without adding to it a political dimension, without satisfying their political needs. Therefore, not only was there a lack of political dimension to the nationality of the minority, but this also conflicted with the political dimension of the nationality of the majority. The result was the unavoidable discrimination against the minority. The fact that the members of the minority had a separate national identity only increased the sense of discrimination against them and of personal bitterness among them. It is no accident that, historically, the existence of multinational states, which granted recognition to the nationality of their minorities, was the outcome of the pressure by national movements in the European empires, the Austro-Hungarian and the Russian. These empires had been ready to recognize the existence of national minorities, while denying them the rights of the national majority, and without granting them any political compensation whatsoever. From the liberal viewpoint, therefore, the federate multinational state is preferable to a national state with a national minority. It is said that from a liberal viewpoint it is preferable not to have a national majority and not to have a national minority, because of the preference of having no nationality at all. This is the view that is unrealistic and thus mistaken. Further, this view rests on the reluctance to try and reconcile nationality with the love of humanity. The coupling of these two errors leads to the refusal to view nationality as a political force that may be harnessed for positive purposes. It is the refusal to admit that nationality can play a positive role as a political factor that caused liberals to overlook the suppression of the nationalist movements. In historical fact, however, the nationalist movement became so strong a political factor that to this day almost every attempt to repress a nationalist movement has failed, except in cases in which the nation that bore the movement was destroyed and the majority of its members killed.

In the modern world, Judaism preceded Jewish nationality. Judaism existed as a religion, as a community, or, in the best case, as a national minority that was discriminated against. Therefore, it was very difficult for the Jewish national movement to develop. The purpose of the Jewish national liberation movement was therefore full normalization, the establishment of the state that belongs to the majority of the people (62). The character of life in the State of Israel was determined to a large extent by the diverse displays of independence (some justified and some exaggerated). Nevertheless the populace fundamentally retained the character of a national minority and not of a liberated nation. The difference between the two is the difference in priorities on the political agenda. The major item on the political agenda of the minority is to cater to the majority (in the present case, to cater to the Jewish people, whose majority belonged to other nations). But the major item on the agenda of an independent nation relates to the present majority. The difference is not in that an independent nation caters only to itself and a national minority caters to others. The difference is in the sincerity of the catering. For, those who claim that they are not catering to themselves first are not honest, and thus not realistic, and thereby not able to cater to others. It is no surprise, therefore, that the policies of the diverse Israeli governments excel in lack of honesty and in lack of caring for others (63).

Israeli Jews see themselves as members of a national minority, both within the surrounding Arab nation and within their own scattered Jewish nation. This inhibits all Israeli responsible political conduct, of the kind that a ruling majority should show towards individual members of the minorities in their midst and towards groups of them. Therefore, the possibility that non-Jews should join the Israeli nation was denied. This is the reason for the existence of strong conflicts in Israel, without any outline of a way of reaching the solution, while holding in vain onto hopes that with time the solution would come by itself. The solution has not come and the postponement became a normal part of life in Israel, breeding frustration and despair as a part of everyday life here.

The position of the citizens of Israel who are not Jews is much more difficult, despite their status as Israelis with equal rights for all intents and purposes. They have the same confusion that the Israeli Jews have, in particular those who view themselves as Arabs in their nationality and Israeli in their citizenship. But because of the attitude of the Jewish public and the Israeli governments towards them, an increasingly large part of them view themselves as Palestinians for all intents and purposes, without taking account of their Israeli citizenship, which looks to them fictitious. And, indeed, as a result of the fact that the State of Israel does not recognize the Israeli nation, the non-Jews in Israel were not asked whether or not they ever accepted membership in the Israeli nation. They were forced to be Israeli citizens. They have no difficulty, therefore, in considering themselves Palestinians. This situation is dangerous for both sides, and it calls for a general and stable solution. But a major condition for the finding of a solution is the recognition of the existence of the very problem.

Should Israel declare that it ceases to be the state of a scattered nation, should it instead become the normal republic that belongs to its own nation, then the question will be open: Who belongs to the Israeli nation? This question ought to be recognized as open, since it still has no clear-cut answer, neither in Israeli law (especially since the Israeli Supreme Court declared the terms "Jew", "Hebrew", and "Israeli" identical), nor in Israeli tradition, nor in other Israeli social and public institutions, nor in the personal feeling of the Israeli citizen. Thus all Israelis, members of the majority and minority alike, have their national identity stolen from them. Who belongs to the Israeli nation, then? If we recognize that this question is open, then we could recognize the right of both the individual and the nation to self-determination. This is the reason that the nation must in principle offer to non-Jews (who to date have officially an alien and doubtful nationality) to decide whether they prefer to join the Israeli nation, or to stay in the country as resident aliens; in principle, it is not in Israel's interest to decide to which nations they belong. Every individual to whom the nation should offer the right to define themselves should be offered proper directives in order to help them understand the meaning of the choice and the benefit and loss that each alternative entails. It would be proper also to let them have all the time necessary to think and consult friends, relatives, and whoever else they may wish to consult. And during the period before they decide, and unless they decide, it should be assumed that they have decided in favor of being resident aliens. This is the central point in the whole of the detailed proposal brought here for consideration. For it is most important that the one who undertakes the initiative should decide what to do if the other side will not respond, or if the other side will respond this or that way.

The law should make it clear that the proposal to join the Israeli nation should be offered first and foremost to all the non-Jews who are today citizens of the State of Israel, since the Republic of Israel will be the legitimate heir of the State of Israel and will therefore inherit all its rights and duties and will honor all the obligations of the State of Israel including those towards its minorities.

What are the rights of the minorities in Israel? What guarantees should be given that they will not be violated? These are legal and social questions that must be examined with all seriousness. I will discuss here only the principle that should preferably stand behind these studies. It is clear that the *a priori* concern is the separation of state and religious institutions — this is the foundation of the New Israeli Republic. The application of this principle, as in all legislation, will concern those who consider themselves hurt by it and who should also have the right to proper compensation. For example, all those religious leaders who have been government officials, directly or indirectly (Jews, Moslems, or other), should have the right to compensation. In addition to this, the way by which the state may cater to the welfare of the diverse religious organizations must be tended to, as is customary in diverse democratic countries in Europe. It is clear from the very start, however, that all in all, both the non-Jewish individual who accepts the proposal and joins the Israeli nation and the one who rejects it and will agree to continue to stay permanently in Israel as a resident alien — both will enjoy a considerable improvement in this area. In addition, and this is no less significant, the membership of the Moslem religion will cease to endow its holder with an inferior status, and the Palestinian ethnic identity should cease to be an intolerable burden, since both religion and the ethnic culture will lose all political weight. Despite the fact that the majority of the members of the nation will be more interested in the support of the Jewish religion than of the Moslem religion, it may be hoped that the rule of tolerance and friendly relations will bring about inter-faith initiatives in Israel in a manner that would impress the whole enlightened world. The same should hold concerning the Palestinian culture of Israelis of Palestinian origin who, like Americans of Israeli or Palestinian origin, should be free to be proud of their origin. It may be hoped that they would view their contribution simultaneously as a contribution both to the ethnic culture and to the national culture — as is customary in the United States (64).

In this way, one of the major foundations of the absurd situation of the State of Israel concerning the equality of Arab citizens would be eliminated, and the distortion that has caused the corruption of the people in Israel would be rectified.

* Regarding the national minority, a severe deterioration took place since the appearance of the first edition of this book. To begin with, the non-Jewish Israelis had a religious and a linguistic — Arabic — identity, as well as an ethnic — Arabic — identity, but no national identity, certainly no Arab national identity. For, even the aspiration for a pan-Arab nationality that was instigated by Egyptian President Gamal Abdul Nasser failed totally. The conduct of Israel's government imposed on the Palestinians, the Israeli as well as the Jordanian citizens, an increased awareness of a Palestinian national identity, though still not clearly, since such an identity is impossible, unless the claim for the Arab national identity is abandoned, as it is utterly fictitious (almost like the Jewish national identity).

* The aspiration for a pan-Arab nationality is thus nothing more than the instrument for the restraint of the nationalist aspirations in all of the countries of the region (Jordan included). The pan-Arab aspiration is expressed by the contention that the full Arab nationality is already in existence, since, to repeat, nationalist movements do not recognize clearly processes of national crystallization. In the name of this nebulous nationality, Iraq invaded Kuwait. This nebulous nationality has prevented, and still prevents, a few Arab states (including Jordan, Iraq and Kuwait) from becoming nation-states, yet it is successful because the likelihood of becoming a nation-state in our region still is too small, since the countries of the region do not excel in their levels of general education, democracy or liberalism. Only Egypt sees the beginning of a national crystallization, despite its past pan-Arab tendencies, and despite its being far from educated, democratic or liberal. Perhaps other Arab countries are undergoing similar processes. This is hard to judge; since doctrines about nationality do not leave room for processes of national crystallization, there is no discussion of such processes and no information regarding them until they are almost completed. Even the concept of nation building that was once commonly used in the United Nations Organization has led to nothing and has now no specific usage, not even when it is used to denote the foundation of a new state that has no nation (as yet).

* The national minority in Israel has a national identity imposed on it, yet this is no sufficient reason for the development of a sense of national identity, and, indeed, only yesterday their sense of identity was limited to the sense of alienation, the sense of being marginal. But they could develop a relatively high standard of living, including education (general, vocational, and political). The little that their Palestinian national identity includes is rooted in the Israeli provocation, especially towards the Palestinians who inhabit the West Bank of the River Jordan, and who are not citizens of Israel. The strange result was that their rebellion was accompanied by a measure of a national awakening among the Arabic-speaking non-Jewish Israelis. Clearly, the current negotiations with the Palestinians who inhabit the West Bank of the River Jordan, who are not Israelis, cannot succeed because of the complications caused by the multiplicity of Palestinian groups and the clash of interests between them. This multiplicity constitutes a constant provocation for one segment to try and attain the advantages of the other. This phenomenon used to be marginal, but today, in the light of the Iraqi and the Yugoslav and the Georgian experiences, it is hard to avoid considering it a general phenomenon that demands attention to the national problem from a liberal viewpoint even when considering chauvinist groups that are devoid of national culture. This is not the place to discuss them.

* The peace talks in accord with the Camp David agreements are conducted in relation to the national aspirations of the non-Israeli Palestinians settled on the West Bank of the river Jordan whereas those settled in the East Bank of the river Jordan and in Israel do not obtain the same treatment. Israel still stresses its demand to negotiate with the non-Israeli Palestinians of the West Bank of the river Jordan on condition that they do not dwell in Jerusalem and do not recognize the Palestine Liberation Organization. It will become ever harder to overlook the other groups, and even those from the Palestinian Diaspora which is increasing in size since there is a great incentive for all displaced persons in the region to declare themselves Palestinians and there is no obstacle to their doing so. Sooner or later the absence of an Israeli initiative will bring about the demand to handle them. Israel will then find it very difficult to find a comprehensive stable solution to the then Palestinian problem because if it will fit one Palestinian group it will not fit another. The whole Israeli effort was wasted in a desperate effort to prevent the participation of the Palestine Liberation Organization in the process. This effort was doomed to failure, of course, since Israel used it merely as an instrument for the prevention of that consequence which that effort has rendered inevitable. An unconditional recognition of the Palestinian nation would have caused that doubtful and lackluster organization to disband or to alter radically. Israel's employment of its existence as an excuse for displaying no political initiative, provides it with distinction and an increase of prestige despite its many weakness.

* All that was said here provides no answer to the question, is the idea proposed in this chapter still viable? The assumption that a national minority in Israel can persist for long is a mere illusion. Therefore, it is clear that in principle normalization is more vital to Israel today than ever before, so that we are constrained to the choice between rendering Israel a normal nation-state and recognizing it as a bi-national state. One way or another, Israel will not be able to disregard the need to abolish the status of a national minority that is so

conspicuous here today. Clearly, a national state is preferable as long as this option is open (without expulsion and without appropriation, of course). As long as we can offer our neighbors a reasonable peace plan, it is possible to reach an agreement that will retain Israel's character as a one-nation state. To that end this discussion will be continued in the next chapter. *

Chapter 27: The Need for an Israeli Initiative to Establish Peace in the Middle East

Theodor Herzl said that the Jewish problem was not the problem of the Jews alone, but the problem of the whole of Europe, since the Jews of Europe constitute a political nuisance for all. This principle has become more and more accepted in diverse places; in the United States, for example, the claim is accepted that the problem of the Blacks is not the problem of the Blacks alone, but the problem of the whole of the American nation regardless of religion, race, or economic status. With the same degree of justice, it may be said that the Palestinian problem is no longer the problem of the Palestinians alone, but the problem of all the inhabitants of the Middle East, perhaps of the whole world. From the viewpoint of the Israeli national interest, the Palestinian problem is first and foremost the problem of Israel. The first political step, therefore, is to undertake the initiative towards recognizing this problem — recognizing not only the discomfort and suffering, but also the fact that these constitute a *political* problem, namely, a task awaiting a political solution. I will try to present what I consider a possible, just solution, even though with no certitude that all the interested parties would accept it. In contemporary Israel, even the presentation of a possible political solution might constitute a radical political change.

Moreover, for moral and political reasons, some facts cannot be overlooked. During the period of the first Knesset, Hillel Kook proposed to Prime Minister

David Ben-Gurion that the problem of the Palestinian refugees be addressed. He said it was impossible that the Jews, a people who had been persecuted for centuries, would not show sensitivity to refugees. Ben-Gurion showed a lack of initiative. He continued to act as a Zionist leader even after he was appointed the head of a sovereign government, thereby overlooking the responsibility of a sovereign government of a sovereign nation to solve the problems and protect the rights of members of other religious congregations and nations. Thus the problems of the Palestinians inside and outside Israel were and still are intentionally ignored. As a result of denying this problem, Israel faces increasing pressure to force it to agree to negotiations with the Palestine Liberation Organization. In order to balance matters, some meaningless pressure is exerted by Israel on the Palestine Liberation Organization to make it recognize the right of Israel to exist. As long as there is no Israeli initiative, the pressure will mount and a compromise solution might be found. The Palestine Liberation Organization will make some unclear declaration as a gesture, and Israel will be called to recognize this organization as a partner to this or that negotiation. Israel will refuse, most likely, and the more it justifies its refusal, the worse her situation will get. This is the reason Israel has to undertake a position of principle concerning the Palestine problem, that will enable it to undertake a unilateral political initiative on the road to peace.

The most common argument against Israel taking any political initiative is the argument that time is on Israel's side. At present this argument vanishes. For the time is short in which to try to prevent the possible damage and to act in the national interest and in humane consideration of the problem of its neighbors. But, to repeat, the obvious duty of every state is first and foremost to cater to the welfare of its own nation. As the theologian Reinhold Niebuhr says (see quote on p. 131), it might be hoped that a reasonable attitude to activity in the national interest will result in intelligent activity in the international interest.

This chapter is written from the viewpoint of the Israeli national interest. Every detail presented here concerning Israel's neighbors is not written out of a desire to intervene in their internal affairs, but out of a desire that Israel should be able to live with them in peace. The search here is for a proposal that will bring these neighbors to a position in which they will recognize their own interest in living in peace and in developing normal neighborly relations, and their own need to act accordingly. The next chapter, on political initiative towards peace in the region, makes two qualifications. First, our neighbors should be brought to this or that situation for one and only one purpose: helping them to recognize their own interest in peace and their need for activity to further it. Second, the proposal relates to our neighbors' existing situation without analyzing that situation and its stability. The proposal, therefore, should be altered in every case of political change in the region.

There is no need to enlarge on the claim that the Israeli national interest calls for peace in the region. The need to live in peace and in a peaceful neighborhood is known to everyone, even to those who hardly care for politics. There is no need to add that Israel has to live in peace with its neighbors, to stabilize normal neighborly relations. The need for normal neighborly relations constitutes an integral part of the proposal for internal normalization, as a normal state caters to the interest of its nation (and peace is a basic interest of every nation). And, of course, another relevant part of the proposal for internal normalization is the change in the status of the Israeli Arabs, who will turn after normalization part into members of the Israeli nation to all intents and purposes, and part into resident aliens, as they wish. Of course, by the idea of unilateral initiative, the prospect should be considered that most Israeli Arabs would become members of the Israeli nation as well as that they will not become Israelis.

The preference of the Israeli political establishment for no political initiative over taking some political initiative is rooted in its endorsement of the New Zionist Myth. This myth perpetuates the abnormalcy (which, to repeat, paralyzes all initiative). Further, the abnormalcy of Israel provides its enemies with propaganda weapons and excuses for their refusal to negotiate peace. This situation is comfortable for the Israeli leaders too, since, among other things, it justifies the perpetuation of the inferior status of the majority of Israel's citizens who are not Jews. The excuse for this is that not all duties of citizens can be imposed on them (not the duty of national military service) as is required in a normal state, since they are recognized as members of an enemy nation. The abnormalcy and the preference for it constitute a positive incentive for the political leadership of the abnormal State of Israel, to avoid exhibiting any political initiative that might further the Israeli national interest by the furthering of peace and sound neighborly relations in the region.

The keen reader will surely notice that some of the claims to be presented in this chapter have already been voiced by people who hold high office in the Israeli political establishment, and even by people who served and are still serving in this or that Israeli government. Yet, it is not the claims themselves that matter, but the use of them as part of a political initiative that will bring the neighbors to recognize that their interest is in peace and to show a readiness to forward this interest. For example, when the previous Egyptian President, the late Anwar Sadat, showed political daring in his peace initiative, many Israeli government leaders and party political leaders said in response that he was forcing Israel to cooperate with him. This is not to belittle the important role of the then Israeli Premier, Menachem Begin, in his having invited President Sadat to deliver a speech before the Knesset in Jerusalem and even expressed his readiness to speak before the Egyptian Parliament. These two moves are certainly exceptional in that they exhibited a dash of political initiative. But in the whole peace affair, Israel did not show much initiative.

Let us now move to a description of the situation in the neighboring countries and to a search for means that would bring them to recognize the interest of peace and to show readiness to promote it. First of all, the most stable factors should be stressed, for example, the fact that Jordan is a kingdom. Even this fact is not so stable, however, as the existence of the Hashemite kingdom for so long is no evidence of stability, since it exists under Israel's protection and by its favor. Israel favors this kingdom only because of its abnormalcy. This situation might change, especially if the proposal for normalization made here will be accepted and Israel will seriously consider the question whether support of the Hashemite kingdom promotes the Israeli national interest. This is no expression of either opposition to or support for the Hashemite kingdom; the principle of unilateral political initiative obliges the political leadership of Israel to bring the view of peace as part of a vital national interest for that kingdom or for factors that oppose it, so that Israel could then support any factor that will view peace as a part of its national interest.

The most stable facts in the region concern the national question. It is impossible to overlook these facts, and it is impossible to change them by sheer force. The desire to alter them must appear in a political plan to that end. The facts will be presented here, as a condition for every unilateral Israeli political plan.

First, the State of Jordan exists, even though there is no Jordanian people or Jordanian nation. This matter is not of principle but of fact: most Jordanians are Palestinians and Jordan claims sovereignty over areas populated with additional Palestinians and thereby claims sovereignty over the greatest majority of the Palestinians who are in the midst of the process of crystallization into a national unit. All this strengthens the Palestinian character of Jordan and has prevented the Jordanians from developing a process of national crystallization. The interesting aspect of this fact is just theoretical, and not practical, but this will not be discussed here.

Second, all denials of diverse Israeli governments and leaders on various occasions do not alter the fact: the Palestinian people are in the midst of a process of national crystallization. (The claim that there is no Palestinian "entity" is rooted in the fact that by bowing to the notion of the Arab nation, different leaders prefer to speak not of a nation but of an entity; this mode of speech displays the adverse influence of pan-Arabism on the development of national movements in the region.) This, too, is no historical necessity. As mentioned above, the plan of the Hebrew Committee for National Liberation had some likelihood for success, and had it succeeded, the majority of the original inhabitants of Palestine would have become Israelis for all intents and purposes; and the development of this national unit might have been prevented. Instead, a national unit might have developed on the east of the river Jordan alone, Jordanian or Palestinian, but not hostile to Israel, and so of no special concern to it. In such a case, Jordan would have been recognized as the Jordanian or Palestinian national state for all intents and purposes, and the terrible bloodshed in the Middle East might perhaps have been prevented. But all this did not happen. Today the Palestinian people are in the process of national crystallization. Nobody knows if it is possible or desirable to try to hold this process back. It is clear that the central factor in the development and the encouragement of this process is the Israeli policy of the systematic lack of political initiative, and it is quite possible that if this erroneous policy ends, the direction of the development will then alter and the whole situation will change.

Third, as to the plan for a Palestinian state in Judea and Samaria, there is no possibility of a stable, lasting state within such boundaries. This is so clear and self-evident that there is no need to discuss it. But in addition to this decisive argument, it may be pointed out that this plan has never been claimed to be a proposal for a solution to the problem of the whole of the Palestinian people but, at most, the solution for the problem of the minority of that nation that dwells in those regions.

* These facts are repeatedly obscured by new ones, but these new facts are in principle insignificant, as they do not reflect the national problem in our region. Repeatedly the Hashemite King of Jordan has washed his hands of the Palestinian people to the west of the river Jordan, in order to distinguish between them and their eastern kin, to stress their dependence on the Jordanian Government, and to present Israel in the position of a foreign conqueror in the whole of the territory of Palestine. Since he has no interest in enabling the Palestinian people to develop a national movement towards independence or to recognize the absence of a Jordanian nation, his declarations have no basic value, as they do not pertain to the national question in our region. The peace talks that were being conducted at the second edition of this book went to press were convened while Israel's demand was accepted to consider the Palestinian and the Jordanian delegations as one body, since Israel supports the Hashemite kingdom only as a means for it to disregard the Palestinian nationalist movement. Of course, even this demand was endorsed as mere fiction, devoid of all basic value, since the aim of the Israeli Government was not to reflect its attitude towards the national question in our region, since to date all Israeli governments took the same stand on the national question in our region, which is a total disregard for it and the denial of its very existence.

* Of course, new facts have to be considered even if they lack basic significance, but they cannot be discussed in this book. Similarly, the possibility should be considered that even far-reaching changes on matters of basic import could occur, since there is no basic reason for the absence of a Jordanian nation. Yet it is doubtful that such a change will occur soon. (The lack of a national crystallization characterizes the whole region, since its inhabitants are steeped in ignorance and their rulers either have no interest in national movements or else they prefer the large-scale, pan-Arab nationalist movement; it is no accident

that the most conspicuous national movement in the region is the Palestinian, as it is an offspring of the Jewish national movement.) If, nevertheless, a Jordanian national movement evolves, the picture here presented will be significantly altered. *

It is interesting to observe, by the way, that the Palestine Covenant, which is the political platform of the Palestine Liberation Organization, declares that the whole of mandatory Palestine (that is to say Palestine on both banks of the river Jordan) is the territory which they demand for themselves. This is, admittedly, boastful, empty verbiage, but it is clear that if this organization receives control over Judea and Samaria, it will try to create a military coup in Jordan, since the majority of the inhabitants of the East Bank of the river Jordan view themselves as members of the Palestinian nation. Afterward, they will try to do all they can to lessen the options open to Israel. It is desirable to assume that this plan of this ephemeral organization is not serious and not realizable; yet more and more states support this organization and its plan. Therefore, unless Israel shows immediate political initiative, it is quite possible that there will be enough folly in the world to support an attempt to execute this disastrous plan.

In mandatory Palestine today, there are two nations and two states, and all in all three entities. The State of Israel and the Israeli nation exist as one entity, but the Kingdom of Jordan and the Palestinian people are separate entities. The problem is not how to make it easy for these latter two separate entities to cooperate, but how to bring about their merger, in order that Jordan should be the state of the nation that dwells in it. The desire to use this merger for the purpose of peace should raise the question, what is the obstacle to this merger? The obstacle is, of course, the tactic used by both Jordan and the Palestine Liberation Organization: the claim that Israel has disinherited the Palestinians of their own motherland, and the use of this claim as an argument to demand the dismembering of the State of Israel. The very presentation of this demand is, indeed, the obvious obstacle to the attainment of peace. Therefore, the very presentation of the opposite, namely, of the fact that the area of mandatory Palestine was in fact divided between two people who live in it, and that the negotiation of its partition may be the basis for peace, is the first step towards the establishment of peace.

This detail deserves great emphasis. The ideological basis of the Palestine Liberation Organization is indeed the Palestine Covenant. This Covenant calls for the annihilation of Israel by unifying mandatory Palestine under the rule of a Palestinian government. Israel justly refuses to legitimize this Organization and justifies this refusal by pointing to this Organization's call to destroy Israel. But Israel itself raises the prestige of the Organization both in its claim that recognizing the existence of the Palestinian entity by itself constitutes recognition of this Organization and in its ignoring the conflict that the Palestine Covenant has created and strengthened between that Organization and the Hashemite kingdom of Jordan. Israel raises the prestige of that Organization because in that way it gains release from the duty of showing a political initiative. In this way, the present conflict between Israel and the Palestinians will stay unresolved.

* Israel demands regularly that the Palestinian representatives in the peace talks should not represent the Palestine Liberation Organization. This demand caused that organization to go to a transparent underground, and this enabled it to supervise the Palestinian delegates openly and to gain prestige during its low ebb, since the governments that are exerting pressure on Israel to continue with the peace talks endorse this organization's stance, all in total blindness to the fact that this organization has no interest in forwarding the Palestinian national interest and that these governments cannot exert pressure on it as they do on Israel. There is no substitute for the recognition of the Palestinian nation that is better coupled with the demand to replace its representation by a more representative and comprehensive one, a representation that will abstain from terrorist activities as long as the talks are conducted. The absence of an Israeli readiness to recognize the Palestinian nation is the sole factor that sustains the prestige of this terrorist organization. Regrettably, even the stand of this organization alongside Iraq during the Gulf War, which weakened it tremendously, did not bring Israel to take steps that would cause its dissolution. This organization exists because Israel insists on ascribing to it the monopoly over the national aspirations of the Palestinian people. Israel insists on this only in order to disregard these aspirations, but it succeeds only in strengthening that organization's position.

* The lack of initiative, then, is excused on the ground of the contention that Israel has no open options. This contention is fairly well justified: the absence of options is indeed a constant political fact. Except that the principle of one-sided initiative is a constant principle of attempts to create new options by effecting changes in the political situation. There is never an excuse for the abstention from taking one-sided political initiative, and certainly the position of the enemy or the neighbor cannot supply such an excuse, since in the absence of any new venues, the leadership always has available a simple option, even a duty, and that is to resign. *

Chapter 28 Political Initiative Towards Peace in the Middle East

Proposal: Israel should undertake a broad political initiative within some international framework, in order to achieve an overall peace agreement with its neighbors with or without the autonomy plan. The proposal has to include many details, and there is no way to mention them all here, especially since, of necessity, these details will be altered in accord with circumstances and the light of the different parties' reactions to them.

The first move of an Israeli initiative should be a declaration by Israel that it takes a solution of the problem of the Palestinian nation as in its own supreme national interest and that it is ready to act decisively to attain this aim quickly. To that end, it should declare recognition of the existence of the Palestinian people living in their country, which is today called Jordan, and that this recognition is unconditional, and depends on no further supposition. In addition, Israel has to call for the creation of a peace conference in which representatives of the Israeli and Palestinian nations should participate in order to discuss the cessation of the long and bloody conflict, that results from the fact that both nations claim sovereignty over the whole or over a part of the territory that is mandatory Palestine, as long as the identities of the sides will be considered not purely on religious or ethnic grounds, but as nations (65).

* As to different peace talks, if they are going on, then there is no need to cancel them, but Israel should either demand specific guarantees to secure that the ongoing talks will bring about a comprehensive and lasting peace or invite the other side to a serious negotiation towards peace, and, of course, this

invitation will by itself neutralize instantly all ephemeral talks. As the second edition of this book is going to press, Israel is doing everything possible to ensure that the peace talks will be of no consequence, as they are imposed on us, and to limit the very possibility that they might be fruitful to the option of creating an autonomous region in Judea, Samaria and the Gaza Strip and no more, even though, clearly, this plan will not solve the national problem, and it will thus only aggravate the situation. Israel is not concerned with such possible aggravation, and thereby it exhibits a lack of national responsibility. *

Israel should invite to the peace conference the government of Jordan, showing that it views the territory of the Jordanian Hashemite kingdom as a territory of the Palestinian people. Israel should also invite a broad representation of the Palestinians living in Judea and Samaria and the Gaza Strip and also as far as possible representatives of the Palestinian refugees who live in other countries.

* Israel is particularly hostile to the very idea of including the Palestinian refugees in the peace talks, and this, again, out of the lack of readiness to deal with the situation in a principled manner in the desire to find a radical solution to our problems. There is no need to examine the Israeli attitude to the problem of the refugees, as the place to deal with it is the negotiation table; Israel's interest is not to shelve the problem but to find a stable solution to it. *

The purpose of the peace conference is to turn the conflict between the Israeli and the Palestinian nations into a border dispute between two neighboring nations which are striving for normal peaceful relations through mutual recognition.

The starting point for the negotiations concerning borders should be the assumption that the Palestinian territory includes the area of the Kingdom of Jordan and that Israel is ready to negotiate about boundaries. The negotiations have to decide the sovereignty over the areas that exchanged hands during the Six Day War and to arrive at agreed borders and agreed security arrangements between the two states within this area. The negotiations should take into account the possibility of a large Palestinian state — seventy-five percent of the area of mandatory Palestine — to provide both for the legitimate right of the Palestinian nation to self-determination and the security needs of Israel through demilitarization of areas as agreed in the conference. This way Israel would not be choked and would have secure borders and would thus be able to satisfy the legitimate security needs of the neighboring country.

From an Israeli viewpoint the emphasis of this plan is on its generality. It does not depend on one or another Israeli position, since the Israeli representatives in the negotiations could represent any opinion accepted by the Israeli government at the time, including extremist attitudes, whether concerning annexation or the return of lands, not to mention other options, such as confederation or federation. From the Palestinian viewpoint, the very acceptance by the Palestinian nation of the proposal for negotiations will supersede the question of whether Israel's right to exist should be recognized, since holding this in question would prevent the Palestinians from developing their own interests. Even if there is no response to the Israeli proposal, the very act of making the proposal will forward the Israeli interest, and the Palestinian interest, and the goal of peace, for the initiative would turn into a challenge for the Palestinian people and their friends and supporters, and especially for the friends of the two peoples. In addition, current international pressure on Israel would immediately be reduced.

* As the second edition of this book is going to press the pressure on Israel is mounting, and the Israeli press plays the role of a pressure gauge reporting daily on its rate of rise or fall, showing no sensitivity to the hard fact that the longer the government postpones undertaking any initiative, the more this guarantees the increase of the pressure exerted on it by Western governments jointly. As the Arab states will recognize this fact, it will be an incentive for them to increase their demands on Israel in exchange for any arrangement. *

This is not the place to study the complex of problems the peace conference would have to examine, such as the problem of the resettlement of refugees, mutual compensation, division of water, free transit to the Mediterranean Sea, and the rights of citizens of both states to visit or reside in the neighbor's country.

Israel should initiate broad diplomatic activity in order to mobilize the support of peace-loving countries — especially the United States, Canada, Egypt, and the countries in the West and North of Europe — for efforts to convince the present Government of Jordan to agree to participate in the conference. Similarly, these countries should be mobilized to help, with the support of countries neutral in the conflict, to form the apparatus that would supervise proper elections of representation for the Palestinians who live outside the area of Jordan, so that they too might join the representation of the Palestinian people at the peace conference. Should the Government of Jordan refuse to join the conference, then such elections should be conducted also among the general public of Jordan. Should the Jordanian Government bar such elections, Israel should then recognize the representatives of the Palestinians outside the area of Jordan elected to participate at the conference as the spokesperson of the whole Palestinian nation.

This plan is proposed at a given stage, mainly as an example of a program initiated by a normal nation that considers intolerable the conditions of siege and permanent war it is living under. And now some brief comments on this program.

First, clearly, it is a program of unilateral initiative, since it takes into account the possibility of diverse responses from the diverse parties with which Israel has to negotiate peace. Similarly, account was taken of the consideration of incentives to encourage the other parties to act in the common interest — the interest of peace — since the representatives of the Palestinian nation at the conference will also be competitors for positions of power in the future Palestinian state.

Second, clearly, the plan fulfills the conditions mentioned in the previous chapter. It is not a plan for a state without basis in Judea and Samaria. It overlooks neither the fact that Jordan is a Palestinian country, nor the existence of the Palestinian people and its national aspirations.

Third, this program is in the interests of Israel. Hence, the abnormalcy of Israel is the major obstacle to attempts to realize it. Those who support the abnormalcy of Israel as a permanent state of affairs should take into account the possibility that, thereby, they support an obstacle to peace. In particular, one should respond to the claim that the plan proposed here is unlikely to succeed since the opposite party will not agree to it at all. This claim, true or false, is not to the point. For even if the plan is unlikely, there would be a dramatic change as a result of a unilateral initiative of the Government of Israel, since, at the very least, Israel's current political isolation would thereby be terminated. Contrary to the present situation, the pressure would be directed at those who refuse to participate in the conference, and they would be the ones to suffer isolation.

As to the plan itself, of course it should be adjusted to changing circumstances. But the specific to it is preferably left unchanged. It is that it is a combination of plans, the Palestine plan, the Jordan plan, as these are called by their advocates, and so it is an Israeli plan. The critic of the plan could say that there is no difference between it and the Jordanian option or the Palestinian option. Clearly, the difference between the proposal made here and the Jordanian option is that the former is also a Palestinian option, and the difference between it and the Palestinian option is that it is also a Jordanian option. More precisely, the plan proposed here is the Israeli option, as it is a program that will impose on Israel's neighbors recognition of her and the readiness to live with her in peace.

* The Jordanian option is a mere excuse. If it means the partition of Palestine between Israel and Jordan, then this option has been realized without solving the burning problems; if it means that cooperation between the two countries is desirable, then this cooperation likewise exists and has not solved any problem; the Hashemite kingdom still rules Jordan only because Israel supports it. Even when Israel declares readiness to withdraw support, the declaration serves no other purpose than to exert pressure on the Hashemite kingdom; in fact — the two coordinate and cooperate ever since they were founded (and even before). And the purpose of the support that all the governments of Israel have lent this kingdom is a matter not of principle but of expediency, of course, and it is none but the vain hope that this kingdom will prevent, or at least delay, the process of Palestinian national crystallization. It is time to ask, what is the value of this kingdom for Israel and is the traditional support for it desirable? The absence of a public debate on this question in Israel is rooted in the conspiratorial atmosphere that surrounds all discussions in Israel about relations with its neighbors; this atmosphere weakens its sovereignty. The fact that all the governments Israel ever had are parties to the attitude of its first government towards the Hashemite kingdom clearly points at the cause of the absence of an Israeli position and initiative regarding the national problem in our region: it is rooted in the abnormalcy of Israel, since any genuine Jordanian option will raise the question, after a solution charted in accord with that option will be realized, what will be the status of Israel's citizens who are not Jewish? Will Israel then allow the transfer of the areas inhabited mainly by non-Jews to pass to Jordanian hands after the Jordanian option will be implemented? But if the Jordanian option is one for the initiating of political action that will bring about the re-partition of Palestine between two nations, then there is no essential difference between the Jordanian option and the one proposed in this book. And if these two proposals are essentially similar, then those who take this option seriously have to say what this difference is and examine it.

The Palestinian option likewise is non-existent. If it is nothing more than the one-sided Israeli retreat, then the question is, what is the worth of such a retreat? The answer will be that it will help the Palestine Liberation Organization, and those who oppose a mere withdrawal are right, since a withdrawal with no arrangement for a stable peace is an invitation for trouble. If the Palestinian option means negotiations, then those who advocate it do not say who will represent the Palestinian nation and what should Israel do if there will be no response to the proposal that she should make, to open peace talks. If those who advocate this option have an answer to these questions, then their proposal is not essentially different from the one made here. If they have an answer and it differs from the one proposed here, then they should explain the difference between the peace talks on the pattern of the Palestinian option and the talks currently imposed on Israel, which are going on with no expectation that they will bring about a viable solution that will not be imposed on Israel. *

This Israeli plan stems from Israel being an accomplished fact, since anyone who discusses an Israeli initiative clearly should assume this fact *a priori*. The plan, to repeat, will bring about the unification of the state of Jordan with the Palestinian people — whether because, in fact, the Palestinian people are the legitimate people of Jordan, and the Jordanian Government is their legitimate government, or because the Palestinian nation, according to its own wish, would change the regime there and thereby create a different legitimate government. In any case, all this should terminate the present undesirable situation for Israel, in which the Jordanian Government claims in one and the same breath both that it is the legitimate government of the Palestinians on both banks of the River Jordan and that the Palestinians are a nation deprived of a motherland, since Israel robbed it of its motherland. In making such a claim,

Jordan deprives the Palestinians of their legitimate right to identify with their own state, and Israel does not point out the lack of logic and decency in the attitude of the Jordanian Government towards both the Palestinian people and towards Israel, because Israel is afraid to recognize the very existence of the Palestinian people.

With no political initiative on the side of Israel, Jordan can indeed use the existence of the Palestinian people as an instrument for putting pressure on Israel. But had Israel showed political initiative, it could very easily reverse the pressure and impose on the Jordanian Government the need to recognize its duty towards its own people, including the duty to advance the cause of peace, since the interest in peace is universal.

Serious readers should not be discouraged from seeking alternative criticisms of the program presented here, or from seeking an alternative plan. On the contrary, they are invited most heartily to do so. Since the plan proposed here is practical, geared to practical conditions, it will naturally require changes and updating until its successful execution.

Readers might have noticed the fact that in the whole of this chapter, and in the whole of this presentation of a plan for peace in our region, no consideration at all was given to the existence of the Palestine Liberation Organization. This is one of the strongest points of this proposal, for the force of this organization is sustained by the policy of Israel which, being devoid of initiative, prevent all initiative on the part of the Palestinians, except being destructive towards Israel. The moment Israel shows any initiative and enables the Palestinians to act in some constructive way, this Organization will either split and disintegrate or change radically by the acceptance of an alternative plan of one kind or another. All that is required of Israel is to propose, in complete accord with the most generally accepted international procedure, that if the supporters of the Palestine Liberation Organization want to participate in the election of delegates to the peace conference in accord with the plan proposed here, they will have to avoid the use of violence. In order to secure the broad participation of Palestinians in the elections of their representatives to the peace conference, the plan might need include a proposal for international supervision of the elections.

To conclude, those who reject this plan as unusual and in the realm of fantasy, and who claim that Jordan would not wish to consider the possibility of viewing itself as a Palestinian state, might be reminded that the King of Jordan has already more or less agreed to this quite a number of times, even though, to repeat, inconsistently so. But the plan does not depend on the wish of this or that individual: the Jordanian King said whatever he said under the pressure of certain circumstances. Israel, too, could create similar circumstances or encourage peace-loving factors to impose on their government readiness for peace or to replace it. After all, the power of the Hashemite regime in Jordan is rooted in the constant support of all Israeli governments. If, instead of that nondescript support, a new plan and a new initiative were to come forth, Israel would find no difficulty in goading the Hashemite kingdom to cooperate, especially if the initiative were for peace and justice. The Israeli interest is chiefly catering to the peace and welfare of the Israeli nation, and it is desirable for that purpose first to bring the Palestinians to the recognition that the existence of Israel might help them in forwarding their own national interest and second to create, thereby, a firm basis for joint interest, which in the course of time will normalize relations between the nations of the region.

* There is no detail more important as to any peace talks whatsoever, including those that are in process as the second edition of this book is going to the press, than the absence of regard of any party for the position and status of the Israeli Palestinians. In private conversations, all parties assert that this matter is not urgent, since Israeli Arabs still prefer their Israeli citizenship over any other option that they consider available. Even were this assertion true, it is no consolation, since it is as clear as day that Israel cannot prefer systematically the status of one Palestinian group over another, since this will be a source of instability and restlessness in the whole region. It is not possible that Israel will allow equal status to all Palestinians without having to choose between relinquishing all areas occupied mainly by Palestinians and seizing the whole of Palestine. Both options are impracticable, as shown by the bitter experience of the remnants of Yugoslavia. It is, therefore, clear that a lasting peace in our region is not possible without a radical solution of the national problem in Israel, and no civilized, humane, solution to this problem is possible except for normalization. However bad the situation may be, and however hard the solution offered here — normalization — may be to implement, it should not be viewed as obsolete until an alternative to it will be proposed. *

Chapter 29: Israel and the Jews of Other Nations

Israel's failure to recognize the Israeli nation is rooted in the fear of weakening ties between Israel and Jews of other nations. This chapter will therefore present a solution to difficult and increasingly severe problems that cloud the relations between Israel and the Jews of other nations, and propose a way to open healthy cooperation between them.

The contribution of Jews of Western nations to the growth and the welfare of Israel deserves profound appreciation. This is not to imply that the relations between Israel and Jews of other nations are normal, or that they have developed in accord with any plan whatsoever. The New Zionist Myth, according to which it is the duty of every Jew to migrate to Israel sooner or later, is not based on the assessment that the Jews of the whole world will migrate to Israel, but on recognition of the fact that such a demand creates a status of permanent and continuing affiliation that Israel sees as financially and politically desirable for itself despite its lack of realism. This is a fictitious affiliation, one that receives a sort of reality by the validity of the Law of Return, which holds the status of a constitutional law in Israel, and permits almost all Jews to become Israeli citizens merely by virtue of their being Jews. This law has no practical meaning for the Jews of affluent countries, since they do not intend to demand this citizenship. And in its present form, its very existence may even harm them. But this law has a practical political meaning for the Israelis who overlook its being impractical for the Jews of affluent countries, as they are not aware of the great price that they themselves pay for it. The Law of Return is an expression of the abnormal situation of Israel, and it thus enables Israeli governments to justify their neglect of their task of catering to the welfare of Israeli citizens, demanding of them not to expect this, as they are allegedly the pioneers who should cater to the Jews of the affluent countries and to their children and grandchildren. Israel thus remains, of necessity, not a nation with a clear size and structure, but the bridgehead for an unspecified number of people from other countries who might turn up in an unspecified span of time to a country with an unspecified territory (66). Hence Israel cannot belong to the region in which it is located, and this will increase the difficulty for Israel to overcome the ongoing state of belligerence with its neighbors. Admittedly, these difficulties are part of the internal affairs of Israel. But the Israelis expect the Jews of other nations to act in accord with this arrangement, to which the Jews of the other nations have never agreed. This fact distorts the relations between Israeli Jews and the Jews of other nations. For instance, Jewish Israeli youths feel resentment towards Jews from other nations because they view themselves as serving them in that they defend their occasional motherland. This resentment is expressed, among other things, in the support that these youths lend to the exaggerated demands that Israel makes of these Jews. Until now, the Jews of other nations have responded to these exaggerated demands of the Israelis with restraint and great tact. They have tried to overlook the resentment. Yet as long as the New Zionist Myth is established, the resentment will increase. Sooner or later there will be no escape from response to it. Jews of the affluent countries may respond by withdrawal from Judaism, as Georges Friedmann expected (see p. 133). And they may respond by withdrawal from Israel while adhering to their Judaism (be it their religious, cultural, or ethnic characteristics).

It is surprising that for the decades of Israel's existence, not even a few thinkers (among the Jews of other nations, particularly in the United States) criticized the Israeli Law of Return in its present wording. There was no one to claim that in its present wording, that law was undesirable, as it puts responsibility on the Jews of other nations for Israel's belligerent and deteriorating relations with its neighbors. The spirit of the Law of Return was just, vital and daring at the time of Israel's establishment. Today it is imposed on Jews of other nations, at least on Jews of affluent countries. It remains for them to disavow it and respectfully decline the doubtful service that Israel offers them — a service that they never requested in the first place. They should declare it preferable for all parties (or, if not for Israel, then at least for them), that the Law of Return be limited, so that it should apply only to those persecuted as Jews. (Israel should, indeed, limit the law to those persecuted as Jews.) A disclaimer coming from Jews of affluent countries will constitute not interference in Israeli internal affairs, but a responsible protest against interference in the affairs of Jews who belong to other nations.

This bears some expansion. It is easy to agree that the Jews are unique; every people is unique. It is easy to agree that, for generations on end, the peculiarity of the Jewish people lay in their abnormalcy, both as a people with no national territory, and as a combination of nation and religious congregation. This state of abnormalcy was terminated, or should have been terminated, with Israel's attainment of independence (when it inherited the achievements of the Jewish national liberation movement). Since independence, the Jews of other nations can have no claim for a national liberation movement. Hence, the Zionist Movement should be dismantled or altered radically. Yet it refused to be dismantled, as was required, and continues to behave as if the independence of Israel has not been achieved. While basing itself on the New Zionist Myth (which is masqueraded as old), it pretends to demand that all Jews should migrate to Israel. This myth is, thus, the refusal to recognize the independence of the Israeli nation and even of its state. This refusal is expressed in the continuation of Jewish ghetto life in Israel. Despite the New Zionist Myth, it should be clearly declared that the abnormal state of affairs has been terminated in all countries that permit free migration. It has been terminated in the victory of the revolution of the historical Zionist Movement, of the Political and Practical Zionist Movements together. Politically, therefore, the Diaspora has been terminated for all Jews whose conditions permit them to migrate to Israel. To be more precise, as long as Judaism was a nationality and a religion, the Diaspora was a national as well as a religious phenomenon — a phenomenon that was both political and religious. From a national-political viewpoint, the Diaspora was terminated by the independence of Israel for every Jew who was able to migrate here. Religiously, the Jewish people as a whole is still in the Diaspora till kingdom come. Therefore, the very fact of Israel's independence has effected the separation of nationality and religion for all Jews in countries that respect the freedom of migration (67). The refusal to recognize this separation perpetuates the Israeli ghetto mentality, which continues to fail to recognize Israel's independence.

Splitting the concept of the Diaspora into two — the political and the religious — was done by the Jewish national liberation movement, in full consciousness, and from its inception. The Hebrew Committee for National Liberation, headed by Peter Bergson, applied and developed this distinction. There is no escape from this distinction. The concept of the Diaspora is deeply rooted in Jewish tradition and is ramified in all areas of Jewish life. For the concept of the Diaspora to have any meaning at all in the modern liberal world, it has to be split every time it appears, into two factors — political and religious. Let us look, for example, at the concept of the Chosen People. It may be a part of the religion of a person or a religious community, but it certainly cannot possibly have place in the modern state without causing a national disaster and an international one as well. The same goes for the concept of the ingathering of the exiles. As a Messianic concept, it must be considered religious, but it embraces a political component as well, the revival of the people in the land of Israel and the creation of political conditions that permit migration to Israel for every Jew who wishes to migrate here. Jewish Messianism was always utopian to the core. From the earliest days of Political Zionism its purpose was not utopian and certainly not religious-utopian, least of all was it the utopia of a society living by purely religious edicts. There is a great danger for the world in every attempt to apply the utopian vision, including a utopia of a world clean of Jews and the utopia of a state clean of non-Jews. Much has been written about this matter and it need not be expanded on here; for obvious reasons it is not very pleasant to expand on it (67a).

The Jewish religion has a utopian component. This component was not rejected when Israel turned into a theocracy; thus Israel unwittingly became a utopian Messianic state. Israel became a theocracy not on the basis of any principle but, on the contrary, for lack of principle. Now Israel accuses the Jews abroad of a non-acceptance of the utopian assignment of the complete ingathering of the exiles, that is to say, of a world free of Jews. The accusers even disingenuously deny the obvious, namely, that this assignment is utopian. The proof of this is in the fact that the New Zionist Myth claims Israel ready to wait for the desired ingathering of the exiles, even for a thousand years, on the excuse that when this is fully realized, then, as is customary in myths, no one will have the choice but to recognize the Israeli nation that today is not recognized even in her own land, as if in consideration for the existence of the Diaspora and in the exhibition of goodwill towards the Diaspora. This excuse covers up the lack of political responsibility. The slogan that Zionism is still in its earliest stages demands that Israeli citizens be pioneers, sacrificing themselves and demanding nothing of their government in return. Therefore, it is to the benefit of diverse Israeli governments to behave as if Israel is not an earthly Israel, a political Israel with daily problems of her own, fighting for her existence. It is to their benefit to behave as if Israel is already today the heavenly Israel, the Messianic state whose citizens make no demands. This explains the lack of political initiative; the lack of action in earthly affairs on the part of diverse Israeli governments; the readiness of those governments to return repeatedly to the ghetto mode of activity while relying excessively on brute force. It is no surprise, therefore, that members of Western nations find it difficult to understand Israel; even Western Jews friendly to Israel find it increasingly difficult to understand what happens here.

Zionism fought for the Jewish individual's right to political self-determination — to live as a member of a normal, free nation. Theodor Herzl stressed that the freedom to choose migration to Palestine also clearly means the freedom to choose to stay in the country of one's origin. He saw in the creation of this freedom, as well as in assimilation and emigration, the abolition of the Diaspora. The New Zionist Myth is piously presented as if it were a part of the Zionist tradition though it is the opposite of the principles of historical Zionism. The logic of it is simple: historical Zionism had to be terminated through victory, yet the termination of historical Zionism was not accompanied by the termination of the Zionist Organization as should have happened, and this Organization sought a new justification for its existence. This justification was found in the claim that Israel is a Jewish state, that Judaism is a peculiar nation-religion, and that it is thus impossible to apply the principle of the separation of political and religious authorities of the modern nation-state to the case of Israel; Israel, it was claimed, must be considered a specific and unique political entity.

Admittedly, the existence of Israel as a sovereign nation-state in which the Jewish religion is the current religion of the majority of its members fully justifies the view of Israel as a Jewish state, in the very same sense in which France is Catholic, England is Anglican, and America is Christian — that is to say, not in any political sense, but in the normal sense in which it is used in Western, liberal, normal countries. (This was meant in Herzl's conception of the State of the Jews.) Therefore, clearly the separation of religious authority and state is no violation of religion but, on the contrary, the freeing of it from excessive dependence on the institutions of government. It is imperative for Judaism to be the religion whose affiliates are members of diverse nations the world over, like the religions of the liberal Western countries. The normalcy of the separation of nation and religion, then, is an integral part of seeing the situation in this way. This situation should be clearly recognized. Israel should declare clearly the separation between state and religious institutions, between secular and religious authorities. For that purpose, Israel must first declare the separation of membership in the Israeli nation and membership in the Jewish religious congregation. In this way the relation of Israel with Israelis that are not Jews and with Jews that are not Israelis will become humane and normal. As to the former, the impossible situation of a national minority that belongs to an enemy nation will be terminated. As to the latter, Israel's unjust and unrealistic demands of them will be terminated, including the demand for Israeli excessive self-sacrifice, which sacrifice is worthless for them. The road will open to healthy and normal relations between the Jews of Israel and the Jews of other nations.

Clearly, the confusion of the Messianic and the temporal is the cause of the unclear relations between the Jews of Israel and of other nations. This confusion has forestalled the reasonable expectations of good and close ties between the two groups. Things have gone so far that Israel, meant to be the solution to the problem of the Jewish people, has become the greatest problem for the Jews of other nations. A new sort of cooperation is required. The Jews of other nations have to be partners from the very start in the debate concerning this new cooperation. To be party to this discussion is not only a right of people sharing an interest, but also a duty that rests on Israel's justification of its abnormal conduct by assuming that it caters to the interests of Jews of other nations. In the long run this is an impossible situation. Unchecked, it will necessarily lead to the separation of Jews from their Judaism and more so to the separation of Jewish communities from Israel. The relations between Israel and Jews of other nations should undergo the process of normalization in order to preserve and develop common interests on diverse levels.

The separation in Israel between nation and religious community, as well as between state and religious institutions, the purpose of which separation is internal normalization, will afford, then, creative cooperation between the Jews of Israel and of other nations — in matters of religion and culture. A general discussion might be conducted concerning the possibility of erecting in Israel a world religious Jewish center or perhaps diverse centers of this kind. Similar options of creating spiritual and cultural centers, secular or religious, would also avail themselves. This way the dream of Ahad Ha'am and Martin Buber and their fellow spiritual Zionists to create in Israel a spiritual Jewish center would be realizable — on condition that it will not be identical with the state and its institutions (it should have no attachment to any government organization and no political character). Cooperation in spiritual, scientific, intellectual and technological matters would also be possible, as the dependence of Israel on Jews of other nations in exchange for self-sacrifice will give way to new horizons for creative initiative in the development of joint interests between organizations and public and private bodies and even between Israelis, Europeans, Americans and others. Herzl's dream that Israel would become an economic meeting-point between East and West would become possible with the establishment of peace in the region. The securing of relations between Israel and Jews of other nations would also terminate the present abnormal situation in which all the public bodies that sympathize with Israel in the United States, for example, are Jewish, and officially so, even though it is in the interest of both Israel and the United States for these bodies to be open to all.

This is not the place to discuss detailed reforms of Israeli-Jewish funds and other mixed bodies. Clearly, the Jewish Agency would have to undergo basic changes; Israel would have to cancel the concord with the Jewish Agency as an agreement that violates its sovereignty. Similarly, Israel must have a new system of relations, a more realistic one, with the World Zionist Organization, the World Jewish Congress, and similar bodies.

Clearly, also, the Jewish National Fund is obsolete and has no place in the new framework. Without going into details, one may observe that the guideline in all these decisions should be the preservation and strengthening of Israel's sovereignty, while upholding that Israel and the diverse Jewish organizations in diverse countries should not violate each other's autonomy and should respect each other's rights.

More generally, to repeat, no details presented in this plan are sacrosanct and the purpose of introducing them here is to illustrate the applicability of the principle in detail, and the need to update any application until the principle is realized. The principle of normalization itself is not a short-range but a medium range and perhaps even a long-range matter, since it concerns normalization of internal political and social structures, and of the foreign relations of Israel with her neighbors and with partners to the historical Jewish religion and culture. Miracles are not to be expected. But the responsibility of politicians to their nation should exceed the four years in which they stay in office. A politician moved by a sense of national responsibility must attend to the problem and struggle with a plan (even if it is not ideal) to bring the State of Israel to a normal state of affairs, even if there is no possibility of its immediate realization. Without medium-range and long-range plans, all short-range plans become petty, and those who execute them turn from politicians into social activists, and from servers of the nation to servers of their own narrow personal interests within some party-political framework. It is no accident that the bitter despair that gnaws at Israel receives its expression in discussions and conversations of relations to the Jews of other nations. Israeli leaders, stuck with no program and with a resultant helplessness, hide behind their demand from Jews of other nations for help and unconditionally loyal support. This requirement spells helplessness. Israel should change this situation and speak to Jews of other nations in a new tone — not from the position of a poor relative whose services are not properly appreciated, but from the siblinghood of proud participants in an ancient religion, a glorious tradition, and a rich culture.

* Since this chapter was written a radical change occurred between Israel and the Jews of other nations, when, in a moment of crisis the Jewish lobby in the United States of America displayed some hostility to Israel and a disregard for its demands. Regardless of whether this deterioration was temporary or accidental and of whether it will be prolonged (and the likelihood is of ups and downs), the myth of unconditional loyalty of the Jews of affluent nations to Israel was shattered, since Israeli Jews did not express amazement or astonishment or aversion; they thereby showed that there is in Israel a readiness to adopt a more realistic perception of the situation, namely, a deviation from the judgment according to a script that expresses a central national myth. This way, an even more important myth was shattered, of the possibility of Israel relying on unconditional loyalty. It is thus clear that Israel ought to consider the possibility of a conflict of interest between itself and Jews of other nations, and this consideration will be expressed chiefly in a new mode of thinking. The same holds for the attitude of the Jews of other nations towards Israel: their attitude towards Israel is still positive and full of goodwill, but a change has started there, a certain maturation, a certain improvement of relations rooted in the recognition of the possibility of separation.

* This is a most important classical liberal idea: cooperation is always better voluntary than imposed. In order to transfer the cooperation from an imposition to self-interest, there is a need for a radical change in this web of relations. To that end it is, of course, imperative for Israel to discuss the national question and the normalization proposed here. *

Chapter 30: The New Zionist Myth

According to the New Zionist Myth, membership in the Jewish people is a duty of every Jew, as is migration to Israel. It is difficult to argue with a myth, especially this one, since it does not clarify what the sense of this duty is — religious or national. Of course, the myth does not clarify this point, since its very purpose is to perpetuate the confusion between religion and nationality, supporting the view of the Jewish faith as simultaneously a faith and a nationality. But experience shows that if one does not take a myth with intellectual seriousness (even if it does not deserve it), it receives the value of legitimate intellectual coinage and imposes its own intellectual patterns. "Myths think for us", says the French thinker Claude Lévi-Strauss. And if a myth does not think for us well, it is better relinquished, and the sooner the better.

The new myth is disguised as traditional Zionist theory. It is easy to show, however, in a manner convincing to every historian, that the traditional Zionist theory was the heir of the theory of auto-emancipation and called for the self-liberation of the individual Jew, and even while emphasizing that it did not deem itself a competitor either to the Jewish religion, or to the nationality of Jews satisfied with their situation as it is.

Advocates of the New Zionist Myth have to admit its novelty. They may view as the source of its novelty the terrible disaster that befell European Jews; in particular, they may note the failure of German Jews to remain members of the German nation despite all their goodwill, effort, and success in disguising themselves well and in generally looking like Germans.

As the New Zionist Myth receives this justification, it changes unrecognizably. This justification does not justify the myth at all, but confuses it with another myth that it does justify. The justified myth is the claim that there is no escape from hatred of Jews wherever they dwell, and that, therefore, all efforts to evade this hatred must fail, except for the return to Zion. The conclusion that this leads to is that sooner or later the Jews of the United States will be meted the same bitter lot as the Jews of Germany, and even Americans not aware of their Jewish descent will be persecuted and forced to seek refuge, and then they will find no refuge except, of course, in Israel.

The first question to ask those who seriously endorse this claim is, why is the wording of the myth cast in the language of duty, and defended in the language of inevitability? This may be done by the claim that, since one has no escape from being a Jew, it is one's duty to recognize it. This claim transfers the duty of individuals to the community to which they belong; it thus belongs to the Romantic Chauvinist philosophy, whereas the philosophy that emphasizes the duty of the individual as the responsibility of individuals to themselves belongs to the Enlightenment Movement. Both have been represented in this book as defective; in their place a new philosophy was presented that emphasizes the duty of individuals as their responsibility to themselves, to their neighbors and to their communities. Therefore, the purpose of the present discussion is not to reduce the responsibility of Jews as members of their religious communities or ethnic culture, nor to reduce the responsibility of citizens to their own countries. But this responsibility of individuals to their communities is a matter of free choice. Therefore, basic to the principle of normalization presented in this book is the recognition that duties and responsibilities are applicable to the individual who freely belongs to a religious community, and the same is true of national culture and of the nation. The myth that imposes on the individual involuntary membership in the nation-religion is the claim that there is no escape from this membership. The proof for this rests on the pathetic assumption that is a mixture of an empirical fact about the Jews in Nazi Germany with crude Romantic philosophy.

Let us leave all this then, and turn to the question, not to the myth presumed to be an answer to it: What would happen if the Jews in Western countries were persecuted as Jews? Today, Israel is their potential state, and therefore they can find refuge here. But should Israel accept the proposal of normalization, will she not, thereby, neglect them?

In fact, it is Israel that insists that the Law of Return should remain valid; Jews of other nations do not require it, and many of them are not pleased with its present wording. The claim that some time or another this law might prove useful to them does not explain why it is desirable to keep it in its present wording when it is not useful, especially since, to repeat, it is harmful. Nor is this the end of the discussion. For one can examine the way Israeli Jews and Jews of other nations respond to the question, what will Jews do in case of persecution in their own countries? When this question is addressed to normal Israeli Jews, they answer with a sense of victory: Of course they will come here, to Israel. This sense of victory testifies that these Israelis do not see themselves as sacrificing themselves for these potential victims of persecution, and indicates that they expect this persecution. This expectation makes the Law of Return dangerous in a few respects. It is what the sociological literature calls "a self-fulfilling prophecy".

When the same question is addressed to American Jews, for example, they answer as members of their nation. They respond as patriots willing to fight any deterioration in their country, and who quite rightly consider the rise of hatred of Jews as deterioration. This response shows that the Law of Return, as now worded, not only enables Jews to become Israeli citizens; it also expresses a refusal to see their belonging to other nations. Indeed, deeming itself the state that belongs to the nation-religion, Israel refuses to consider Jews as belonging to other nations.

It is self-evident that when a part of the nation is persecuted, that part may escape, as individuals or as a group, and even as a group that will develop a new national sentiment. This is what happened to the English Puritans who escaped to New England and this is what happened to the Jews in Europe. Is it possible to surmise what would happen if and when American Jews will be persecuted to the point that they will have to escape and will be willing to do so? Is it so clear that they will then be willing to escape to Israel? Is it already so clear today that this move would be wise? Let us assume then, that around the year 2,000 apocalyptic events on the North American Continent will bring the Jews there to a situation similar to the one German Jews found themselves in. Will the concentration of the greatest majority of the Jews of the world in a small territory like the State of Israel be a practical solution even in such an apocalyptic situation?

The New Zionist Myth gives rise to these hard questions. Anyone who sees in this myth a workable positive idea should consider them seriously. The fact that in Israel nobody studies them proves that nobody here takes the New Zionist Myth seriously. This is not to say that it has no weight in the cultural life of Israel. It is repeatedly stressed as a serious argument against the idea of normalization whenever someone tries to speak in its favor. It is time to discuss the proposed normalization seriously and not to reject it out-of-hand on the mere basis of a deceptive and dangerous myth.

Therefore, Hillel Kook proposes a new wording of the Law of Return as a constitutional law that would guarantee refuge in Israel for all those who are persecuted as Jews, and would leave the matter of the right of immigration of Jews who are not persecuted to immigration laws in any form decided by the constitution. I do not know if his suggestion is the best but, clearly, as a normal sovereign state Israel may make a law to express readiness to extend refuge to the persecuted as Jews.

* Till now Israel showed no readiness to reject willfully any project for massive immigration of Jews who wish to immigrate. But already now the beginnings of such an attitude appear, and even were this not so, the question should be asked, what is the guarantee that future Israeli governments will not refuse entry to Jews? For the demand to retain the Law of Return unaltered is endorsed by many Israeli Jews who are not happy about it, just because they find in it the required guarantee for the right of return for every Jew, regardless of the government and its short-range needs.

* There is some logic in this attitude, yet it is erroneous, especially because in the absence of normalcy the Israeli attitude to democracy is not healthy. Obviously, there is no way to guarantee that Israel will never prefer to prevent the entry of more Jews, and that the Law of Return will not stop this preference, as Israel is an autonomous state that can alter any of its laws. Being abnormal, Israel can even leave the law as it stands and suspend its application in specific cases, even for no better reason than convenience, as it does in many cases even today, though such conduct endangers its very existence as a law-abiding state

(and there is no democracy without the rule of law). Israel keeps some laws on the books more as declarations of intent than as rules to be obeyed. And the Law of Return is kept this way, on the pretext that it is incumbent on Israel as the unique country of all Jews. It is as clear as day, however, that Israel is an autonomous state where Jews of other nations have no right to vote or legislate or influence the sovereign state. Admittedly, the abnormal character of Israel is legally expressed in its belonging not to its citizens, but due to circumstances it does not belong to the Jews of the world either, and as Hillel Kook stresses, the absence of normalcy invites irresponsible conduct on the part of its government: Israel is not a free country as it is enslaved by a myth. It is, therefore, clear that were Israel's government to decide that it should delay a wave of mass immigration, it will not find it difficult to do so. It is known that to maintain its character as an immigration country it needs education to that end, and such education should be democratic. This requires normalization and frankness as to the position of the Jewish and Zionist leadership towards the destruction of the Jews of Europe during World War II, so that when we say "Never again!" it should be clear to us that we do not mean that we will stand up against the whole world and prevent the slaughter of Jews, since we do not know how to do that, but that we mean that we will not permit our own leadership to display helplessness in the face of a national disaster, Heaven forbid. To that end clear speech must be adopted and every important issue must be raised clearly and put on the public agenda for public debate, even in unpleasant cases. This is the character of democracy. *

PART FOUR

Conclusions

The theoretical and historical parts of this book present the background to the situation in Israel in accord not with Hillel Kook's ideas but with my own ideas and researches. My presentation is in the spirit of his ideas and his philosophical contribution to my researches in the field in which I had worked and published a few studies that are not unknown in professional circles. It was clear to me from the start that it is possible to view human collections or groups from social, cultural, economic, and political viewpoints. By custom, the social group is called a society, a stratum, a national society, or even a tradition. The cultural group is called a culture, a sub-culture, a sub-sub-culture, or an ethnic group. The economic group is called an economy, a market, a class, or an economic organization. The political group is called a nation, a political party, or a pressure group. For my own part, until I met Kook, I refused to call any political group by the name of a nation. For this I had good reasons and bad, and I will return to them later in this discussion. Kook corrected me, and this correction is presented in this book. Similarly, I have tried to emphasize a single, or perhaps dual, philosophical peculiarity in his thought. The one is the concept of the autonomy of the individual, who has the right both to liberty and to self-determination, including the right to national self-determination, which contributes to the right of the nation to its national self-determination. The other is the concept of the political autonomy of individuals as initiators, as actors responsible for their own activities. It is well known that in the theory of action a supreme significance is attached to the purpose ascribed to actors and to their understanding of the situations in which they act. Not enough attention was paid in the professional literature to the very important possibility of interaction of the aims of an activity with actors' assessments of the situations within which they act. There is a desired goal that does not change with the situation. Economists call this the long-term goal, students of logistics call it strategy, philosophers call it the ideal or the guiding principle, and political scientists call it utopia or aspiration. There is also the short-term goal or tactic or the immediate goal of action. Whichever name it has, it presents immediate targets in accord with the long-term goal, that is to say, in accord both with the strategy and with the details of one's assessment of the situation within which one acts. But Hillel Kook's thought is placed in particular in the range most interesting from the theoretical point of view, the medium range, which is almost entirely missing in the theoretical literature (68). The medium-range of strategy is of great theoretical interest, for in this range the goal strongly interacts with the assessment of the situation. The strength of the theory in the medium range is this. The goal and the assessment of the situation influence activity and, moreover, the assessment of the situation itself becomes a major factor in the determination of the goal (the possibility of attaining a goal in real terms), though not necessarily of the immediate goal. The theory deals here with bootstrap operations, or with people who pull themselves out of the morass by their own hair, as the famous Baron Münchhausen has done. For the assessment of the situation alters radically by the very invention of means for the goals' possible realization (69). One way of summing up Part Three above is to say, its purpose was to show that all the steps proposed by Hillel Kook have the character of bootstrap operations.

* To my regret, most of the scholars who have commented on the first edition of this book responded to the practical proposals in it and claimed that they are not sufficiently practical, or that they are no longer practical, even if they once were. Yet this book stresses that all the practical proposals in it are mere illustrations of two basic ideas in it that are important both theoretically and practically, as new ideas that are absent from the theoretical and the practical literature, and whose significance does not depend on changing details. The one is the liberal idea of the two-way principle of national self-determination (of the individual and the collective), that sanctions liberal nationalism (both theoretically and practically). The other is the idea of one-sided political initiative, which is the principle of practical politics; while politics and political life last it cannot be extinguished. *

Chapter 31   *Personal Summary: Concerning Israeli National Identity*

With the reader's permission, I start this chapter with some autobiographical details. Perhaps they do not belong here, perhaps they do — I defer to the reader's judgment. In my adolescence I participated in the political activities of youth movements, including the one whose graduates joined the Irgun National Military Organization. I detested their nationalist fervor, which I found opposed the idea of the unity of humanity, and soon I distanced myself from them. I participated in activities of other youth movements, most of whose graduates joined the Haganah Defense Organization, and believed that nationalism is permitted only to the extent that it does not contradict the principle of the unity of humanity. Eventually, I detested them too, because their behavior did not conform to that principle. The matter is of the absence of conformity concerning political questions, as they constantly discriminated between Jew and non-Jew. The same holds for social questions, as the whole of the Jewish settlement in Palestine, then and now, offered no chance of entry into society except to members of "our crowd" — those who belong to one establishment or another. One not trusted by one's superior was doomed, and neither competence helped one then, nor excuses, nor even connections. I never belonged to "our crowd", certainly I was never deemed trustworthy, nor did I try to be. Thus, I found no place in recognized frameworks or networks. Consequently, I was attracted to independent thinking, and to Marxism. I did have an intense desire to be accepted, but not as a member of "our crowd" nor as a trusted member of the establishment, but merely as a civilized human being. I had no chance. My life as an adolescent and as a youth was very painful. I remember as a particularly painful blow the fact that I did not succeed to integrate myself militarily, whether in the Irgun Military Organization, the Palmach Shock Troops, the Haganah Defense Organization, or even the Israeli Defense Force, despite my qualifications. During the War of Independence, I was the only parachute instructor who remained without a role and only because I identified with the Hebrew Communists (70). I remember, as an additional blow, the damage done to me some time afterward by an intervention of the Israeli Ambassador in London. He was on sufficiently friendly terms with me, but he found it necessary to prevent private financial support from going to an Israeli student from a local Jewish benefactor. He demanded forcefully that the person who had promised to help me revoke his promise. This was done for the utterly impersonal reason that the arrangement was not made through proper channels. This is no complaint, since sooner or later I was very lucky. I have two reasons for telling all this. First, I want to draw attention to the damage to the individual caused by abnormalcy. Second, I want to illustrate in a personal manner the crucial difference between Hillel Kook and myself. He was involved with the public to which he belonged, and drew great personal and national pride, support and strength, from being in his youth a member of the Haganah and the Irgun (since at a very early age he was a member of the headquarters of the latter). I remember again the opinion of Charlie Chaplin that only those who had a peaceful and cheerful youth become patriots. His opinion is false, but it provokes thinking. In any case, apart from my private life and my academic career (the latter is summed up mainly by my teaching and in my publication list), I have no more personal, biographical details to tell. My teaching, studies and research do connect with my political reasoning, and thus they do link with the topic of this book, but I have already mentioned them at the early part of this book, and all that remains for me to do is to conclude. But my wish is that the conclusion should be personal, and so I chose to speak personally in this paragraph.

Though I was always interested in politics, I used to look with suspicion, and even hostility, at the feeling of national pride, since many a time it meant discrimination in favor of those who belonged to the cream of the nation. It meant discrimination, especially between those who are thought to deserve privileges, "our crowd," and those who, not belonging to "our crowd," could be rejected despite their suffering and with no consideration of the injustice thus incurred. In addition, members of "our crowd," instead of protesting against discrimination, express pride at their belonging to the discriminating group (and perhaps even pride in the affiliation of the discriminating group with the nation that has created a great culture, even though this culture is a closed book for those who are proud of it). I cannot describe my feelings of displeasure towards the Israeli International Bible Quizzes, which in their great popularity conceal enormous public ignorance and display frivolity by considering knowledge to be the ability to recall trivial details from a text that is a spiritual creation of great magnitude and egalitarian character; they have turned a great cultural treasure into a collection of chauvinistic faded coins. Perhaps the feelings I have had that come closest to national feelings relate to the joy I have felt about Israeli cultural achievements of one kind or another, as also the shame I have felt whenever I have witnessed Israelis exhibit their cultural poverty (at home or abroad). I always felt that Israel's cultural achievements are mere confection and luxury that do not reduce the suffering of the second Israel [Jews of non-European descent] and the third Israel [non-Jewish Israelis], that did not make these sufferings less harsh or less troublesome for the conscience of people who possess a conscience. Thus I noted, with a sense of helplessness, my inability to participate in Israeli political activity. And since religion has become increasingly a political force in Israel, I find it increasingly difficult to say in Israel that I am a Jew, though in other places I declare myself a Jew without difficulty. In retrospect I could see this frustration, and the intellectual and emotional system that this frustration blocks, as a strong nationalist attitude. But only in retrospect, and only with the help of my friend Hillel Kook, who declares himself as one hundred percent Jewish and one hundred percent Israeli. Had I been informed of his way of thinking before the establishment of Israel, or immediately afterward, perhaps I would have become a different person.

Why did I not know? How did it happen that Peter Bergson (Hillel Kook), who was contemptuously declared a merely successful public relations person, failed in Israel in the minimal public-relations activity of appearing within the range of vision of young people interested in our national crisis? Why did all my complaints about the ghetto character of Israel, which I voiced among friends and acquaintances for decades, not meet even the beginning of a proposal that I should try to meet Hillel Kook? There is evidence here, to a large extent, of the strength of a society enclosed in its own ghetto, in a voluntary ghetto, to defend itself against spiritual influences that would threaten its tenets. Omissions of this kind are as old as the Talmud which has lost all memory of the ideas that the Talmudic rabbis considered harmful, and even the Maccabees are mentioned in the whole of the Talmud only once and incidentally. Of the opinions of the Sadducees there is almost nothing in the Talmud. As for the Essenes, the situation is even worse: their very existence is not mentioned in the Talmud (we know of them from other sources). From antiquity to the beginning of Zionism is a long distance. Zionism itself was radical and to a large extent deviated from Jewish tradition and was even often hostile to it. Nevertheless, the diverse strains within the history of Zionism and the history of the Jewish settlement in Palestine were forgotten. The story of the disarming of the first defense group, Hashomer, for example, was forgotten, though it was an admired organization, only because it was a dissident group. Other organizations not acceptable to the establishment were likewise consigned to oblivion. Today there is much to remedy in the official history taught to the sons and daughters of Israel.

There is here, to a large extent, a cover-up under a cloak of secrecy, excused as allegedly required by national security. I have tried not to discuss questions of national security in this book, since this is a political book, not a military one, and since the tendency of the liberal, democratic idea, accepted throughout this book's discussion, is towards maximal openness to as broad a public debate as possible, and towards trust between ruler and ruled, whereas the tendency of military theories is, with almost no exception, to endorse this or that level of secrecy. Admittedly, from time to time, the claim is heard, which seemed to me so reasonable, that following a successful armament, or as a part of it, care should be taken to see to it that the restrained party should know, as much as possible, the strength of the force that restrains it. But in Israel, even the weakest appeal to national security usually suffices to justify secrecy. In Israel secrecy is exaggerated beyond imagination. Immediately after the establishment of Israel, military censorship was used to screen more than military information. Even the report of the Agranat Commission, which studied Israel's failures and helplessness prior to the Yom Kippur War disaster, is still mostly kept classified, despite its having lost all military import.

This is one example for my claim — and it is the claim of Hillel Kook — that a ghetto with an army is more of a ghetto than a traditional defenseless ghetto. When the military is itself a ghetto, then it is a harsher ghetto than usual. This is dangerous, because Israeli education presents military service as a supreme goal to every boy and girl in elementary, middle and high school. This enables and even tempts educators, teachers, and youth leaders to introduce conformism into the educational system in the name of the national interest and for the sake of national security. This holds true particularly forcefully in the *Gadna*, the paramilitary youth organization under military aegis. The *Gadna* may easily raise militaristic aspirations in an educational organization, while evading public criticism under the excuse that it is a military organization. The paramilitary youth organization in Israel thus constitutes a danger to the peace of Israel. The new Israeli republic will have to handle this matter decisively and swiftly. Despite secrecy, some information about the Bergson Group did appear in the daily press in Palestine. This information was marginal and gossipy and so it did not reach my ear. Much later, in April 18, 1975, Hillel Kook and Shmuel Merlin published a full-page advertisement in various leading Israeli newspapers. The advertisement set off no echoes. At least such echoes never reached my ear — until I met Hillel Kook himself. Israel is a ghetto, a ghetto with almost no reprieve. This is why I discussed, at some length, the question, is Israel a normal state that is abnormally oppressed and has to be liberated, or is it an abnormal people who refuse to be a normal nation? There are so many ghetto phenomena, I think, in the Israeli public arena, in Israeli workshops, in Israeli schools, and in the Israeli legislature, that perhaps there is no hope left, and perhaps this book is one person's attempt to make peace with oneself and nothing more than that.

I do not wish to close this summary conveying the feeling that the place of the Jewish religion is necessarily in the ghetto. On the contrary, I think that the offense that the State of Israel commits towards Judaism (Judaism as a faith that I am not bound by and as a culture with which I am affiliated) is its behaving as if Israel and the Jewish people are obliged to live in the ghetto till kingdom come. The Jewish faith is a matter of at least two, if not four thousand years. The ghetto is clearly the product of the European Renaissance, at most one form of a traditional Jewish way of life. But there are many traditional ways of life within Judaism, all of them cultural and humane, and the ghetto way of life in its achievements is only one of them — one that was imposed on its residents. It may serve as a source of pride despite its narrowness. But as a sovereign nation we cannot be proud of voluntarily accepting it as an imposed, narrow formula. The separation between nation and religion is advantageous from the viewpoint of religion, for it permits the blossoming of Judaism, which in turn will serve as an inspiration to the developing Israeli culture of a renewing sovereign nation.

In my outlook I am no optimist. For I see the world as a set of neglected opportunities. But I do think that it is the duty of all humans to give their neighbors the benefit of the doubt, and this means that I have the duty to look at my neighbors with an optimistic eye. I also think that the great political revolutions were all failures, and yet they have nevertheless contributed to the achievements of humanity, because of their moral-educational value (71). Therefore, it is desirable to initiate great political revolutions in order to offer the nations participating in them the opportunity for moral education. These words are written in dark and bitter days. During these dark moments, when many of the intellectual and political leaders in Israel comfort themselves with minutiae, I found in myself a very strong desire to dissociate myself actively and clearly, to disengage, to distance from Israel, to entertain the very thought of emigrating; except that I have had an equally strong desire not to run away.

Through this refusal to run away, a shocking and joyful occasion presented itself to me, the opportunity of meeting Hillel Kook and learning that my refusal is nothing but the legitimate national sentiment, namely, the national attitude or position that does not render its holder suspect as a chauvinist, because it involves dealing sensibly with the question, are the narrow national interest and general human interest identical, do they limit each other, or do they conflict with each other? In the legitimate national sentiment, the desire to abolish discrimination and to bring peace to the region are central to the national interest and to the general human interest simultaneously. To see the deterioration of the State of Israel as harmful to members of the Israeli nation, members of neighboring nations, and humanity at large. The question, therefore, is, how can one harness the members of the nation to the national interest in the name of decency and of the right of all the members of the Israeli nation to national identity and even, like all nations, to national uniqueness and national pride while showing concern for the peace and the welfare of the nation and hope for a better future? A person with a sufficiently clear national identity, who is part of a sufficiently clear national entity, will find it easier to seek and find solutions to the whole set of difficult national problems on the national agenda, and thus even transcend them towards a global solution (72).

Chapter 32 Cultural Conclusion: Concerning the Unity of the Jewish People

The political corollaries should be noted for the disregard of the Israeli national identity and the diminution of the Israeli national sentiment. There are many arguments for this. The most common among them is that there is no room for Israeli nationality because there is room only for stress on Jewish nationality and its grounding. Of course, this Jewish nationality should apply not only to Israeli Jews but also, allegedly, to Jews of other nations. Does this mean that the Jews who live in other countries are not members of the nations of their countries? This is true of the Jews of the Soviet Union and her satellites, but not of the Jews of Western countries, since these Jews generally belong to the nations of their countries. The claim for Jewish nationality, then, may contend that Western Jews have dual nationalities. If so, then why should there not be Israeli nationality, so that the Israeli Jew might have a dual nationality, just like a French Jew? Why, then, is it not possible for a person to be both an Israeli and a Jew (72a)? This question can be answered as follows. The French nationality of the French Jew, as much as the Israeli nationality of the Israeli Jew, says the defender of the *status quo*, is a mere administrative affair, whereas the nationality of all the Jews is a matter of profound roots that leave no room for an additional nationality.

This opinion prevails in Israel, but not systematically and consistently. On the contrary, when Israeli Jews meet Jews of other nations, at times they tend to emphasize what they have in common and ignore the difference quite out of hand; at other times they tend to emphasize the difference and deny the common — sometimes so much so, that they express the readiness to identify themselves as Israelis who are not Jews. Of course, swinging from one pole to the other this way is a confusion rooted in the New Zionist Myth, since the myth does not allow one to consider a national variance coupled with a religious-cultural similarity. The myth, then, imposes the choice between admitting national unity coupled with religious unity, and national difference coupled with religious difference.

In fact, people from different countries may share the Jewish religion and differ in their nationalities, and this difference is not a mere administrative matter but a significant political matter. To overlook it is to be politically irresponsible and religiously intolerant. Let us hope that there is no need to repeat that the New Zionist Myth robs Israelis of their national identity and Jews of other nations their right to national self-determination.

There is a simple political sense to the imposition of the New Zionist Myth of an Israeli national identity on the Jews of the other nations and to its identification of the terms "Jew" and "Israeli." The same holds for the New Zionist claim that Zionism and Judaism are in principle identical. All those who are hostile to Israel for any reason whatsoever, and all those who are hostile to Zionism for any reason whatsoever, are made by this myth, and as a result of this myth, into persons hostile to the Jews of their own countries. Hence, the identification of the nation and of Zionism with the Jewish religion is no defense of the Jewish religion, nor a defense of the unity of the Jewish people. Rather it is the irresponsible introduction of an element of a possible disunity. This irresponsibility is a political affair, both because it is based on denying the Jews of other nations the right to individual self-determination, and because it introduces religious discrimination into other nations. For, it is the right of Jews to define themselves as members of their own nations, and this right should become a part of the law that forbids religious discrimination there. Hence, the Israeli contention that Western Jews belong not to their own nations but to the Israeli nation which is Jewish, constitutes an invitation for religious discrimination in the West.

Nevertheless, this is the place to ask, if the separation of religion and nationality is effected in Israel, and if the Judaism of the Jews of the other nations is considered a matter of religion and national origin alone, what will happen to the Jewish people? Is it not the case that the presence of the Jewish people refutes the idea of the separation of religion and nationality, since the Jewish people are simultaneously a nation and a religion? And what will happen to the Zionist Movement? Will it be possible to maintain it after Israel accepts the separation of religion and nationality?

Consider the Jewish people first. Let us admit that the Jewish people is an ancient people that has developed a national movement, that in due course this movement brought about the independence of Israel and the renewed nation, and that not all members of the people became members of the nation. Every honest, right-thinking individual would recognize these as matters of uncontroversial facts (72). (Hence, the New Zionist Myth that contradicts them is not just an opposite opinion but also sheer myth.) What has happened to the Jewish people or to the part of the Jewish people that did not join the renewed nation? Does the renewed nation abandon them? Is the renewal of the nation meaningless for all members of the people who did not join the nation? These are two extreme options, and they are both utterly unsatisfactory.

Clearly, the facts are between these two extreme options: the Jewish people were influenced by the renewal of the nation, and by the fact that in this way its national aspirations were fulfilled and realized, since the Israeli nation is the legitimate political heir of the Jewish people; but the Jewish people does not thereby cease to exist as a religion and as a historical entity. Comparing the American Italian with the American Jew, and the Catholic American with the Jewish American, indicates a significant difference here: Catholics do not have to be Italian even though most Italians are religiously Catholic (if they have a religion or any religious education at all). American Jews are different from the Italian Americans; in the case of the American Jews, the religion and ethnic culture go hand in hand. We may, therefore, speak of the Jewish people in contradistinction to the Israeli nation — since the nation dwells more or less within its own national territory. In principle, the distinction here is possible and has much more meaning for the Jews of other nations who do not feel a strong religious identity, but who do feel a strong ethnic identity, which they ascribe to the unity of the religious, ethnic Jewish aggregate. The affinity of the people to the nation, as well as the religious and cultural ties between the scattered people and the nation that dwells on its land, may become very desirable, but of course only on the condition that the national identity of the member of the nation will not be constrained, as it regrettably is in Israel today.

Just on this point the problem seems unsolved and insoluble. Notoriously, cultural links between Israel and the Jewish people proceed mainly through the apparatuses of the Zionist Movement and the Jewish Agency and with the help of Zionist activists from Israel. Might not the normalization of Israel as proposed in this book, then, damage the unity of the Jewish people?

There is justice in this question, but also confusion that rests on the wish to maintain the unity of the Jewish people, or the cultural ties between Israel and the Jewish members of other nations who see themselves both as members of the other nations and as Jews — whether religiously or culturally. The confusion was expressed in David Ben-Gurion's advocacy of normalization in the early days of Israel's Independence: he did it by demanding a reform of the Zionist Movement and a limitation on its leadership — since these leaders, Ben-Gurion assumed, preached others joining the nation, without themselves showing readiness to join. He demanded that the Zionist Movement split into two bodies, one of the friends of Israel and the other of people who would join the nation, and only the latter group should be called Zionist, and membership in it should be limited to only a few years, which is the reasonable time span for preparing to migrate to Israel. Ben-Gurion's tragic mistake was in that, instead of declaring the existence of the Israeli nation and fighting in Israel for normalization of the nation, he preached to Jews of other nations concerning their organizations. Ben-Gurion lacked the courage to prescribe normalization openly and in a normal fashion. He failed to appeal to those to whom the matter means most, namely, to the members of the Israeli nation. While preaching normalization, he thus strengthened the abnormalcy of Israel. For he acted then on the assumption that Israel can be normalized only after the World Zionist Movement was reformed. In this way, he violated the principle of national auto-emancipation (self-liberation), and Israel sank deeper into the abnormal situation from which she has still not emerged.

(Ben-Gurion himself sank into dangerous pseudo-religious messianic mysticism that then heralded the acceleration of the socio-political deterioration that continued after his demise and that is still at its peak.)

It is difficult to know when exactly the abnormal situation of Israel was established. To repeat, the Jewish national movement, including the Zionist Movement, was indeed an abnormal movement of a nation living in abnormal conditions and seeking normalization. The Declaration of Independence of Israel was not a declaration of the independence of a normal sovereign nation. This was understandable and even, perhaps, somewhat justifiable in the light of the fact that Israel's independence was declared in the middle of the process of mass migration of Jewish refugees from Europe and from Arabic-speaking countries. But with the termination of this process of mass migration, the lack of normalization of Israel became intolerable. The need to remedy it increased with time, and the distortions that come in its wake prevent normal relations between Israeli Jews and Jews of the other nations. Ben-Gurion's stricture against the World Zionist Movement was made in recognition of both the need for normalization and of the helplessness of a national leadership. It was a transition period. The leadership should have arisen to lead the nation on the road to the desired normalization by updating Israel as an independent nation. This would have enabled the nation to maintain good and normal relations with the Jews of all other nations while relying on shared religion, culture, and history.

In this way and only in this way can the Jewish people reach a stable cultural unity. The denial of the Israeli national identity of the Israelis, and the oversight of the non-Israeli nationality of the Jews of other nations, do not serve the cause of unity, but do lead to the disregard for some facts of life which leads to a conflict of political interests that sooner or later would of necessity receive some political expression. This expression may prove very dangerous both to the Israeli nation and to the whole of the Jewish people. When the desired normalization takes place, Israel will continue to be the state of the historical Jewish people, since the majority of its citizens will be adherents of the Jewish faith, and in an extensive growth of the historical traditional Jewish culture, but without the Jewish people constituting a political entity.

* Some people fear that normalizing Israel might alter its religious character, whether through reform of the Jewish religion or through the affiliation of most of Israelis with some other religion. These people ignore some facts. The character of the Jewish people has already altered by the very fact that Israel is Jewish in character, and the abnormalcy of Israel adversely affects Israeli and non-Israeli Jews — as has been observed by Georges Friedmann (see p. 133). One way or another, it is clear that every preference has a price, and that a public democratic debate is required on the basic question, is this or that preference desirable despite its price? There is no escape from the conclusion that decency and democracy demand a discussion on the basic question, is the present abnormalcy desirable for Israeli Jews and/or Jews of other nations? It seems that all things considered, the normalization of the Israeli Republic is preferable both to Israelis and to Jews who value the preservation of religious values more than the survival of Israel. *

Chapter 33 — A Political Conclusion: Towards a Transition Period

This book contains a presentation of a new integrated view of philosophy, political theory, the history of the Zionist ideology, the state of the Israeli nation, and more. The author does not expect to find agreement with the readers on every point. Even readers who sympathize with the viewpoint of the author and who have read carefully everything presented here will have much to disagree with, and much that requires further clarification and fresh critical examination. The immediate aim of this book is practical, not intellectual. This is not to say that the author looks for agreement with the readers, in order to undertake certain activities. On the contrary, the first required activity is public debate. This does not require agreement about this or that thesis. The required agreement is only on a change in the national agenda.

The question of agreement is theoretical-philosophical as well as practical-philosophical; it will not be discussed in this concluding chapter. After all, Israelis interested in the political problems of Israel, even if only slightly, are sufficiently familiar with this question, since the distinction is generally recognized in Israel, since its establishment, between questions the answers to which demand a national consensus and questions the answers to which may, perhaps even should, be disputes. This is not to say that the Israeli national consensus was unproblematic. It was particularly problematic because in the early years the Israeli Parliament, the Knesset, included two political parties — Begin's Herut Party and the Communist Party — which were not parties to the national consensus. (Afterward, only the Communists were left out.) Today, the national consensus is presented as minimal, and it includes only agreement concerning the importance of the survival of Israel and whatever is linked with agreement concerning major problems of security.

To my regret, I cannot agree. In principle I tend to agree that it is desirable that the national consensus should be minimal in order to prevent any imposition of opinions, and I do agree that survival is a minimal requirement. But it seems to me that before the nation is defined, a national consensus is impossible, and that without the existence of a national framework, the danger is so great, that even agreement about matters of national security does not suffice, unless it be recognized that a chronic state of war without political initiative for peace constitutes a danger to the national security and even to the very survival of the nation. Clearly, we are approaching a very dangerous situation, one in which political debates are heard more and more as a collection of empty formulas that nobody believes in, that the national helm is left without direction, and the nation is no longer guided. Since even a minimal national policy is absent, the danger of disintegration is on the increase.

Let me present an utterly new approach to the national consensus. Let me do so before it is too late, before the disintegration is so great and so obvious that any alternative to it will seem preferable. For then innocent people are ready to support demagogues who promise to hold the helm with strong hands and one way or another replace democracy with a dictatorship of one sort or another. Assuming that the present situation is dangerous, and that it is desirable to stop the disintegration before the democratic system is lost, the desirability will be recognized of finding within the democratic system the ruinous factor in the consensus, which could be presented as the major enemy to be jointly assaulted.

The first priority on the national agenda should be to the question, what is the root of the evil? We may wish to reach a consensus about this matter. The democratic process is the public control over the national administration, and this control is in the hands of the body that determines the national agenda (the leadership of the parliament, the parliamentary steering committee, or something of the sort). It is well known that in a seemingly or insufficiently democratic regime, the tyrant will be content with control over the bodies that steer the parliament, leaving all other political processes to proceed democratically. For in controlling the parliamentary steering bodies, tyrants can prevent parliamentary discussions about questions that endanger their control and their plans.

To a large extent, the Israeli establishment controls public life here with the aid of these simple tactics of eliminating from the agenda details they deem dangerous (not only political items but also historical ones). This is done successfully, without national notice. Until today, there was no public debate on the report of the Agranat Commission [which reports on the negligence that led to the disaster of the Yom Kippur War, and which is still classified though its military relevance is long expired]. Similarly, not even a trace of public debate has taken place concerning the responsibility of the national leadership at the time of the mass murder of the European Jews and their abstention from declaring a national state of emergency at that time.

The purpose of this book, as that of this concluding chapter, is to call the Israeli citizens who are aware of the severity of the situation and who suffer the pain of the nation, to fight for putting on the national agenda details that the establishment as a whole rejects in a consensus of a bunch of community activists who pose as politicians. This pseudo-national consensus of these activists should be repudiated. A program for a new national consensus should be formulated and promoted. It should express democratically the national interest. In my view, naturally, a discussion is called for primarily of the fact that there is no political initiative in the Israeli political leadership, that there is no discussion even of medium-range interests, not to mention the long-range ones, and that there is no debate on the question of whether the abnormalcy of Israel is desirable, whether it is not preferable to move towards normalization.

My proposal is to fight for placing on the national agenda as the most urgent point of top priority the question of whether normalization is desirable. If my proposal is accepted, it will possibly bring some public support to the idea of normalization. If this happens, then supporters, or some of them, will generate a new kind of political involvement that will come from a new part of the public and will have a new character. In this way new people will enter the Israeli system of party politics, which is thus far practically closed to this public. Thus, a new process of basic change might occur on the Israeli political scene. The new people might try to come to terms with the national agenda (whether on the lines described in this book or on other lines). And if the normalization plan will be brought to public debate, it will have to undergo changes at every stage, until it will be executed. For normalization is not a light matter, even with a national consensus. The problems that it raises are complex in every one of its many aspects, social, legal, economic and much more. Clearly, this will not happen overnight.

In the Jewish national revolution of the nineteenth century, a process began of absorption of a mixture of theoretical and practical influences from the Western world. The revolution incorporated the historical Zionist revolution, which was political in character, and sought the normalization of the Jewish people in its historic homeland. The Zionist Movement deemed self-evident that its aim was normalization. Thus the movement was political and saw itself as such. This does not mean that the movement did not aspire for more than national independence. On the contrary, the idea was essential to enlightened nationalism that a free nation can and even should create for its sons and daughters a high quality of life (economically, socially, culturally, etc.). The fact that the Zionist Movement demanded from its members sacrifices and heroism, including the sacrifice of life, is not contrary to this, as every national movement requires sacrifice. But the idea of the chronic abnormalcy of the State of Israel created the illusion that the state requires constant sacrifice as a substitute for a high quality of life. How did this happen? How did the idea of normalization, which was so central in the traditional historical Zionist Movement, deteriorate so far as to become the New Zionist Myth?

I do not know. It seems to me that there are a few answers to this. First, there is the anti-political, theocratic Jewish tradition, discussed at great length in Gershon Weiler's book, *Jewish Theocracy* (73). Second, there is the system of economic support of members of a political party who toe the official party line, a sort of a translation of the institution of financial support of the old Jewish settlement in Palestine to the Zionist framework of the new Jewish settlement, described at length by the sociologist Yonathan Shapiro, in his *Formative Years of the Israeli Labor Party: The Organization of Power* (74). Third, the change from the old to the new myth is based partly on the threat that is known in the Western world as the credibility crisis.

Let me conclude this book with a specific political discussion concerning the character and origin of the credibility crisis in the modern civilized world. Hopefully this discussion will explain

(a) why this crisis is so dangerous for human civilization in general;
(b) why Israel, more than other countries, is a victim of this crisis;
(c) how Israel can become a pioneer in the international political struggle for the elimination of the present crisis.

The origin of the crisis of credibility lies, I think, in a philosophical theory known as *Realpolitik*, which means realistic politics. The best known expression of it in the post-World War II world, in Israel and elsewhere, was the sarcastic, rhetorical question that Stalin asked Roosevelt and Churchill during the Yalta Conference: How many divisions does the Pope have? The idea behind *Realpolitik* is simple: if an agreement is kept, it is kept because the power that is interested in keeping it is stronger than the power that is interested in revoking it. For if the stronger power revokes an agreement, the weaker can do nothing about it (protest is possible, but it has no influence on real political situations). Therefore, what matters is not agreement but power, not words but deeds. So much for the malignant philosophy that justifies and encourages lies in the guise of realism.

The theory of *Realpolitik* is sham. People who are excited by an idea are ready to sacrifice themselves for it. Nations convinced of the justice of the weak party may be willing to support and strengthen it. Clearly, when strong nations are convinced that *Realpolitik* is right, or when they show moral weakness, or when despite their recognition of the justice of the weak they do not defend them, they thereby testify in support of the idea of *Realpolitik*. Experiencing such treachery tends to render the idea of *Realpolitik* a matter of self-evident fact. But one has to distinguish clearly between two very different cases, the case of the strong who recognizes the injustice of the assault on the weak and who nevertheless does not volunteer to help, and the case of the strong who are aware of the situation but, in addition to their refusal to help, deny that they have the duty to do so. The refusal of the one who recognizes the facts could be justified or not. The unwillingness of the one who denies the facts creates a credibility crisis, and the credibility crisis mobilizes support of the idea of *Realpolitik*.

The theory of *Realpolitik* disregards the case in which agreement expresses the interests of different parties to it. The theory assumes that in every agreement there is a compromise at least from one side, and that when the side that compromises becomes stronger, it shows a readiness to revoke the compromise. Such cases do indeed occur, but they are not the norm. They are problematic because those who revoke compromises lose thereby their credibility, and usually the gain is smaller than the loss, since the loss is of the possibility of further cooperation. The exception is the agreements that incur such far-reaching compromises that they create situations in which the gain from the revocation of the compromise is bigger by far than the loss of credibility involved in that revocation. The interest of the one who compromises in that case will naturally be to give up credibility and revoke the compromise. The 1919 Versailles Treaty was like that, and the temptation for Germany to withdraw from that agreement was so strong that there was enormous support in the German people for the Nazi Party, which in turn openly made light of its own credibility. The disaster of the credibility crisis is that it causes a general reduction in the moral level of international politics, in the same manner in which crime reduces the moral level of a society which is not capable of handling it properly. Those Romantic philosophers who preached *Realpolitik* saw a crucial difference between the community of nations and the community of individuals of one and the same nation, because they saw every nation as one organic unit and hoped that individual members of the same nation would share the trust rooted in their joint fate. These philosophers saw no need for trust between two nations with no common fate, especially since one might conquer the other and then justify the conquest by arguments from *Realpolitik*. Today the situation is different: joint fate does not lead to trust even within the same nation, certainly not between activists and their public, whereas in concrete fact, all the nations of the globe have today a joint fate and a joint interest in the survival of the human race. The first difficulty, which those who show concern about the fate of humanity face, is the credibility crisis (74a).

In the history of the Zionist Movement the idea of *Realpolitik* has played a chronic, significant role, even though, of course, the movement was largely idealistic and so opposed to the cynicism that characterizes this idea. Nevertheless, the general cynicism that was at its peak in the heyday of the Zionist Movement and the popularity of *Realpolitik* then made their mark. In addition, the socialist movement inherited from the Romantic Movement the idea of *Realpolitik* and used it to justify the idea that there is no escape from civil war for the realization of its aim. This idea had a profound influence on the theory of Practical Zionism, since according to this theory, there is no sense to political arrangements unless they are backed up by facts. This is not to say that the doctrine of Practical Zionism includes the erroneous, evil idea of *Realpolitik*, since the Zionists never expected that the desired state would have a considerable military power. Nevertheless, support for this erroneous, evil idea was voiced, within both the Practical and the Political stream of Zionism. Today, when Israel is a considerable military power, this fact brings many Israelis to support this evil idea.

The credibility crisis is devouring Israel. The basic assumption in Israel is that there is no trust and no basis for trust in politics or in social life, when every citizen must try to penetrate a screen of untrustworthy words in order to find out what one's neighbors think. We must terminate this situation. We must assume that citizens say what they mean and exhibit responsibility for their words. I will not expand on this, since in my opinion it is clear and self-evident that Israelis who agree that the country is in bad shape and who are concerned about the fate of the nation should learn to speak responsibly and precisely, and seek partners on this matter and discuss with them the question of what is the root of the evil, and discuss the possibility that the true answer is that the root of the evil is the abnormalcy. They should then try to bring all this to the political parties that they and their friends sympathize with and vote for (75). Perhaps this will permit one to hope that the situation will alter, that credibility will be renewed, that politics will cease to be a scorned activity of activists devoid of credibility, who employ big empty words, that politics will be reinstated within a responsible public of citizens who care about the fate of their nation. Then the Israeli public could force its leadership to declare a transition period towards normalization or else help a new leadership emerge, one that will express the desire to be a free, normal nation living in its land in peace.

Notes

N.B. All translations here are mine, unless otherwise indicated.

01. ∗ See David A. Hollinger, *Postethnic America: Beyond Multiculturalism*. New York: Basic Books, 1995. Chapter 6. ∗

02. ∗ Fortunately, there is a decline of support for the erroneous identification of the demand for the normalization of Israel with the demand for its dissociation herself from the Jewish people. The New Zionist Myth is the claim that normalcy in Israel is impossible because Israel represents the Jewish people. The myth thus constrains the available options to only two: the acceptance of the current situation or detachment from the Jewish people. A myth imposes the *status quo* by a threat that otherwise the linkage will be severed between Israel and the rest of the Jewish people. The opposition of this book to the New Zionist Myth is expressed as the plan for normalcy through the reaffirmation of Israel's alliance with the Jewish people due to its Jewish character.

    ∗ Secularization in the sense of normalization is no rejection of religion, but the neutralization of the religious dimension of all political authority in order to facilitate the endorsement of the political goal of restraining religious discrimination. Thus, as long as the Law of Return refers to Jews as a religious group, it invites the fusion of religious and secular authorities and thus prevents normalization. The advocates of the New Zionist Myth consider this inevitable; clearly, the requirement to secularize the Law of Return is the demand that it refer to Jews as a group of a distinctly political character (for example, as victims of the persecution of Jews), inviting a political solution to their political problem.

    ∗ The group which suffers most from the confusion that rests at the base of the abnormalcy of Israel is the one labeled "Canaanites." See Boas Evron, *The National Balance Sheet* (in Hebrew, Tel Aviv: Dvir, 1990), for example, p. 356: "There is no 'common platform' to a Jew and a Hebrew. These are different modes of being that are on different existential plains. The Hebrew has no need for the Jew...." Compare this with Hillel Kook's declaration that he is fully a Jew and fully an Israeli, since, normally, his being a Jew is a religious-ethnic-cultural matter, and his being an Israeli is a matter of national affiliation alone, even though the Israeli nation adheres to the Jewish faith. ∗

03. ∗ The letter from Peter Bergson to Chaim Weizmann is in the Weizmann Archive. Copies are found in many libraries. See also Note 1 below.

* Perhaps it is time to have it published in a new edition since, as will be explained below, its practical and historical value have not diminished. *

04. * Not being a student of American history I wish to mention only one autobiographical book, which mentions Peter Bergson and which advocates the separation of church and state from a religious point of view; Stuart E. Rosenberg, *The Real Jewish World: A Rabbi's Second Thoughts*, New York: Philosophical Library, 1984, pp. 228-24. Let me also mention a few new books on the United States attitude to the destruction of the Jews of Europe: David S. Wyman, *The Abandonment of the Jews: America and the Holocaust*, 1941-45. New York: Pantheon Books, 1984. Deborah E. Lipstadt, *Beyond Belief: The American Press and the Coming of the Holocaust, 1933-1945*, New York: Free Press, 1986. Irving Abella and Harold Troper, *None is too many: Canada and the Jews of Europe, 1933-1948*, Toronto: Dennys, 1983 and 1991. *

1. Extensive documentary material concerning the topic is kept in a special library at Yale University. Only a small part of it appeared in diverse publications in the United States, and part of it will be mentioned in Part Two of this volume. Interest in this affair was revived and a documentary film sympathetic to Bergson's Group was screened on a national television channel in the United States on February 19, 1983. In addition, a Jewish public commission to study the attitude of the Jewish leadership towards the mass murder of the Jews was set up (see page 1 of the *New York Times*, January 4, 1983, and page 7 of the *Los Angeles Times*, January 12, 1983).

    Additional documentary material can be found in David Niv's bokk, see Note 23, in *Irgun, National Military Organization*, in Hebrew, Jabotinsky institute, Israel 1990 et seqq., and in *Jacob (Yoel) Amrami, Useful Bibliography, Nili, etc.*, in Hebrew, Tel-Aviv, Hadar 1975.

2. J. Agassi, *Towards Rational Philosophical Anthropology*, The Hague: Nijhoff, 1977.

3. J. Agassi, *Faraday As Natural Philosopher*, Chicago and London: Chicago University Press, 1971.

4. J. L. Talmon, *The Origins of Totalitarian Democracy*, London: Secker and Warburg, 1955.

5. Elie Kedourie's opinion is more complicated than Karl Popper's. This book is not the place to give this a proper expression. The interested reader should consult their books. Here suffice it to observe that both emphasized the principle of autonomy and the arbitrariness in the foundation of diverse nations. They conclude from this — quite rightly — that the Romantic concept of nationality has no historical basis. From this they conclude further — wrongly — that nationality is impossible. (See Elie Kedourie, *Nationalism*. London: Hutchinson, 1960. See also his *Nationalism in Asia and Africa*, London, 1970. See also, Karl R. Popper, *The Open Society and Its Enemies*, London: Routledge, 1945 and many other editions.)

    The literature concerning nationalism is immense, of course, and there is no point in giving a list of additional references here. But since the viewpoint proposed here is so unusual, I would like to recommend two instructive articles concerning nationalism by E. Gellner, in his two collections, *Contemporary Thought and Politics*, London: Routledge, 1974, and *Spectacles and Predicaments*, Cambridge: Cambridge University Press, 1979, as well as his *Nations and Nationalism*, Oxford, 1983.

    The difficulty of grasping the concept of nationality which breaks away from the two classic traditions is well expressed in Dov Ronen, *The Quest for Self-Determination*, New Haven: Yale University Press, 1979. See my review of it in *Philosophy of the Social Sciences*, 13,

1983, 126-8. The same difficulty is more emphatically expressed by the very absence of a theory of the rise of nations. See, for example, Mancur Olson, *The Rise and Decline of Nations*, New Haven: Yale University Press, 1982, which, being apolitical, cannot deal with the topic announced in its title.

6. This idea is presented extensively in the seventh chapter of Karl Popper's important *The Open Society and Its Enemies* (see previous note). Popper's idea is new, important, and revolutionary. It is limited, because he overlooks the importance of political leadership though he should suggest that the duties of democratic political leaders should be democratically determined. This is its limitation.

7. The refusal of President Lincoln to recognize the right of the South to secede is in profound discord with the ideas of the Enlightenment, on which the original constitution of the United States is based. See, in this connection, Thomas J. Schlereth, *The Cosmopolitan Ideal in Enlightenment Thought*, South Bend: University of Notre Dame Press, 1977, especially p. 105. The book is valuable, even though the author is not sufficiently systematic, since he relies on conflicting views concerning nationality, as is reflected in his notes 28 ff. on p. 206.

8. J. Agassi, "Liberal Forensic Medicine", *J. of Medicine and Philosophy*, 3, 1978, 226-41.

9. J. Agassi, *Letters to My Sister Concerning Contemporary Philosophy*, in Hebrew, Sarah Batz, Beer-Sheva, 1977.

10. Yoram Dinstein, *The Defense of "Obedience to Superior Order" in International Law*. Leyden: A. W. Sijthoff, 1965.

11. J. Agassi, "Rights and Reason," *Israel Yearbook of Human Rights*, 9, 1980, 9-22.

12. Reinhold Niebuhr, *Moral Man and Immoral Society*, New York and London: Scribner's Sons, 1932. Chapter 9.

13. Moshe Sharett and his associates who were incarcerated in Latrun at about the same period were released when they asked for a reprieve, and they even reached the Zionist Congress where he did not tell the story of his request for a reprieve from the British but reported that he was released after negotiations with them. He used this as proof that one can negotiate with the British (see p. 187).

14. The revival of the Hebrew language as an everyday language only began at the beginning of the twentieth century, of course. The discussion here concerns Hebrew secular literature, that is, one devoid of religious contents. Such literature is perennial, but its appearance and blossom 19th century Europe was a revival of the language in clear, varied senses that will be ignored here, since this book is limited to the political import of this literature. The earlier secular Hebrew literature had no political import.

15. It is interesting here that the cultural component of a society united not with its political component but with its religious ones.

16. As for the United States, it is a limiting case, and one may claim that the American nation did not grow from a people but grew as a nation from its very start. But perhaps one might also claim the opposite. This is a very interesting theoretical question, but it has no place in this book.

16a. * Buber did not study the national question; he took for granted that two people inhabit Palestine. In this way he supported the abnormalcy that characterizes Israel without noticing this fact. Though he distinguishes between society and state, he did not examine the distinction between community, society and nation, and thus also nor between nation and state, though he recognized, of course, that the state is a mere instrument. *

16b. * The Al-Demi (= No Reticence) movement was founded by Yehoshua Radler-Feldmann (alias Rabbi Benjamin), who was a close associate of Buber. See also references in Note 33a.*

17. Shlomo Avineri, *The Making of Modern Zionism: The Intellectual Origins of the Jewish State*, New York: Basic Books, 1981. This book is the latest and best expression of the Practical Zionist philosophy as it is understood in Israel today, and it is justly a popular book, accepted almost universally. I have tried to limit the information concerning the history of Zionism as much as possible to details mentioned in Avineri's book and only when he omitted a vital detail have I deviated from this rule. See also my review of the book, "Nationalism and the Philosophy of Zionism", *Inquiry*, 27, 1984, 311-26.

18. Herzl gave in to his colleagues, the Practical Zionists, who opposed the founding of the bank in Jerusalem. He considered this a diversionary tactic. He emphasized the location of the bank in order to deflect the discussion from the question, should the bank be founded. It is difficult for me to free myself of the impression that the whole story is somewhat ludicrous, even when considering its background.

19. Avineri praises Herzl's utopianism more than anything else Herzl has contributed, despite the known fact that this utopianism had no influence.

20. The Zionist Directorship agreed to accept mass migration only after the mass murder of European Jews became public knowledge. The Practical Zionists had intended to organize only the migration of Zionists, whereas the Political Zionists had intended to organize the migration of persecuted Jews. The mass migration was not primarily Zionist; the percentage of Zionists among the immigrants to Israel was always very small. The leadership felt the need to maintain the superiority of the Zionists by all sorts of undemocratic means. The means that were available reflected the ghetto mentality, and they are largely responsible for the ghetto character of Israel today. This character was masked during the early days by the guise of pioneering and progressive socialism. But with Israel's independence, the unwillingness of the political parties to give up their power in the national interest became conspicuous — such as their unwillingness to nationalize the medical service of the labor unions. (See Yonathan Shapiro, *Formative Years of the Israeli Labor Party: The Organization of Power, 1919-1930*. London: Sage, 1976.)

20a. * There is almost no literature on the history of the illegal immigration organized by the Haganah, especially by the Mossad. The little extant literature on it is cryptic. See for example, Dalia Ofer, "Why was the 'Aliah B [Haganah organized illegal immigration]' stopped and then renewed", *Ha'apalah*, in Hebrew, Tel Aviv, 1990, pp. 178-210. The author begins with a description of Ben-Gurion's position as struggling Zionism — struggling against the British policy that limited immigration, but on p. 102 it becomes clear that in 1940 Ben-Gurion hesitated and at most expressed readiness to approve of the infiltration of a small groups of pioneers who were in great trouble, whereas for the problems of most of the pioneers who were ready to escape "the Mossad found no solution"; "the ill-success deterred support for illegal immigration" (pp. 202-3). The discussion itself begins on page 204, in the sub-section on the causes of the renewal of the illegal immigration in 1944 (!), in which the author notices "three components: the comprehension of the extent and the meaning of the final solution, the efforts to crystallize a rescue policy, as well as the recognition of the limitations and the poverty of achievements of the then Zionist policy." The rescue operations of the Mossad in the years 1941-42 are described on page 207. In the opinion of the Mossad people, the author adds on page 209, in the year 1943 "the limitations of the illegal immigration were not objective but stemmed from the lack of an adequate support of the politicians." Hopefully the reader notices that the evidence here quoted does not include the claim that the illegal immigration began against explicit instructions but that this is implied in the text cited. The text deserves careful study and examination that has no room here, especially since, surprisingly, the author cites here a document from August 1943, presumably produced by Haganah commander-in-chief Eliahu Golomb, in which a daring plan for mass immigration is proposed akin to the plan of Peter Bergson and similarly justified, except that Golomb was establishment, unlike the dissident Bergson. Golomb himself, it might be added, was not sharply hostile to the dissident military organizations. In the conference of the Labour Party of Palestine on 28 September 1941 he said, "I cannot honestly say that all these years we did all in order to have security in Palestine one and unified." (Sabetai Nadiv, *Burning Fire*, in Hebrew, 1991, p. 404). Had this information been available to me when I wrote the first edition of this book, I would have been more positive and more decisive in my judgment of the significance and likelihood of success of Bergson's plans. Despite the sharp criticism of the Zionist establishment that appeared already in the first edition of this book, until I prepared its second edition I was not sufficiently free of doubts whose source is misinformation produced by the Zionist establishment of that time.

* Let me end this discussion by reference to the preface of Anita Shapira to the volume from which most of the quotes in this note are taken. In the second paragraph there Shapira describes in general outline the policy of the Zionist establishment to illegal immigration during the War, and it is easy to document the refutation of claims she presents there and show that the policy she ascribes to the Zionist establishment is the one that the Committee to Save the Jews of Europe had advocated and the Zionist establishment denounced all along in a denunciation that has still not been rescinded. These days even East European countries rehabilitate those who had been denounced during the Communist regime; it is much more reasonable to expect a rehabilitation of the Bergson Group. At least the denunciation of the Zionist Congress of 1946 (see pp. 188-9) demands correction, if not by the state then at least by the Zionist Organization. It stands to reason that the rehabilitation of Bergson's committees is not only a matter of justice, even though belated, but also a matter of clearing the air. *

20b. * See in this connection the speech of Chaim Arlosoroff in Warsaw in 1933, *Works*, in Hebrew, p. 130: "The war to extinction against the Jews of Germany presents the whole world... the tragedy of the German Jews renders Zionism a burning problem.... Of necessity a radical change of attitude towards Zionism will appear..." and there is no more radical change within Zionism than that its Practical Stream would adopt attitudes of its Political Stream. See also p. 132: "Transjordan has to become, and will become in due course, an arena of activity of Zionist settlement."

* See also the letters of Chaim Arlosoroff to Chaim Weizmann of June 10, 1932, November 12th, 1932, and February 2nd, 1933. See Chaim Arlosoroff, *Jerusalem Diary*, in Hebrew, 2nd ed., Tel Aviv, 1949, pp. 327-359, quoted by Yigal Eilam, *An Introduction to a Different Zionism*, in Hebrew, 1975. See also Note 37a below.

* In the absence of discussion of the views Arlosoroff advocated before he was murdered let me present abstracts of these letters since they indicate that he began to develop an attitude more expressing sovereignty than that of his colleagues, thereby opening the road to a bridge between the ideologies of practical Zionism and of political Zionism, though it was no more than a preliminary foray. Arlosoroff endorsed with no hesitation a "maximalist formula" of "a Jewish state on both banks of the river Jordan" (p. 333); he raises the problem as that of a struggle between two nations, and considers the Jewish nation as having a slight advantage, one that does not suffice as long as the Zionist movement clings to its current strategy (p. 334) unless that strategy will be backed by the British Government, yet, clearly, such a backing is not to be expected (pp. 335-6), just as it is not to be expected that Zionist policy will manage to mobilize British support for mass migration or a Jewish readiness for it (pp. 358-9). Therefore, he concludes, assuming that the problem is soluble, then it is either a partition of the land or its full conquest by force (pp. 339-41). But not in the pattern of the Revisionist Party, which is erroneously based on expectations of British support and in that it arouses needless Arab hostility, in addition to the empty rhetoric of its founders (p. 343). Later on Arlosoroff admits that his policy is also based on the erroneous assumption of the British Government's cooperation (p. 350). (He was clearly unaware of the option of engaging world public opinion as a tool for putting pressure on the British Government to cooperate with the Jewish nationalist movement, though he came close to it. This is a central item in the doctrine of Peter Bergson, as will be explained later on; I do not know if activity in that direction was at all feasible before World War II.) In any case, in this letter Arlosoroff declares that in the country there are two nations (despite his awareness of the presence of the pan-Arab movement that opposed local nationality; see p. 286), and that the British Government should endorse the parity plan, so-called (of equal representation on the Palestinian legislative council). Arlosoroff complains about two merchants who plan "to manage a political action towards the conquest of Transjordan" prior to his completion of his effort to achieve superiority in the internal Jewish struggles (p. 356). He also complains about the Zionist leader Nahum Sokolov's refrain of an explicit opposition to them. The correspondence ends with Arlosoroff's claim that in order to further the cause of the settlement in Transjordan it is necessary to avoid confrontation with Arab public opinion and with the British Government and by avoiding public statements before the matter is concluded (pp. 357-9). In sum, Arlosoroff expresses discomfort at the absence of a political program, in cognizance of the transitory character of his own activities towards a crystallization of such a program. It is clear that he denies that the Revisionists have any political program, and particularly that he is revolted by their Chauvinism (without saying so explicitly); and of course he has no clear picture as to the national question and he does not ask, do the local inhabitants constitute a nation? This is so partly because his hopes for cooperation with the Emir who rules Transjordan concerning his plans for Jewish settlement there — with no sensitivity to the fact that the Emir was a foreign ruler, though he was well aware of this fact (see p. 250), since he considered this fact the possible basis for the readiness of that Emir to cooperate with the Jewish settlers there. See also Note 37a. (Half a year later, on June 6, 1933, Arlosoroff was murdered.) *

21. See Note 12 above.

21a. * An addendum concerning the relations between the Revisionist Party or the New Zionist Organization and the Irgun National Military Organization. Much material was recently published on this, and much more is on its way, which does not seem to me to be too credible. (See next note.) I need not enter the thicket of details of relations between these bodies, since no one has raised any doubt as to the following three general points made in the second part of this book, which, after all, concerns a different matter (that of the normalization of Israel).

* First, at the time the Zionist leadership presented to the Jewish public the Haganah Military Organization as under its own command and the Irgun National Military Organization as under the command of the New Zionist Organization. Hillel Kook was, and still is, of the opinion that the Zionist leadership ceased to represent the national interest and thereby lost the mandate that it took upon itself to speak in the name of the nation. In more detail, it lost its mandate when it gave up the nation's right over Transjordan not in exchange for any advantage and for no reason and decided to prefer selective immigration over mass immigration. Moreover, in Kook's opinion, the leadership of the New Zionist Organization likewise lost any mandate that it took upon itself, despite its pretense, after David Raziel died, to have a monopoly over the Irgun National Military Organization.

* Second, and contrary to the official position of the Zionist leadership, the official position of the Irgun National Military Organization was of utter sovereignty: officially the Organization declared itself a national body, an a-political representation of the nation as a whole. Kook always deemed of central importance its official position as an a-political national body. (As to the view of its members concerning the significance of this item see the biography of David Raziel by Arieh Naor, published by the Ministry of Defense in 1990.)

* Third, the Irgun National Military Organization did exhibit a strong separatist tendency, the tendency to endorse the narrow party-political position ascribed to it by the Zionist leadership. As that body was an underground military organization, there is no need to discuss the details of its positions; suffice it to relate to its official position and to the position of its command. Its commander-in-chief, David Raziel, saw the body as national (see his biography mentioned above). After his death, Hillel Kook was the commander of its remnants. The delegation of the Irgun National Military Organization in the United States decided to renew hostilities against the British Government of Palestine in protest against its cruel attitude towards the destruction of European Jewry. To that end, Kook sent Arie Ben Eliezer to appoint a local commander to the Irgun. (Recent publications indicate that Kook's position in the remnants of the Irgun was more significant than it seemed to me when the first edition of this book appeared.) Since then, Menachem Begin was its commander. His attitude to Kook and to the committees that Kook organized is discussed in sufficient detail in the body of this book. This discussion is still not publicly commented on, though there were comments on other aspects of this book — that is proper and understandable — especially on its attitude towards normalization.

* So much for the position of Hillel Kook on the three points raised here. As to myself, I have expressed no attitude regarding them, since I was never a Zionist and I was very far from being a fan of the Irgun National Military Organization. Though I learned from Kook to view Zionism as a part of the Jewish national movement regardless of the conduct of the Zionist leadership in Palestine, and though I learned from him to appreciate every national movement as an expression of a need and an aspiration of a broad public, I still have no position of my own regarding many issues in the history of Zionism, since matters are very hard to judge, as explained in the first part of this book. Moreover, till I met Kook in person, I had no knowledge of the official view of the Irgun about itself as an apolitical national organization, and I consider this fact a serious defect of the propaganda apparatus of that body, a defect that is possibly explicable as rooted in the ambivalence of its command towards the Committee for National Liberation headed by Kook, who was the commander

of its delegation in the United States, as described and documented here. In any case, this matter is marginal in this book, whose chief concern is the need for the normalization of Israel as a tool for the reconstruction and renewed foundations of its sovereignty and of its self-liberation from that communalism that was introduced into its very structure ever since its establishment as an abnormal state. This communalism increasingly governs political life here. It could perhaps be totally avoided had Begin accepted Kook's proposal to declare a government in exile. As explained here, Begin had his own significant considerations, yet these were communalist in spirit. Communalism has its place in the life of a religious community, but not in the life of a healthy modern state, which Israel should hopefully soon become. *

22a. * As the second edition of this book is being prepared for the press, the traditional bickering takes place behind the scenes as to the way to describe the history of the Jewish settlement in Palestine: after scores of years in which the official history was written uncritically by followers of the Palestine Labor Party and its heirs and of the Haganah Military Organization, a significantly sharp turn was made as the pen was passed on from them to the followers of the Revisionist Party and its heirs and of the dissident military organizations. The conduct of both sides testifies to their view that recent history still has political implications. Hence, a change is required: instead of quarrels and of hiring scribes to write uncritical histories, it is preferable to bring matters to public debate. And the item that should be put as first on the agenda of the debate is my proposal to rehabilitate the Bergson Group. All those who deem themselves heirs to the classical Zionist movement have to debate the denunciation of the Group by the last Zionist Congress prior to Independence.

22b. * Nevertheless, I wish to mention one detail, the official Obituary in the U. S. Senate of the former president of the League of Free Palestine, former Senator Guy M. Gillette: 93rd Congress, First Session, Senate Document No. 93-14; *Memorial Addresses and Other Tributes in the Congress of the United States on the Life and Contributions of Guy M. Gillette*. Washington: U. S. Govt. Printing Office, 1973, especially pp. 37-40 and 41-3. *

22. For the chronicle of these committees and documentation concerning them see Isaac Zaar, *Rescue and Liberation: America's Part in the Birth of Israel*. New York: Bloch Publication House, 1954. See also a brief and sympathetic description on pp. 68-73 of the *American Jewish Yearbook*, 1982.

23. David Niv, *The History of the Irgun National Military Organization*, in Hebrew, 1965-1980, in six volumes.

24. Walter Laqueur, *A History of Zionism*, London: Weidenfeld and Nicholson, 1972.

24a. * Historians who mention the activities of the committees of the Bergson Group add that at the time the organization of mass movements was a novelty, so that these committees acted with a force scarcely imaginable these days, after the mass movements and the mass marches became routine in the sixties. The individual most active in these matters was the celebrated English philosopher Bertrand Russell. He certainly was aware of the early marches on Washington by the unemployed, but these differed from the protest marches in that they involved the victims themselves and not protest marches of protesters concerned with public affairs. I do not know if and how much Russell learned from Bergson in this matter, but it is known that he was in the United States during the war and it is hard to imagine that he did not hear about the organization of the march on Washington of 500

Orthodox rabbis that was involved in the institution of the War Refugee Board. That was the first mass march, but it was not as massive as those organized by Russell. On mass protest and Russell's contribution to their evolution, see my *Technology: Philosophical and Social Aspects*. Dordrecht: Kluwer, 1985, final chapter. *

25. The interested reader may look at the informative if unexciting article by Eliahu Matz, "Political Action Versus Personal Relations", *Midstream, a Monthly Jewish Review*, April 1981, pp. 41-8. It refers to the literature concerning the War Refugee Board and discusses its political and practical importance as well as the distortion in the Jewish literature concerning whatever relates to the contribution of Bergson and his friends and the Committee for the Rescue of the Jews of Europe in the process of establishing the Board. The literature is broad and this is not the place to review it.

26. See N. N. Penkower, "In Dramatic Dissent — the Bergson Boys", *American Jewish History*, 70, 1981, 281-309.

27. A number of national movements passed significant stages of development in the United States. See Stuart E. Rosenberg, *America Is Different*, 1964, Chapter 3.

28. Robert E. Sherwood, *Roosevelt and Hopkins*. New York: Harpers, Bantam Books, 1948 and many reprints; see especially Chapter 28, pp. 325ff.

28a. * For the official attitude of the United States Administration to the British rule over Palestine, see Carl J. Friedrich, *American Policy Towards Palestine*, Published under the auspices of the American Council on Public Affairs Press, Washington, 1944; Greenwood Press, 1977. I cannot properly discuss here the question that this book raises, and which is clearly asked here: could Bergson declare a government-in-exile? I categorically reject the received notion that historians should not ask hypothetical questions: no inquiry is forbidden, and the lesson from inquiry into hypothetical questions may enlighten — assuming that the investigator has no interest in accusing or praising anyone on any matter that is a *fait accompli*. See notes 37a and 40 below. *

29. It is difficult to translate into Hebrew the word "assimilate": assimilation may be religious, national or other, but in contemporary Hebrew the word always connotes religious assimilation, at least the way I learned the language in my youth. Hebrew usage indicates, of course, the opinion, popular among speakers of modern Hebrew, that religion has a value that eclipses that of nationality, and that Jews constitute a nation-religion.

30. According to Shmuel Merlin, Senator Harry S. Truman was a relatively enthusiastic supporter of the Bergson Group, and yet he was the sole senator who for a time dissociated himself from it, even though reluctantly. Perhaps his change of heart was the result of the effect of the Zionist propaganda. According to Merlin, however, it was because of the hatred of the Bergson Group rampant in the State Department, even without the help of the Zionists.

31. The report quoted above is not necessarily trustworthy, since it was written by individuals whose hostility to the Bergson Group was no smaller than that of the Jewish leadership. There are other testimonies, however, independent of this report, that repeatedly describe the same details. One crude example from the report is Dr. Goldmann's claim that an American Senator, who was a supporter of Bergson, was a fanatic; it hints that the wife of that Senator was in love with Bergson. This is not the level of a proper political discussion and certainly not of a report by a high official in the State Department.

This report is an expression of a situation that is both pathological and pathetic. The President of the World Jewish Congress devoted much time together with the head of the Middle East desk in the Department of State in the middle of World War II. The topic: a group of foreigners who were visitors for about four years, who were allegedly drawing money by deception. As if getting money by deception bothered this Zionist leader more than mass murder. The report concerning the conversation sounds more like gossip than anything else, but, to repeat, there is no want of documents about Dr. Goldmann himself in this connection. The report by Isaiah Berlin to the Foreign Office in London, F0371 35041 XCA 047702, dated November 15 1943, corroborates the State Department report at hand, as well as the claim that the War Refugee Board was established because of public pressure.

32. Sarah E. Peck, "The Campaign for an American Response to the Nazi Holocaust, 1943-1945", *The Journal of Contemporary History*, Volume 15, Number 2, pp. 367-400, whose editor, Walter Laqueur, was mentioned above as an important historian who himself expressed the establishment view of the whole affair.

33. Amos Eilon, *Zero Hour*, in Hebrew, 1980.

33a. * In this book there is no discussion of the national leadership in Palestine concerning the Nazi atrocities, since this is an emotionally charged item that is not closely related to the story of the activities of the committees that Bergson organized. Nevertheless, I would like to refer to one clear item. The delegation of the Irgun National Military Organization in the United States that Hillel Kook headed decided to take active part in the revival of that Organization by appointing a new commander in chief in order to implement its policy of committing acts of hostilities against the British authorities in Palestine because of its prohibition of rescue operations. Were the national leadership in Palestine ready to deal with the problem in any possible way, there would be room for organizing a national protest movement instead of reviving the Irgun National Military Organization, and then the attitude of the Zionist Organization in the United States of America to the Committee to Save the Jews of Europe would have been more humane. It is therefore clear that there is no sense in attempts to present the history of the Jewish settlement in Palestine officially, once from the viewpoint of those who deem themselves heirs to the official Zionist leadership, and once from that of those who deem themselves heirs to the dissidents, as is the custom in Israel today, but that it is required that a search should commence for a political consensus on the matter, and the natural starting point of such a search should be none other than the rehabilitation of the Bergson committees.

* As to the attitude of the national leadership towards the Nazi atrocities at the time, sufficient accusation is found in a paper that defends it, written by Dina Porat, "'Al-Demi' — Intellectual Leaders in Palestine facing the Holocaust, 1943-45", in Hebrew, *Hazionuth*, 5, 1983, 245-75. The most up-to-date material on this matter is Tom Segev's book, *The Seventh Million: The Israelis and the Holocaust*, 1991, English version, New York: Hill and Wang, 1993. It contains much material and many significant references and harsh discussions; it directs almost no accusations against the Haganah, and even its passing reference (silently omitted from the English version) to the Committee to Save the Jews of Europe includes no mention of the hostility to it of the Jewish and the Zionist Establishments, though the first edition of this book was already published by then. Segev refers to the book by Dina Porat, *Trapped Leadership*, in Hebrew, 1986, p. 493 of which he quotes (p. 466): "The Jewish settlement did not alter its way of life and did not change course because of the Holocaust." I find this shocking, because behind it stands Porat's standard claim that we are too prone to self-

accusation, since, anyway, nothing could be done: the aim of her discussion is to save the reputation of the national leadership at any cost. She would not even consider the alternative possibility that the Jewish settlement could not be mobilized for action because it had a defective leadership. Nevertheless, all things considered, Segev is right in suggesting that her book is important (*loc. cit.*). He also refers there to the moving book of S. B. Beit-Zvi, *Post Ugandan Zionism in the Crisis of the Holocaust*, in Hebrew, 1977 (which describes the very same "Al-Demi" movement as Porat does, but honestly). Segev also cites what Ben-Gurion said in an interview that he, Segev, had organized and from another interview with Saul Friedlander. I do not know how such severe self-accusations do not sound traumatic. Yet Nahum Goldmann did the same in an interview that appears in the television film mentioned in Note 1 above and in his autobiography, mentioned in Note 34a below.

* As to the philosophical aspect of Porat's views, and more so of the views of her predecessor Yehuda Bauer, the amazing thing about them is that they rely on a philosophical thesis advocated by Hannah Arendt, in the very opposite direction, the thesis of the banality of evil. This thesis is nothing but a disclaimer: there is no room for any complaint, as the matter is commonplace and of no specific significance. In general, this disclaimer is amazing as it involves the refusal to admit that the specific in the evil of the destruction of Europe's Jewry is precisely in its being far from the banal; especially this disclaimer is amazing in that it unintentionally obliterates the obvious fact that the neglect and indifference to suffering, as exhibited both by the Jewish leadership and by the leadership of the Allies, do not approach the severity of the crime and brutality of the Nazis. It is therefore very clear that the *apologia* of Yehuda Bauer and Dina Porat for the Jewish and the Zionist leadership does not serve them particularly well. They will be considered less culpable and more human if and when their heirs will officially give up this apologetic attitude that Bauer and Porat ascribe to them.

* As to Segev's book, this is not the place to respond to the relevant material it contains. I should only respond to its discussion of the court case of Rudolf Kastner, and to its response to the protest of Yehuda Elkana regarding the Israeli use of the Holocaust (in Hebrew, in the daily newspaper *Haaretz*, March 3, 1988). Elkana's admonition, that was expressed nobly and frankly, should not be overlooked, and, of course, his recommendations should be accepted that when the Holocaust is mentioned one should not lose all sense of proportion and it should not be used to strengthen the Masada complex. Regrettably, however, his proposal is not a plan for action. Israel cannot escape the thicket of its confusions and inhuman conduct (including, let me add, the murder of Kastner) that is encouraged by the misuse of the memory of the Holocaust, which pains Elkana so, without a frank and broad discussion of unpleasant facts — especially the negative attitude of the Jewish leadership in general and the Zionist leadership in particular to the committees for the rescue of the European Jews that Bergson instituted — distantly, and with no self-incrimination and no apologetics, with a measure of what historians call historical distance or scientific objectivity. *

34. Thirty years later, one of these officials remarked, in a telephone conversation with Peck, "Bergson was one of our small group who tried to do all that was possible" (p. 388 note 60).

34a. * More about the absence of expression of remorse in the face of the Holocaust. Nahum Goldmann's autobiography appeared years after Sarah Peck's paper. He says there that what prevented the rescue of Jews was the absence of a Jewish lobby and a lack of imagination.

There is justice to his claim that he had been unimaginative, no doubt, and this explains both his inaction and his lack of sincere expression of remorse. But of course this does not explain his resentment of the efforts that other people exerted to organize help. More interesting is his excuse by reference to the absence of a Jewish lobby at the time. For, the explanation of the resentment of the leadership of the American Jewish community to the rescue was linked to their fear that they had of the establishment of a Jewish lobby, as the quotation from Sarah Peck indicates, which quotation is also repeated in the opening of this chapter, regarding the declaration of patriotism by Rabbi Stephen Wise. The attitude in the United States towards lobbies was negative ever since its establishment but, nevertheless, before World War II there was more activity of a Jewish lobby, of Jewish pressure groups, than in the period under discussion here. The picture altered after the war, in the period in which the ideology of the Founding Fathers was replaced with a new one.

* There is a severe and strange defect in all the discussions regarding the matter of pluralism that students of sociology, political science and political philosophy have published to date: whereas generally there are many who claim paternity for every popular idea, the idea of pluralism is an orphan, and no notice is taken (and there is even an indirect denial) of the fact that it is the child of the remorse that soldiers of the Allied armies in Europe felt when encountering the Nazi atrocities. In this respect the activities of the Bergson Group are of great importance, of course, in that they did organize a *de facto* Jewish lobby exactly as their opponents feared (because of the traditional hostility to all lobbies). At the time Bergson himself appreciated this fear, but declared that the rescue of European Jews took priority over the prevention of anti-Semitism in the United States. Behind this assessment there was both a power of the imagination that his opponents lacked and a high regard for American democracy that they also lacked. The absence of regard for western democracy is a severe defect in Israel, which lives in the shadow of the Dreyfus affair, of the collapse of democracy in Germany, and of the destruction of Europe's Jews. As is explained in the discussion of the new Zionist myth (pp. 278-82), this myth is the contention that a sharp rise in anti-Semitism is sooner or later to be expected all over the world, as well as the view of Jews as aliens in the lands where they happen to dwell. In this respect Bergson's activities and the rise of pluralism certainly refute this contention (assuming it can at all be tested by empirical means). *

34b. * The claim that secrecy conflicts with democracy rests on general considerations (which obtain despite arguments in favor of secrecy) of the view that secrecy is essential for productive negotiations. I was therefore disagreeably surprised when I found support for my view in Tom Segev's *The Seventh Million, op. cit.*, p. 21, the story of the negotiations between the Jewish Agency for Palestine and the Nazi Government of Germany, when the Germans were surprised to discover that the conflict of interest between the Jewish delegates was fierce, "threatening the entire agreement". Segev refers to information found in Edwin Black, *The Transfer Agreement*, New York: Macmillan, 1984. I therefore do not know if the explanation I gave to the preference of secrecy holds; quite possibly this preference is merely an expression of the well-known phenomenon of the persecuted endorsing the complaint of the persecutors, even if it makes little sense and is but an excuse. For, anti-Semitism, contrary to the traditional hatred of the Jews, was always accompanied by the complaint that the Jews are too conspicuous in public life. I was greatly surprised to read in the autobiography of my admired teacher Karl Popper, who is of Jewish descent, the contention that the assimilation of Jews in the Austro-Hungarian Empire was insufficient, even were it more massive, but that they had to do so quietly, without drawing attention to themselves. See Chapter 21 of his autobiography, published in Paul Arthur Schilpp, editor, *The Philosophy of Karl Popper*, LaSalle, IL, Open Court, 1974, and also as a separate volume, *The Unending Quest*, London, Fontana, 1977 and other editions. He expresses there a definite view of the duty of the socialist Jews in the Austro-Hungarian Empire early in the twentieth century. In his view their duty was clearly to keep silent. I find it hard to understand why the demand to be quiet is limited there to socialists alone, since from their own viewpoint nothing is more significant than political action and nothing is less significant than religious origins, whereas from different viewpoints there is hardly a difference between socialist and other political activity. I read Popper to say, first, that all Jews (the assimilated included) should have kept silent as long as anti-Semitism was not intolerable — so as not to increase the hostility towards them — and, second, that this requirement applies particularly to those whose views might annoy the public that might become anti-Semitic (and socialism is such a view). He expresses puzzlement at the fact that this requirement was not generally received. Obviously he is unaware of the fact that it is traditionally Jewish. Of course, it is not reasonable to complain about its acceptance in the mediaeval society in which it evolved and took root. Not so in twentieth-century Austria, and definitely not in the Zionist movement. Nevertheless, the Zionist movement regrettably did endorse the policy of restraint and secrecy. *

34c. * Tom Segev's book, mentioned in the previous note, documents in some detail (pp. 55 ff.) the spread of the information in Palestine about the dimensions of the catastrophe and the response of the national institutions that was a sort of announcement of the facts to the Jewish public. But, Segev concludes (p. 67 of the Hebrew edition, silently omitted from the translation, p. 76), "Except for those few months of organized mourning, no one directed the editors of the daily press as to how to handle the story of the destruction of the Jews" and that the shocking information was silenced by the excuse (stressed by chief labor leader Berl Katznelson) that the public was indifferent to it. On page 78 Segev discusses the Revisionists' accusation that the leaders were concealing information, their response to that accusation, and so on. He concludes (p. 79): "Perhaps the [Jewish] Agency feared damaging the chance for rescuing more Jews. But it may be that the Agency concealed information in an attempt to moderate the public response so as not to lose control over it." (The last words are from the Hebrew version, p.69; they are omitted from the English translation.) He adds a note that documents somewhat the fact that the leadership forbade publication of information about the dimension of the catastrophe.

* When the first edition of this book appeared I had no secondary information about the situation in Palestine similar in credibility and detail to Segev's discussion which is valuable as the beginning of a relatively open discussion, despite the fact that its information is not always clear and not always accurate, and it is hard to suppose that it covers the whole affair. Segev does not ask if it was the duty of the Jewish national leadership to mobilize Jewish public opinion in Palestine in support of the European Jews (even were that public indifferent to their fate). In my opinion this is exactly the role of a responsible political leadership, since an amorphous public cannot possibly initiate political action. In my opinion it is clear that had the leadership shown even a little concern, Bergson would have attempted to organize a national protest movement rather than reconstruct the Irgun National Military Organization, as he did in despair, after the national leadership in Palestine sabotaged every possibility of cooperation between the delegation of the Irgun Military Organization and the Zionist leadership in the United States. (Presumably a

necessary condition for such cooperation was clear pressure from the Zionist leadership in Palestine.) ∗

35. Historians praise Jabotinsky in this connection, without explaining, and without discussing the matter presented in the explanation here.

36. A funny example of this dangerous, anachronistic attitude is the proposal of Israeli political leaders to appoint Simone Weil to the Israeli Presidency. After she was convinced that the proposal was not a joke, she rejected it by explaining that she was French (see the Israeli press on February 14, 1983, especially the daily *Haaretz*).

37. Of course this is a normal step in public activity, done whether negotiation is in principle possible or not.

37a. ∗ These days historians, especially those who side with Practical Zionism and with Ben-Gurion, see the seed of sovereignty in his approach already in his very early steps. I should therefore remind the reader of the fact, explained in the first part of this book, that, in contrast to Political Zionism, Practical Zionism opposed sovereignty as long as one could distance oneself from it, and that in the opinion of Ben-Gurion, secrecy was the necessary condition for success. From the very early days of British rule in Palestine, when the Haganah Military Organization was founded, Jabotinsky demanded that it operate in the open whereas Ben-Gurion preferred it underground. Jabotinsky acted on his views, but without support from the national organizations his action was doomed to failure and he was exiled. In 1940 he fought for a Jewish Army, that is to say, for the legalization of the Irgun National Military Organization. Ben-Gurion repeated his demand for secrecy in the last Zionist Congress before Independence, in 1946. See next chapter.

∗ In his *Introduction to a Different Zionism* [in Hebrew], 1975, Yigal Eilam stresses the difference between openness and secrecy, and the fact that, unlike Ben-Gurion, Jabotinsky sided with openness from the very start; but he also argues differently: he says (p. 133), contrary to known facts, that "already in 1931 the Zionist leadership proved that it was able to break its relations with the British Government" and he endorses (p. 133) the opinion of Ben-Gurion who, said that "in retrospect... in 1933... we did not fix new aims for our policy... but we had a different grasp of the political ways. We did not think that political action is talks between delegates, as all of Arlosoroff's predecessors did,... but in the mobilization of the public and activating it politically." In addition, Eilam himself stresses (p. 136) that in the opinion of Ben-Gurion the Zionist Congress that preceded World War II was a waste of time as that Congress failed to decide that the aim of Zionism was "the establishment of a Hebrew state in Palestine." The idea of "the mobilization of the public and activating it politically in opposition to the British Government" was initiated by Jabotinsky, and Bergson attempted to realize it — with ill-success, and this time due to the absence of support (not of the Zionist directorship but) of the command of the Irgun National Military Organization, as is explained in the next chapter but one. The reference of Ben-Gurion to Arlosoroff in this context indicates that in his opinion Arlosoroff endorsed (a short time prior to his murder) ideas of Political Zionism that his predecessors considered heretic and a betrayal of Practical Zionism. (Ben-Gurion was among these, of course, and only in retrospect did he choose to view Arlosoroff as his predecessor, and not Jabotinsky, nor Bergson, and this only because he wished to credit his own party.)

∗ Arlosoroff did recommend a demand for independence long before his colleagues in his party agreed to it: they endorsed only in 1942 the recommendation that he had made at least a decade earlier. See his Jerusalem Diary (referred to in Note 20b above), p. 260.

* Clearly, then, the different Zionism that Eilam discusses is a fusion of views of the Practical and Political Zionists, and a blurring of the gap between theory and practice. See more in Note 22a above. The writing of history with hindsight is a habit that is hard to kick, and if it is done openly and frankly, it may even have some value. When it is done unannounced, readers are bound to receive distorted views of history (and here this practice is meant to vindicate both Ben-Gurion and Eilam), especially when an ideological group rewrites history in an attempt to achieve self-vindication. Consequently, errors are left uncorrected — regarding both the past and the future, as many historians and philosophers have observed. *

37b. * Bergson's questions clearly indicate how little the Zionist leadership was concerned with independence, since every sincere concern would have raised them as well as efforts to answer them. Answers were given to some of them *ad hoc*, in efforts to avoid confrontation. The most obvious example was the abolition of the Constituent Assembly, and, still worse, this was done on the excuse that it was transformed into the first Knesset, the first Israeli Parliament which was incapable of handling Bergson's questions properly. And so of necessity the Knesset is irresponsible and frustrated.

* The inner logic of Bergson's questions to Dr. Weizmann was so strong that the confusion that prevented their being answered imposed step-by-step the identification of the Israeli nation as a Jewish community. And as the identification of the Israeli nation with the Israeli Jewish community was unacceptable, the view was developed step-by-step that Israel belongs to the whole Jewish community, past, present and future. This is the New Zionist Myth that will be discussed later on in detail. This myth should be viewed as the logical corollary of the refusal to answer Bergson's questions, that is, as the consequence of the lack of interest in independence, namely, of the fact that the leadership of a community preferred the preservation of its own status over the national interest. Thus, when American advisers came to Israel with far-reaching proposals, instead of responding to the proposals themselves (as they were quite objectionable), national leaders said they refused to entertain any proposal that might change Israel's social structure. In other words, their stay at the helm seemed to them so significant, that they found a priori objectionable any proposal that might unhinge their status as leaders, so that they rejected it without prior public debate. The import of such details is that they indicate the road to change: the genuinely interested in sovereignty might find it profitable to respond to Bergson's questions even though this may demand the replacement of their party-political leadership. *

38. See the book by Isaac Zaar, mentioned above in note 22.

39. Apart from this there were the minutes of the meetings of the diverse committees, twelve in all, the Directorship, and the Executive, not to mention the many separately prepared minutes of the diverse bodies of the Zionist organization.

40. The Revisionist delegates at the Congress proposed that it should decide on the establishment of a temporary government (see p. 499). In addition they proposed that the Congress should decide to abolish the Zionist Shekel (which was the membership fee for the Zionist organization and granted its owners the right to vote) and grant the right to vote for the Zionist organization to all the Jews in Palestine and in the refugee camps (see p. 532).

Since the only person in the Zionist establishment to mention the possibility of a temporary government was Dr. Zelig Brodetzky, perhaps his contention should be examined. He rejected it on the ground that no country that would play host to it (p. 120 of the minutes; see p. 185). I do not know if this was an excuse or the result of some inquiry; it seems to me that the Administration of the United States of America might have done so, however reluctantly, especially after it has established the War Refugee Board.

* A quasi official document concerning the Government of the United States regarding the British rule in Palestine is the authoritative book by Carl J. Friedrich, mentioned above, in Note 28a *

41. According to David Niv, an agreement was drawn between the Irgun National Organization and the Revisionist Youth Movement, Betar, in the year 1939 after what he calls the Paris Conference, namely the meeting between David Raziel and Vladimir Jabotinsky in Paris at the beginning of 1939. In April 1939, Niv claims, David Raziel appeared as the commander of he organization in Betar uniform. Nevertheless, he agrees that this is exceptional and contrary to the tradition of the Irgun National Military Organization. He quotes the testimony of Professor H. S. Halevi (who was present at the meeting in Paris): "The main cause for the meeting [in Paris] is rooted somewhere in the past in the fundamental education of the members of the Organization since the [earliest] days of Gideon [Tehomi]. The organization is an army, and an army cannot belong to any one party. This education was never completely eradicated in the life of the Irgun National Military Organization, even though its command was to the largest extent composed of members of Betar. Unconsciously — and in the minds of some of the command in clear consciousness — there was a tendency to assert the independence of the Irgun National Military Organization, even though nobody doubted that the head of Betar [Jabotinsky] was also the Chief Commander of the National Military Organization."

    Kook denies Niv's story and claims that to the best of his knowledge, during the time of David Raziel, there was no organizational contact between the Irgun National Military Organization and the Revisionist Party but that this connection was made after his death in 1941 and was disconnected after the appointment of Menachem Begin to the command of the Organization in 1943.

    * The biography of David Raziel by Arieh Naor, mentioned in Note 21a agrees with all this. *

42. It is not the purpose of this book to discuss Begin's opinion concerning the history of the Irgun National Military Organization, but since the public naturally identifies the official ideology of that Organization with his opinions, it may be worth mentioning that while he was in command, he disconnected his relations with the Revisionist movement. Even though in the eve of his life he referred to the past without mention of this fact, it accords with Kook's claims.

43. David Niv, Volume 5, p. 208.

44. Since his meeting with Bergson, Ben-Gurion became aware of this fact. Testimony of this is to be found in his speech at the Twenty-Second Zionist Congress. See p. 189.

45. Among Ben-Gurion's victories, it is well known, are also brilliant military ones. The political end of the War of Independence was clear — survival. This was the only one of Israel's wars that had a clear political end, as distinct from a clear military end. Ben-Gurion's political retreat, and his leaving the state of the nation in a cloud, did not facilitate the clarification of the situation, and the presentation of a political purpose of medium range or of long range. Israel thus lost the political initiative and has not regained it to this very day.

46. Amnon Rubinstein, *Constitutional Law in Israel*, in Hebrew, first edition, 1974, p. 21. [In the fifth edition, alas! he took this back.]
47. Since Israeli law does not recognize the Israeli nation, the Israeli identity card decides the nationality of its bearers and the greatest majority of Israelis are thereby declared members of the Jewish nation or the Arab nation.
48. See Rubinstein, *op. cit.*, pp. 84-94.
49. Shlomo Avineri is praiseworthy for the concluding chapter of his book (see note 17 above) which presents these details explicitly and frankly. In that chapter he defends Israel's abnormalcy from the viewpoint of a secular Zionist position.
50. A. B. Yehoshua, *Between Right and Right*, (in Hebrew) 1980. The chapter in defense of normalcy defends not normalization but the uniqueness of Israel; the book proposes to institutionalize this uniqueness and make it the accepted norm; that is to say, the author recommends that Israel's abnormal situation be seen as the national norm for Israel forever and a day. In this way he defends the New Zionist Myth (p. 118): "After the state was founded one could say that Zionism was over because its task was completed. One who climbs a mountain ceases to be a climber the moment he reaches the peak and indeed the definition of Zionism has to be altered." Thus, Yehoshua like Avineri (see previous note) recognizes that the New Zionist myth differs from the traditional Zionist attitude. Here is his new definition, which he italicizes (page 119): "*A Zionist is a person who recognizes the principle that the State of Israel belongs not only to her citizens but to the whole Jewish people.*"

    As a corollary, he proposes that there should be Zionists even among the Arabs of the State of Israel (p. 125), and he claims quite erroneously that this is a normal definition, which applies "to every other nation in the world," identifying this alleged technical fact with the national Israeli identity without using the word "national". Here the author simply overlooks the fact that in liberal democracies nationality and citizenship are identical. At the end of his book, he appears as a victim of all the confusions and absurdities that in this book he considers the result of the abnormalcy of Israel. He should be praised, however, for his awareness of the confusions and absurdities that exist in Israel and for his having presented in his book a proposal to overcome them. But it is very sad to see how obvious his failure is. To repeat, there is no escape from this failure except by a true normalization.

50a. * Gershon Weiler, *Jewish Theocracy* (see note 56 below). The description conveyed here in a brief survey is far from sufficient. It has to be supplemented by many details, which invite a broad social research, and I cannot enter into the matter here. Most research in this area does not pass the minimal criteria accepted in the research community as a matter of course. To mention a small project that I was personally involved in, a study performed by Moshe Berent, Judith Buber Agassi and myself concerning national awareness (and supported by the Sapir Foundation, Tel Aviv University), which incidentally exposes the weakness of other researches in the same field. This fact was not noticed by Israeli reviewers of our output (*Who is an Israeli?* in Hebrew, 1991), and the reviews it did receive are defensive, as are the researches on the status of women in Israel, on the relations between Jews and non-Jews since independance. (Among these are political, social and labor relations.) It may be mentioned here that despite their low credibility, the Israeli researches about Israel have a high status. Hopefully more credible ones will soon replace them. See also Note 17 above *

51. Israel will become a commendable religious center if a sufficiently large number of Jews will show interest. This is a distinct possibility, both because of the sanctity of the Holy Land for all Jews and because the Jewish religion will be the religion of most Israelis, as a matter of course.
52. See Yonathan Shapiro's book mentioned above, note 20, especially pp. 218-25 and 241-51, concerning the long tradition in Jewish Palestine of the undemocratic control of activists over the political parties by rather unacceptable means.
53. The absurdity and deception on which the character of the Israeli Parliament, the Knesset, rests are conspicuous. Some members of the Knesset are non-Jews; by law, they have equal rights and yet they cannot utilize this equality even within the Knesset.
54. This confusion makes it difficult to maintain a clear national identity, when the national identity is an integral part of the existence of the modern normal nation-state. The idea that Israel is an oppressed nation, despite the absence of a foreign oppressor, is to be found in the writings of Dan V. Segre, who uses the expression "self-colonialization", which has already been accepted in the literature. See Dan V. Segre, *A Crisis of Identity: Israel and Zionism*, London, Oxford University Press, 1980, pp. 8, 9, and passim.
55. Even though Israeli economic initiative is bound to fail because of the absence of Israeli political initiative, its very existence should not be overlooked, as it is a repeated phenomenon on the Israeli scene. It is the initiative itself that is here noticed, not its success or failure.
56. Gershon Weiler, *Jewish Theocracy*, Brill, The Hague, 1988 (Hebrew edition, 1976).
57. Demands made before the establishment of Israel were certainly political, such as the demand to establish a Hebrew army, the demand from the American Government to consider the rescue of the European Jews as one of the war efforts, the demand to declare independence unilaterally, and, of course, finally, Ben-Gurion's declaration of independence on May 14, 1948.
57a. * Reviewing the first edition of this book Yehoshua Rash claimed (*Kivvunim: A Periodical for Zionism and Judaism*, in Hebrew, 27, 1985) that my proposal was not realistic since the western type liberal nation-state is not ideal, and it is therefore not worth having in exchange for Jewish ideals. In my response (*ibid.*, 28, 1985) I agreed that the modern liberal nation-state is not ideal, and added that I suggest giving up nothing in exchange for it except the confusion between religious and secular utopianism. *
58. The victory of the minority plan could happen even in a democratic society and in a democratic state, and for the reason of a clear inner logic: when action is required in an emergency and only one plan is available, its acceptance is a foregone conclusion, and there is no time to change it.
59. This is, of course, in addition to the fact that an enlightened state allows resident aliens the option of joining the nation, naturalizing and becoming a citizen with equal rights and duties.
60. Benjamin Disraeli claimed (in a political novel, incidentally) that there are two nations in England: the poor and the rich. In contradistinction, Marx claimed later on that there is no English nation at all but only two nations in the whole of the modern world: the poor workers and their rich employers.

61. Judaism as a nation-religion was not an exception, not abnormal, in the social and political structure that was accepted in medieval Europe, but Judaism is abnormal today. Those who blame the abnormalcy of Judaism on its uniqueness ignore this fact.

62. This opinion was expressed both in the writings of Pinsker and in the speech of Ben-Gurion at the last Zionist Congress, which as referred to in Chapter 18 above. Nevertheless, there was no normalization. Ben-Gurion himself abstained from declaring normal independence in Israel, and the Jews of the State of Israel still behave as if they were a national minority in their own country. They do not identify their nationality and citizenship as is customary in independent nation-states of the type that the Jewish national liberation movement attempted to achieve from its very beginning, and which it expressed in the idea of auto-emancipation.

63. This is so because the abnormalcy became normal in Israel, and life in a permanent state of war also became the accepted norm here. Instead, the termination of the state of war should be high on the national agenda and in the center of the national concern.

64. The existence of two official languages in Israel is part of the cloudy situation in which it is not clear whether Israel is a national state or a bi-national state [or perhaps a bilingual one]. In the United States foreign languages are blooming without their being official, whereas in Israel the situation is the reverse. The liberal writer A. B. Yehoshua complains about the fact that some poets among the Israeli Arabs write in Hebrew and in his opinion they should write in Arabic. In the Israeli republic proposed here the situation would be clear. There would be one national language, but the Arabic language would be respected and encouraged as the language of ethnic minorities.

65. When these lines went to press, the possibility of realizing this idea improved and it is a pity that the current Government of Israel shows the same lack of initiative as its predecessors, but invites others to show initiative.

66. This unclear situation feeds the hostile propaganda of the governments of the Arab states concerning Israeli expansionism.

67. The problem of Soviet Jewry is unique both because the Jews there were (and still are) a recognized national minority and because the Soviet Union did not permit emigration. Such a situation calls for special considerations. * After the collapse of the Soviet Union the problem was greatly simplified, but has still not been solved, and this is not the place to deliberate about it. *

67a. * Messianism played an important role in secular politics as Romantic thinkers tried to mobilize sympathy for nationalism by appealing to the feeling of uniqueness of their people. The strong religious appeal of the idea of the siblinghood of humanity upset these thinkers, and in order to overcome it they addressed their people as the Chosen People. There is no harm in the fact that the Blacks of the United States, for example, often used the slogan "Let my people go!" but today there is scarcely a need to point out the great evil of the German Romantic thinkers' description of their own people as the Chosen People, while expressing contempt for their neighbors and raising false messianic political hopes. I will not refer here to the rich literature in political philosophy about secular messianism and its dangers. (Perhaps the most significant among these is Karl Popper's book mentioned in Note 5 above; the works of Jacob Talmon and Uriel Tal deserve mention too.) Israel suffers a traditional confusion of secularism and hostility to religion. This confusion conceals the possibility of secular messianism even well within religious circles, despite the fact that in

Israel secular messianism has a specific expression, and it is "hearing the footsteps of the Messiah". Nevertheless, this messianism is popular in non-religious circles, and even in some quite anti-religious ones. Historically, secular messianism, introduced in Israel in intellectual circles in the Hebrew University of Jerusalem, spread to pseudo-intellectual circles and from there the affliction diffused unchecked.

* The researches of Uriel Tal are particularly significant in the present context, since he deemed secular messianism a political threat to Israel's survival, especially when masked as religious. The religious philosopher-scientist Isaiah Leibovitch was the main public opponent of secular messianism. Since it is customary to associate secular messianism with so-called right-wing circles, it should be noted that it is a new phenomenon, not influenced by Zionist right-wing writings; even the religious right wing in Palestine was not afflicted with it. *

68. The only book that comes close to discussing the topic is Craig C. Pinder and Larry F. Moore, editors, *Middle Range Theory and the Study of Organizations*, the Hague, Nijhoff, 1980, which intentionally confuses the idea of development in the middle range with the middle stage in the development of an idea, and is therefore not an excellent book. * The reason for the absence of middle range policies is discussed in my "Rationalizing Politics" in N. Oren, *Intellectuals in Politics*, Jerusalem, The Magnes Press, The Hebrew University, Jerusalem, 1984, pp. 82-100. *

69. This throws some light on a variety of factors that touch on problems of legislation presented in a confused manner in the theoretical legal literature, whether political, social, or legal. Some of these laws cannot be implemented, whereas others can. Similarly, there are laws that are difficult to introduce into the system and there are laws that become valid the moment they are enacted, becoming broadly accepted by the whole nation and effecting changes in the system. To this last kind of law belong the pulling oneself up by one's bootstraps. A clear example is the Declaration of the Independence of Israel, but not all the declarations of independence are of this character, as the bitter experience in the African continent has shown.

70. I know of no secondary literature that deserves mention concerning this political body. The original literature includes the original pamphlet *On Our National Future* and the weekly of that movement, *Ahduth* (= Unity), all in Hebrew, 1946-1948.

71. I should mention, as an example, the movement of Bergson and his group. Though it was voluntarily dismantled, leaving no heir in the United States, the group has contributed much to the development of the Jewish ethnic group there, because there was not sufficient readiness among American Jews before World War II to recognize themselves without qualification as an ethnic group.

    This is contrary to Goldmann's excuse, in his autobiography, that, in addition to the lack of courage and imagination, the inaction of the Jewish leadership in America during the mass-destruction of the Jews of Europe is explicable by the absence of a Jewish lobby in the United States: it was not the absence of a Jewish lobby that led to inaction; it was rather, action, however constrained, that has led to the creation of the Jewish lobby and thus it contributed also to the recent blooming of ethnicity in the United States and the disavowal of the former national ideology of the melting pot. * See also Note 34a. *

72. The logical strength of this discussion rests on the very existence of the State of Israel and is expressed by its not resting on the claim, sometimes made and sometimes denied, that the Jews of other nations are, in effect, Israeli citizens.

72a. * The claim that the Jews of the normal nation-states have no nationality is basically different from the claim that they have dual nationality, and the confusion between the two is rooted in the fact that, contrary to the normal nation-states, in which nationality and citizenship are identical, in Israel nationality is deemed basic and significant, whereas citizenship is deemed a mere technicality. There is a disastrous confusion in the Israeli usage of the word "citizenship" in two different senses, one in accord with Western usage and one in opposition to it. In the present discussion the confusion is avoided by taking the choice between the two kinds of usage as open. One option is that Jews have no nationality. This option rests on the claim that the Jewish people did not fully undergo the process of national development and therefore did not become a nation proper. Contrary to this claim, one might observe that Israeli nationhood is to be recognized as a process, even if it is not completed, and to ask, how can it be used as a positive political instrument. The Jews of other nations are not partners in this process of the development of the Israeli nation. The refusal to recognize this fact perpetuates the confusion. The other option is that the Jews of the other nations have a dual nationality, which raises the question, why are Israeli Jews deprived of this right to this same dual nationality? For such a dual nationality (known as nationality plus ethnic identity) is possessed by the Irish Americans and the Italian Americans, and why should not an Israeli nationality of this sort also hold for Israeli Jews and Israeli Christians? Hence, the refusal to recognize the possibility of Israeli nationality for a non-Jew robs the Israeli Jews of their nationality. An additional option is that Jews of other nations are citizens of their own nations and Jews by nationality. The refusal to recognize the affiliation of Jews outside Israel with different nationalities is the full recognition of anti-Semitism as an accomplished fact. When, against this, it is claimed that Denmark is not anti-Semitic, the retort to this is with the metaphysical claim that all non-Jews are somehow anti-Semitic — even if their conduct is exemplary. Alternatively, it is said that Denmark is an exception that does not refute the rule. This is illogical, as in this way the defenders of the contention in question simply declare their refusal to change their minds in the light of contrary evidence. The right to cling to views despite all arguments should be defended, but not exercised, as it is unwise.

* There is, nonetheless, a kernel of truth to this confusion, and even an important one; it is that whereas the Italian identity of the Italian Americans differs from their Catholicism, the Judaism of the American Jews is both ethnic and religious, akin to the Italian-Catholic identity of Italian Americans. This explains the tendency in the United States to speak of the American Jews, as having an Israeli origin — even if their origin is not modern Israel. *

73. See note 56 above.
74. See notes 20 and 52 above.
74a. * As to the unity of the fate of humanity deriving from the possibility of humanity's self-destruction, see my book, *Technology: Philosophical and Social Aspects*, Dordrecht, Kluwer, 1985. *
75. It is well known that political parties in Israel do not function in a normal manner; this is not the place to discuss this significant fact. It should be noticed, however, that normal activities of rank-and-file party members in Israel are limited to canvassing before elections. The phenomenon of canvassing is well recognized in the Western world, but the extreme character that it has in Israel is explained by the abnormal situation in Israel in general.

Name Index

A
Abella, Irving, n04, n1c
Acawi, Mustafa, 233
Agassi, Judith Buber, 26, n50a
Agnon, S. Y., 107
Agranat, Shimon, 290, 301
Ahad Ha'am, 108-10, 115-16, 275
Amrami, Yaakov, n1
Arendt, Hanna, n33a
Arlosoroff, Chaim, 191, n20b, n37a
Avineri, Shlomo, 111, 113, 147, n17, n19, n49, n50

B
Balfour, Arthur James, Lord, 117, 124
Barchin, Michael, 143
Bauer Yeuda, n33a
Begin, Menachem, 32, 137, 147, 193-97, 199-200, 205, 255, 299, n21a, n41, n42
Beit-Zvi, S. B., n16b, n33a
Ben-Ami, Isaac, 143
Ben-Eliezer, Arie, 143, 193, n21a
Ben-Gurion, David, 32, 118-20, 133, 168, 172, 182-91, 198-99, 205-6, 253, 296-97, n20a, n33a, n37a, n44, n57, n62
Benjamin, Rabbi (Yehoshua Radler-Feldmann), n16b
Ben-Yehuda, Eliezer, 107, 109
Berent, Moshe, 26, n50a

Berlin, Sir Isaia, n31
Bevin, Ernst, 195
Black, Edwin, n34b
Böll, Henrich, 15
Bonaparte, Napoleon, 64, 69
Brandt, Joel, 163
Brodetzki, Zelig, 185, n40
Buber, Martin, 108-10, 115, 275, n16a

C
Chaplin, Charlie, 243, 287
Churchill, Sir Winston, 303

D
D'Israeli, Benjamin, n60
Dinstein, Yoram, 89, n10
Dostoevsky, Fiodor, 98
Dreyfus, Alfred, 95-96, n34a

E
Eban, Abba, 10
Eden, Anthony, 155
Eilam, Yigal, n20b, n37a
Eilon, Amos, 163, n34
Einstein, Albert, 244
Elkana, Yehuda, n33a
Eshkoli, Hava, 19
Evron, Boaz, n02

F
Faraday, Michael, n3

Friedlander, Saul, n33a
Friedmann, Georges, 133, 270, 298
Friedrich, Carl J., n28a, n40

G
Gandhi, Mohandâs K., 90, 93
Gellner, Ernest, 7, n5
Gillette, Guy, Senator, n22b
Goldmann, Nahum, 132-33, 156-60, 162, 165-57, 183. 186, n31, n33a, n34a, n71
Golomb, Eliahu, n20a
Graetz, Heinrich, 106
Grossmann, Meir, 188
Gruenbaum, Ytzchak, 187, 190
Grunner, Dov, 91

H
Habib, Absalom, 91
Halevi, H. S., n41
Halifax, Edward, Earl, 155
Hall, Cordell, 155
Hastings, Adrian, 7
Hazan, Yaakov, 185
Hegel, Georg, Willhelm. Friedrich, 94, 243
Herzl, Theodor, 102-3, 108, 111-15, 121, 147, 189, 252, 273-75, n18, n19
Hitler, Adolf, 156, 159, 243
Hobbes, Thomas, 61, 86
Hollinger, David A., n01
Hopkins, Harry Lloyd, 155, n28

J
Jabotinsky, Aeri, 143, 200
Jabotinsky, Vladimir, 33, 39, 109, 111, 115, 121-22, 139, 142-43, 169-70, 176, 187, 192, n1, n35, n37a, n41
Jarvie, I.C., 19
Jefferson, Thomas, n7

K
Kastner, Rudolf, n33a
Katzenelson, Berl, n34c
Kedourie, Eli, 74, n5
King, Dr. Martin Luther, 89-90

Kissinger, Henry, 10
Kohn, Hans, 173
Kopilovicz, Aharon, 143
Krochmal, Nachman, 97, 106

L
Lankin, Eliau, 197
Laqueur, Walter, 147, 173, n24, n32
Leibovitz, Isaiah, n67a
Lévi-Strauss, Claude, 278
Lewis, Sir Arthur, 17
Lilienblum, Moshe Leib, 107, 109,
Lincoln, Abraham, 72, n7
Lipstadt, Deborah E., n04
Locke, John, 59

M
Marshall, George C., 18
Marx, Karl, 59, 77, 81, 92, 243, n60
Matz, Eliahu, n25
Meir, Golda, 172, 184
Mendili Mocher Seforim (S. J. Abramowitz), 98
Merlin, Shmuel, 31, 143, 150, 156, 200, 290, n30
Montor, Henry, 150-51, 155
Moore, Larry F., n68
Morgenthau Henry, 163, 174
Münchhause, Baron Hieronimus, 285

N
Nadiv, Sabetai, n20a
Naor, Arie, n21a, n41
Nasser, Gamal Abdul, 248
Newton, Sir Isaac, 59
Niebur, Reinhold, 90, 131-32, 253, n12
Niv, David, 146, 194-97, n1, n23, n41, n43
Nordau, Max, 108, 111, 169-70

O
Ofer, Dalia, n20a
Olson, Mancur, n5
Oren, Nissan, n68

P

Peck, Sarah, 161-63, 190, n32, n34, n34a
Penkover, N. N., 26
Peres, Shimon, 18
Pinder, Craig C., n68
Pinsker, Leo, 102, 107, 109, n62
Plato, 59, 62, 243
Popper, Karl R., 19, 74, n5, n6, n34b, n67
Porat, Dina, n33a
Pralong, S., 19
Priestley, Joseph, 99

R

Rabin, Yitzhak, 10
Rabinowitz, Baruch E., 150
Radler-Feldmann Yehoshua, (Rabbi Benjamin), n16b
Rafaeli, Alexander, 143
Rapoport, Louis, 19
Rash, Yehoshua, n57a
Raziel, David, 136, 142, 192, n21a, n41
Ronen, Dov, n5
Roosevelt, Franklin D., 155, 157, 161-62, 303, n28
Rosenberg, Stuart, n04, n27
Rothchild family, 243
Rousseau, J. J., 63, 67-68
Rubinstein, Amnon, 206-7, n46, n48
Russell, Bertrand, 3, 109, n24a

S

Sadat, Anwar, 255
Schleret, Thomas, n7
Segev, Tom, n33a, n34b, n34c
Segre, Dan V., n54
Shapira, Anita, n20a
Shapiro, Jonathan, 302, n20, n52
Sharett, Moshe, 182-83, 187, n13
Sherwood, Robert, 155, n28
Silver, Abba Hillel, 163, 166, 172, 190
Smith, Adam, 59, 62, 66
Smolenskin, Peretz, 97
Sneh, Moshe, 187-88
Socrates, 62
Sokolow, Nahum, n20b
Spinoza, Benedict, 99
Stalin, Joseph, 81, 303
Stern, Abraham, 138

T

Tal, Uriel, n67a
Talmon, Jacob, 49, 77, n4, n67a
Tehomi, Abraham, 141, n41
Tolstoy, Leo, 98
Toth, Imre, 19
Troper, Harold, n04
Truman, Harry S, n30

V

Viroli, Maurizio, 7

W

Wallenberg, Raoul, 146
Weil Simon, n36
Weiler, Gershon, 219, 228, 302, n50a, n56
Weizmann, Chaim, 28, 147, 175-79, 182-83, 185-86, 195, n03, n20b, n37b
Wells, Somner, 155
Wise, Stephen, 159-60, 162-63, 166, 178, n34a
Wyman, David, S. n04
Yehoshua, A. B., n50, n64

Z

Zaar, Isaac, n22, n38
Zerubavel, Jacob, 185
Ziff, William, 18

Subject Index

A
Abnormalcy, Israel's, *see* Normalization
Agenda, 17, 27, 42, 203, 229, 245, 300
Altalena, 32, 198-200, 205
American Civil War, *see* War
American Revolution, *see* Revolution
Anarchism, 58-59, 109
Anti-Semitism, 112, 159, 162, 172-73, n34a, n34a, n34b, n72a
Arab Ntionalism, *see* Nationalism,
Assimilation, n29
Autoemancipation, 112, 207-8, 212, 278, 196, n62

B
Bergson Group, 140, 143, 144-68, 173-74, 192-97, 290, n1, n20a, n22a, n24a, n25, n26, n30, n31, n71
"Biltmore Plan", 176
British Mandate for Palestine, 105, 124, 182, 185, 193, 258, n20b, n21a, n28a, n33a
Bund, 102

C
Canaanites, n02
Chauvinism, *see* Nationalism
Citizenship, *see* Nationality; Naturalization; New Zionist Myth

Civil rights Movement, 114
Civil War, *See* War
Clericalism, 112
Collectivim, 50, 52, 109, 279
Colonialism, 109-3
Committees of Bergson group, 31, 33, 119, 141, 143, 145-64, 168, 171, 175, 180-81, 188-200, 205, n20a, n21a, n22, n24a, n25, n33a
Communism, *see* Socialism
Conflict of Interests, Israeli-Jewish, 132-34, 153, 169-71, 277, n34a
Congregation, *see* Nation and Congregation
Consensus, *see* National Consensus
Constituent Assembly, 17, 22, 32-33, 200, 207, 221, 223, n37a
Cooperation, 153, 199, 277
Credibility Crisis, 303-5

D
Declaration of independence, 20-21, 118-19, 129, 190, 198-200, 205-6, 240, 297, n57, n69
Definitions, 85
Democracy, 11, 17, 53, 59, 77-80, 85, 89, 138, 220, 228, 239, 300, n6, n20, n34a
Denunciation of the Bergson Group, 31, 35-36, 188-89, 195, n20a, n22a, n33a

Deterioration, Israel's, 22, 129, 146, 233-35, 239, 248, 300
Diaspora, 9, 107, 110, 116, 151, 169, 209, 250, 271-73
Discrimination in Israel, 7, 9, 11-13, 16, 130, 244, 291; National, 130, 246; Religious, 18, 213, 217-19; of Women, 218-19, n50a

E

Emancipation, 81, 95, 101, 112-13, 212, 220
Emergence of Nations, 82-85, 96-100, 108, 249
Empires, 57, 172, 244
Enlightenment Movement, 44-45, 48-50, 53, 55-59, 63-67, 69-74, 77-79, 81-82, 84, 112, 243; Jewish, 97-98, 113
Ethnic Minorities, *see* Minorities
Ethnicity, Ethnic Identity, *see* Identity
Exodus, 19
Expulsion, 232-35

F

Fighters for Freedom of Israel, 137-38
Foreign Aid, 17

G

Ghetto, 209-111, 226-8, 271, 290-91, n20, n52
Glorious Revolution, 59, 66
Goals and Interests, Short, Long and Medium Range, 14, 121, 212, 276, 285, n45, n68
Government in Exile, Temporary, 33, 157, 180-81, 188, 193-95, n21a, n28, n40
Great Rebellion, 66
Guerilla Warfare, 15, 187-88, 194
Guiding Ideas, 48
Gulf War, 13, 18-19, 259
Gush Emunim, 16, 117, 127, 223

H

Haganah, 118-19, 138-39, 141, 187, 194, n20a, n22a, n37a
Hashemite Kingdom, *see* Jordan
Hashomer, 118
Hebrew, 72, 107, n14, n29, n64
History, 30, 108, 144-48, n22a, n28a, n33a, n37a
Holocaust, 10-11, 124-26, 139, 149, 156, 158, 161, 282, n1, n20a, n21a, n33a, n34a, n34b

I

Identity, 26, 108, 110, 130, 132-33, 152-53, 173, 176-77, 204, 208-11, 216, 231, n50, n54, n72a; Ethnic, 176-77, 211, 216, 231; Jewish, 110, 113, 133, 152, 176-77, 215, 217-19, 223-26, 230-31, 234-35, 245, 293-98; National, 244-48, 292, n50, n54, n72a; Israeli, 177-78, 215, 224, 230, 246, 288-92, n50a, n54; Palestinian, 204, 215, 246, 248-50
Identity Card, Israeli, n47
Ideology, Zionist, 30, 111, 273
Imperialism, 57, 93, 172, 244
Individualism, 48-49, 57-58, 109-10, 243, 273; *see also* Self Determination
Initiative, 34, 47-48, 54, 117-18, 124, 126, 146, 148, 204-5, 228, 231, 261, n55, n65
Interest, National, 132, 133-34, 253-54; *see also* Goals
International Law, 88-89
Irgun, 13, 15, 30, 32-33, 90, 118, 136-43, 146, 150, 156, 166, 181, 192-200, 205, n1, n21a, n33a, n34c, n37a, n41, n42,
Irrationalism, *see* Romanticism,
Israel as heir to Jewish Nationalism, 230, 171
Israeli non-Jews, 215-16, 233-5
Israeli Republic, 108, 202, 226, 232, 241, 247, 246-47, n64

J

Jerusalem Plan, 225
Jewish Brigade, 145, 168
Jewish Center in Israel, 220, 225, n51
Jewish National Movement, 96-99, 106-10
Jewish Nation-Congregation, 133, 217-22, 240, 273, 275, n61
Jewish Problem, 81, 94-105, 111-14, 121, 127, 252
Jews, non-Israeli, 132-33, 151-52, 162, 171-73, 177-79, 213, 216-18, 224, 269-77, 293; Russian, 216, 293, n67
Jordan, Transjordan, 204, 255-57, 262-68, n20b

K

Kibbutz, 116, 123
Knesset, 32, 200, 207, 210, 221, 223, 240, 255, 299, n53

L

Language, National, 72, 107, n29, n64
Law of Return, 11, 27, 213, 242, 269-71, 280-81
League of Nations, 121
Legal Reform, Legislation, 89, n69
Liberalism, 109-10, 131, 244-45
Lobbies, 167, n34a, n71
Lovers of Zion, 107, 109, 114, 116

M

Marxism, 59, 77, 81, 92, 243, n60
Masada Complex, 214, 33a
Melting-Pot, 167, n71
Messianism, Utopism, 49, 80, 122, 272, 274, 297, n19, n67a
Migration, 62-63, 83, 108, 130-31 216-17, 241; Jewish, 115, 116142, 150, 155, 175, 279, 296-97, n20, n20a; from Israel, 133, 215-16, 238; Mass, 19, 93, 103, 119, 121, 124-26, 160, 175, 185, 194, 297, n20, n20b; Selective, 19, 150, 169, n20

Militarism, 199-200, 289-90; *see also* Gush Emunim
Minorities, Ethnic and National, 81-82, 130, 204, '215, 232-33, 247-51, n62, n64
Mossad, n20a
Multi-National State, 9, 244

N

Nation and Congregation, Distinction between, 103-4, 107-8, 125, 176-77, 129-30, 132, 153, 160, 166-68, 177, 188-9, 240, n16a
Nation, 71, 73-74, 85, 88, 131, 152-53
Nation Building, 82, 84, 249
National Character, 84
National Consensus, 34, 40-42, 299-301, n33a
National Language, see Language
National Liberation Movements, Nationalist Movements, 80-81, 87-88, 94-97, 165, 245, 271, n21a, n27
National Minorities, *see* Minorities
National Problem, 44, 80
National Self-Determination, *see* Self-Determination
National Unity, 72, 83, 107, 170, n7
Nationalism, 39-40, 45, 243, 215, n5, n21a; Arab, 14, 248; Chauvinist, Romantic, 45-46, 49-50, 52-53, 65-79, 81-82, 84, 99, 104, 123, 171, 243, 279, 304, 67a; Jewish, 14, 74, 97, 106-9, 245; Liberal, 8, 17, 45, 77-88, 136, n5; Palestinian, 13, 248, 256
Nation-State, 9, 86, 125, 129-30, 221-26, 273-72, n57a, n62
Naturalization, 230-31, 248, n59
New Left, 15
New Zionist Myth, 8-10, 12, 26-27, 35, 105, 134, 206-211, 230, 234, 269-71, 273, 278-82, 294-95, 302, n02, n34a, n37a, n50, n72

SUBJECT INDEX

Normalization, 19, 26-27, 37, 41, 51, 100, 105, 124-25, 129-30, 134, 182, 211, 212-42, 246, 254, 270, 274, 296, 302, n02, n21a, n49, n50, n54, n63, n72a
North America, 755
Nuremberg Trials, 89

O
One-sided Initiative for Peace, 252-60

P
Palestine Covenant, 13-14, 258-59
Palestine Liberation Organization, 13-15, 19, 250, 253, 258-59, 267
Palestinian Authority, 13-14, 16, 19
Pan-Arabism, 75, 248-49, 256
Pan-Slavism, 75
Passive Resistance, 89-90, 93
Pax Romana, 57
Peace, Peace Process, 14-16, 203, 250, 257, 261-62
Peasant Revolt, 87-88
Piedmont, 74-75
Pluralism, 19, n34a
Poland, 244
Political Parties in Israel, n75
Political Theory, *see* Social Science
Political Zionism, *see* Zionism
Post-Zionism, 158, 173
Practical Zionism, *see* Zionism
Public Debate, 237-40
Public Opinion, 93, 113, 147-48, 175, 186, 193, n20b, n34c

R
Radicalism, 96
Rationalism, *see* Enlightenment
Reaction, *see* Nationalism
Realpolitik, 303-5
Refugees, 23, 155, 195, 253, 262, 297
Rehabilitation, *see* Denunciation
Religion in Israel, 8, 217-19
Religious Toleration, 78, 112, 247-48, 294

Resistance Movement in Palestine, 118, 139, 187-88, 194
Responsibility, 50-54, 124-25
Revisionism, *see* Zionist Movement
Revolution, 291; American, 91, 108; English, 66; French, 44-45, 49, 64, 67, 70, 74, 77, 95. 108; Glorious, 59, 66; Jewish, 219, 291, 302; National, 225, 291; Russian, 93; Socialist, 92-93, 103; Zionist, 207-8, 271
Romanticism, *see* Nationalism
Rule of law, 133

S
Science, *see* Social Science
Scotland, 95, 131
Season, The, 118, 138, 187
Secrecy, 138-39, 289-90, 301, n34b, n37a
Secularism, 103-4, 107
Self-Determination, Individual and/or National, 70, 73-74, 154, 165-74, 179, 244, 247, 285
Separation of Church and State, 11, 37, 210-11, 224, 238, 291, n04
Separatism, 11, 16, 17, 37-38, 41, n7, n21a
Settlers, Israeli, *see* Gush Emunim
Social Contract, 17, 55-64, 66-67
Social Science, 45, 47, 78-79, 82, 148, 277-78, 280, n6, n34a, n68, n69
Socialism, 16, 77, 102, 108-9, 116, n20
Sovereignty, 72-73
Spiritual Zionism, *see* Zionism, Spiritual
Spring of Nations, 104
Stability, social, 112-14
State, Bi-National, Multi-National, 9, 109, 130, 186
Suffering of the Jews, 111-15, 121, 125, 153
Survival, 125, 300, 304, n45

T
Territory, National, 14, 76, 81, 242, 261, 263, 270
Terror, French, 68-69

Terrorism, 13-14

U

Underground Movements in Palestine, 138
See also Fighter for Freedom; Haganah; Irgun; Hashomer; Mossad; Resistance Movement

United Nations Organization, 82, 133, 178, 182, 186, 249

United States of America, 67-8, 68, 71, 75, 83, 89, 91, 127, 130, 136, 176-77, 248, 252, n04, n16, n34a, n64, n67a

Utopism, *see* Messianism

V

Versailles Treaty, 304

Violence, 15, 58-64, 68-69, 89, 92

W

War Refugee Board, 146-49, 158-50, n24a, n25, n31, n40

Wars of Independence, 87-93; Civil, 66, 72, 85, n7; Israeli, 210, n45; Religious, 66; Gulf, 13, 18-19, 259

Warsaw Ghetto Uprising, 63, 126

Z

Zionism, 20-21, 40-41, 67, 104, 106-7, 120-28, 134, 206, 271, 273, 305, n20a, n20b, n21a

Zionism as Judaism, 133, 222, 294

Zionism, Political, 104-5, 108-9, 111-15, 118, 122-28, 168-69, 272, 305, n20, n20a, n20b, n47a

Zionism, Practical, 104-5, 108-9, 115-27, 146, 148, 150, 168-69, 187, 305, n20, n20a, n20b, n37a

Zionism, Spiritual, 109-10, 115-16, 275

Zionism-in-quotation-marks, 206, 222

Zionist Dream, 275

Zionist Leadership, 119, 123-26, 133, 137-38, 142. 146-51, 155-61, 167-70, 172-73, 189, 300-1, n1, n20, n20a, n21a, n33a, n34c, n37a, n71

Zionist Movement, 108-9, 114, 120-27, 176, 183-85, 296, 302

Zionist Movement, New (Revisionists), 109, 122, 187125, 137, 139, 142-43, 176, 194-96, n21a, n40, n41, n42